Handbook on Constructing Composite Indicators

METHODOLOGY AND USER GUIDE

OECD

ORGANISATION FOR ECONOMIC CO-OPERATION AND DEVELOPMENT

The OECD is a unique forum where the governments of 30 democracies work together to address the economic, social and environmental challenges of globalisation. The OECD is also at the forefront of efforts to understand and to help governments respond to new developments and concerns, such as corporate governance, the information economy and the challenges of an ageing population. The Organisation provides a setting where governments can compare policy experiences, seek answers to common problems, identify good practice and work to co-ordinate domestic and international policies.

The OECD member countries are: Australia, Austria, Belgium, Canada, the Czech Republic, Denmark, Finland, France, Germany, Greece, Hungary, Iceland, Ireland, Italy, Japan, Korea, Luxembourg, Mexico, the Netherlands, New Zealand, Norway, Poland, Portugal, the Slovak Republic, Spain, Sweden, Switzerland, Turkey, the United Kingdom and the United States. The Commission of the European Communities takes part in the work of the OECD.

OECD Publishing disseminates widely the results of the Organisation's statistics gathering and research on economic, social and environmental issues, as well as the conventions, guidelines and standards agreed by its members.

This work is published on the responsibility of the Secretary-General of the OECD. The opinions expressed and arguments employed herein do not necessarily reflect the official views of the Organisation or of the governments of its member countries or of the European Commission. Neither the European Commission nor any person acting on behalf of the Commission is responsible for the use which might be made of this publication.

FOREWORD

This Handbook aims to provide a guide to the construction and use of composite indicators, for policy-makers, academics, the media and other interested parties. While there are several types of composite indicators, this Handbook is concerned with those which compare and rank country performance in areas such as industrial competitiveness, sustainable development, globalization and innovation. The Handbook aims to contribute to a better understanding of the complexity of composite indicators and to an improvement in the techniques currently used to build them. In particular, it contains a set of technical guidelines that can help constructors of composite indicators to improve the quality of their outputs.

It has been jointly prepared by the OECD (the Statistics Directorate and the Directorate for Science, Technology and Industry) and the Econometrics and Applied Statistics Unit of the Joint Research Centre (JRC) of the European Commission in Ispra, Italy. Primary authors from the JRC are Michela Nardo, Michaela Saisana, Andrea Saltelli and Stefano Tarantola. Primary authors from the OECD are Anders Hoffmann and Enrico Giovannini. Editorial assistance was provided by Candice Stevens, Gunseli Baygan, Karsten Olsen and Sarah Moore.

Many people contributed to improve this handbook with their valuable comments and suggestions. The authors wish to thank especially Jochen Jesinghaus from the European Commission, DG Joint Research Centre; Tanja Srebotnjak from the Yale Center for Environmental Law and Policy; Laurens Cherchye and Tom Van Puyenbroeck from the Catholic University of Leuven; Pascal Rivière from INSEE ; Tom Griffin, Senior Statistical Adviser to the UNDP Human Development Report; and Ari LATVALA from the European Commission, DG Enterprise and Industry.

A special thank goes to Giuseppe Munda (Universitat Autònoma de Barcelona and European Commission, DG Joint Research Centre) who supplied all the material for the chapter on aggregation methods and the box on measurement scales and to Eurostat (Unit B5-'Methodology and research', DDG-02 ' Statistical governance, quality and evaluation' and other members of the Task Force on Composite Indicators) for the useful comments and the improvements they suggested. We are also grateful to the Statistical Offices of the OECD Committee on Statistics whose comments contributed to enhance the quality of this handbook.

Further information on the topics treated in this handbook and on other issues related to composite indicators can be found in the web page: http://composite-indicators.jrc.ec.europa.eu/

The research was partly funded by the European Commission, Research Directorate, under the project KEI (Knowledge Economy Indicators), Contract FP6 No. 502529. In the OECD context, the work has benefited from a grant from the Danish Government. The views expressed are those of the authors and should not be regarded as stating an official position of either the European Commission or the OECD.

TABLE OF CONTENTS

TABLES

FIGURES

BOXES

LIST OF ABBREVIATIONS

AHP   Analytic Hierarchy Processes

BAP   Budget Allocation Process

BOD   Benefit of the Doubt

CA   Conjoint Analysis

CCA   Canonical Correlation Analysis

CI   Composite Indicator

C-K-Y-L   Condorcet-Kemeny-Young-Levenglick

CLA   Cluster Analysis

DEA   Data Envelopment Analysis

DFA   Discriminant Function Analysis

DQAF   Data Quality Framework

EC   European Commission

EM   Expected Maximisation

EU   European Union

EW   Equal weighting

FA   Factor Analysis

GCI   Growth Competitiveness Index

GDP   Gross Domestic Product

GME   Geometric aggregation

HDI   Human Development Index

ICT   Information and Communication Technologies

IMF   International Monetary Fund

INSEE   National Institute for Statistics and Economic Studies (France)

JRC   Joint Research Centre

KMO   Kaiser-Meyer-Olkin

LIN   Linear aggregation

MAR   Missing At Random [in the context of imputation methods]

MCA	Multi-Criteria Approach
MCAR	Missing Completely At Random [in the context of imputation methods]
MCMC	Markov Chain Monte Carlo
MC-TAI	Monte Carlo version of the Technology Achievement Index
MI	Multiple Imputation
ML	Maximum Likelihood
MSE	Mean Square Error
NCMC	Non-compensatory multi-criteria analysis
NMAR	Not Missing At Random [in the context of imputation methods]
OECD	Organization for Economic Co-operation and Development
PC	Principal Component
PCA	Principal Components Analysis
PISA	Programme for International Student Assessment (OECD)
R&D	Research and Development
RMS	Residual Mean Square
SEM	Structural Equation Modelling
SII	Summary Innovation Index
TAI	Technology Achievement Index
UCM	Unobserved Components Model
UN	United Nations
UNDP	United Nations Development Program
VIF	Variance-inflation factor
WEF	World Economic Forum
WHO	World Health Organisation

INTRODUCTION

Composite indicators (CIs) which compare country performance are increasingly recognised as a useful tool in policy analysis and public communication. The number of CIs in existence around the world is growing year after year (for a recent review see Bandura, 2006, which cites more than 160 composite indicators). Such composite indicators provide simple comparisons of countries that can be used to illustrate complex and sometimes elusive issues in wide-ranging fields, *e.g.*, environment, economy, society or technological development.

It often seems easier for the general public to interpret composite indicators than to identify common trends across many separate indicators, and they have also proven useful in benchmarking country performance (Saltelli, 2007). However, composite indicators can send misleading policy messages if they are poorly constructed or misinterpreted. Their "big picture" results may invite users (especially policy-makers) to draw simplistic analytical or policy conclusions. In fact, composite indicators must be seen as a means of initiating discussion and stimulating public interest. Their relevance should be gauged with respect to constituencies affected by the composite index.

Pros and cons of composite indicators

In general terms, an indicator is a quantitative or a qualitative measure derived from a series of observed facts that can reveal relative positions (*e.g.* of a country) in a given area. When evaluated at regular intervals, an indicator can point out the direction of change across different units and through time. In the context of policy analysis (see Brand *et al.*, 2007, for a case study on alcohol control policies in the OECD countries), indicators are useful in identifying trends and drawing attention to particular issues. They can also be helpful in setting policy priorities and in benchmarking or monitoring performance. A composite indicator is formed when individual indicators are compiled into a single index on the basis of an underlying model. The composite indicator should ideally measure multi-dimensional concepts which cannot be captured by a single indicator, *e.g.* competitiveness, industrialisation, sustainability, single market integration, knowledge-based society, etc. The main pros and cons of using composite indicators are the following (Box 1) (adapted from Saisana & Tarantola, 2002):

Box 1. Pros and Cons of Composite Indicators	
Pros:	**Cons:**
• Can summarise complex, multi-dimensional realities with a view to supporting decision-makers.	• May send misleading policy messages if poorly constructed or misinterpreted.
• Are easier to interpret than a battery of many separate indicators.	• May invite simplistic policy conclusions.
• Can assess progress of countries over time.	• May be misused, *e.g.* to support a desired policy, if the construction process is not transparent and/or lacks sound statistical or conceptual principles.
• Reduce the visible size of a set of indicators without dropping the underlying information base.	• The selection of indicators and weights could be the subject of political dispute.

Box 1. Pros and Cons of Composite Indicators	
Pros:	**Cons:**
• Thus make it possible to include more information within the existing size limit. • Place issues of country performance and progress at the centre of the policy arena. • Facilitate communication with general public (*i.e.* citizens, media, *etc.*) and promote accountability. • Help to construct/underpin narratives for lay and literate audiences. • Enable users to compare complex dimensions effectively.	• May disguise serious failings in some dimensions and increase the difficulty of identifying proper remedial action, if the construction process is not transparent. • May lead to inappropriate policies if dimensions of performance that are difficult to measure are ignored.

Composite indicators are much like mathematical or computational models. As such, their construction owes more to the craftsmanship of the modeller than to universally accepted scientific rules for encoding. With regard to models, the justification for a composite indicator lies in its fitness for the intended purpose and in peer acceptance (Rosen, 1991). On the dispute over whether composite indicators are good or bad *per se*, it has been noted:

The aggregators believe there are two major reasons that there is value in combining indicators in some manner to produce a bottom line. They believe that such a summary statistic can indeed capture reality and is meaningful, and that stressing the bottom line is extremely useful in garnering media interest and hence the attention of policy makers. The second school, the non-aggregators, believe one should stop once an appropriate set of indicators has been created and not go the further step of producing a composite index. Their key objection to aggregation is what they see as the arbitrary nature of the weighting process by which the variables are combined. (Sharpe, 2004)

According to other commentators:

[…] it is hard to imagine that debate on the use of composite indicators will ever be settled […] official statisticians may tend to resent composite indicators, whereby a lot of work in data collection and editing is "wasted" or "hidden" behind a single number of dubious significance. On the other hand, the temptation of stakeholders and practitioners to summarise complex and sometime elusive processes (*e.g.* sustainability, single market policy, etc.) into a single figure to benchmark country performance for policy consumption seems likewise irresistible. (Saisana *et al.*, 2005a)

Aim of the Handbook

This Handbook does not aim to resolve the debate, but only to contribute to a better understanding of the complexity of composite indicators and to an improvement in the techniques currently used to build them. In particular, it contains a set of technical guidelines that can help builders of composite indicators to improve the quality of their outputs.

The proposal to develop a Handbook was launched at the end of a workshop on composite indicators jointly organised by the JRC and OECD in the spring of 2003 which demonstrated:

- The growing interest in composite indicators in academic circles, the media and among policy-makers;

- The existence of a wide range of methodological approaches to composite indicators, and;

- The need, clearly expressed by participants at the workshop, to have international guidelines in this domain.

Therefore, the JRC and OECD launched a project, open to other institutions, to develop the present Handbook. Key elements of the Handbook were presented at a second workshop, held in Paris in February 2004, while its aims and outline were presented to the OECD Committee on Statistics in June 2004. This version of the Handbook is a revision of the document published in 2005 in the OECD's statistics working paper series and contains an update of current research in the field.

The main aim of the Handbook is to provide builders of composite indicators with a set of recommendations on how to design, develop and disseminate a composite indicator. In fact, methodological issues need to be addressed transparently prior to the construction and use of composite indicators in order to avoid data manipulation and misrepresentation. In particular, to guide constructors and users by highlighting the technical problems and common pitfalls to be avoided, the first part of the Handbook discusses the following steps in the construction of composite indicators:

- *Theoretical framework.* A theoretical framework should be developed to provide the basis for the selection and combination of single indicators into a meaningful composite indicator under a fitness-for-purpose principle.

- *Data selection.* Indicators should be selected on the basis of their analytical soundness, measurability, country coverage, relevance to the phenomenon being measured and relationship to each other. The use of proxy variables should be considered when data are scarce.

- *Imputation of missing data.* Consideration should be given to different approaches for imputing missing values. Extreme values should be examined as they can become unintended benchmarks.

- *Multivariate analysis.* An exploratory analysis should investigate the overall structure of the indicators, assess the suitability of the data set and explain the methodological choices, *e.g.* weighting, aggregation.

- *Normalisation.* Indicators should be normalised to render them comparable. Attention needs to be paid to extreme values as they may influence subsequent steps in the process of building a composite indicator. Skewed data should also be identified and accounted for.

- *Weighting and aggregation.* Indicators should be aggregated and weighted according to the underlying theoretical framework. Correlation and compensability issues among indicators need to considered and either be corrected for or treated as features of the phenomenon that need to retained in the analysis.

- *Robustness and sensitivity.* Analysis should be undertaken to assess the robustness of the composite indicator in terms of, *e.g.,* the mechanism for including or excluding single indicators, the normalisation scheme, the imputation of missing data, the choice of weights and the aggregation method.

- *Back to the real data.* Composite indicators should be transparent and fit to be decomposed into their underlying indicators or values.

- *Links to other variables.* Attempts should be made to correlate the composite indicator with other published indicators, as well as to identify linkages through regressions.

- *Presentation and Visualisation.* Composite indicators can be visualised or presented in a number of different ways, which can influence their interpretation.

The first part of the Handbook also offers a thorough discussion on the quality framework for composite indicators, in which the relationships between methodologies used to construct and disseminate composite indicators and different quality dimensions are sketched.

The second part of the Handbook, the "Toolbox for Constructors", presents and discusses in more detail popular methodologies already in use in the composite indicator community.

For explanatory purposes, a concrete example (the Technology Achievement Index - TAI) is used to illustrate the various steps in the construction of a composite indicator and to highlight problems that may arise. The TAI is a composite indicator developed by the United Nations for the Human Development Report (UN, 2001; Fukuda-Parr, 2003). It is composed of a relatively small number of individual indicators, which renders it suitable for the didactic purposes of this Handbook (Box 2). Moreover, the TAI is well documented by its developers and the underlying data are freely available on the Internet. For the sake of simplicity, only the first 23 of the 72 original countries measured by the TAI are considered here. Further details are given in the Appendix. A warning: the TAI (like any other composite indicator mentioned in this Handbook) is not intended to be an example of "good practice" but rather a flexible explanatory tool, which serves to clarify some of the issues treated.

The following notation is employed throughout the Handbook (more formal definitions are given in the Second Part: Toolbox for Constructors):

$x_{q,c}^t$: raw value of individual indicator q for country c at time t, with $q=1,...,Q$ and $c=1,...,M$.

$I_{q,c}^t$: normalised value of individual indicator q for country c at time t.

$w_{r,q}$: weight associated to individual indicator q, with $r=1,...,R$ denoting the weighting method.

CI_c^t: value of the composite indicator for country c at time t.

For reasons of clarity, the time suffix is normally omitted and is present only in certain sections. When no time indication is present, the reader should consider that all variables have the same time dimension.

Box 2. Technology Achievement Index (TAI)

The TAI focuses on four dimensions of technological capacity (data given) in Table A.1

Creation of technology. Two individual indicators are used to capture the level of innovation in a society: (i) the number of patents granted per capita (to reflect the current level of innovative activities), and (ii) receipts from royalty and license fees from abroad per capita (to reflect the stock of successful innovations that are still useful and hence have market value).

Diffusion of recent innovations. Diffusion is measured by two individual indicators: (i) diffusion of the Internet (indispensable to participation), and (ii) exports of high- and medium-technology products as a share of all exports.

Diffusion of old innovations. Two individual indicators are included: telephones and electricity. These are needed to use newer technologies and have wide-ranging applications. Both indicators are expressed as logarithms, as they are important at the earlier stages of technological advance, but not at the most advanced stages. Expressing the measure in logarithms ensures that as the level increases, it contributes less to technology achievement.

Human skills. Two individual indicators are used to reflect the human skills needed to create and absorb innovations: (i) mean years of schooling and (ii) gross enrolment ratio of tertiary students in science, mathematics and engineering.

What's next

The literature on composite indicators is vast and almost every month new proposals are published on specific methodological aspects potentially relevant for the development of composite indicators. In this Handbook, taking into account its potential audience, we have preferred to make reference to relatively well established methodologies and procedures, avoiding the inclusion of some interesting, but still experimental, approaches. However, the Handbook should be seen as a "live" product, with successive editions being issued as long as new developments are taking place. On the other hand, this version of the Handbook does not cover the "composite leading indicators" normally used to identify cyclical movements of economic activity. Although the OECD has a long-standing tradition and much experience in this field, we have preferred to exclude them, because they are based on statistical and econometric approaches quite different from those relevant for other types of composite indicators.

The quality of a composite indicator as well as the soundness of the messages it conveys depend not only on the methodology used in its construction but primarily on the quality of the framework and the data used. A composite based on a weak theoretical background or on soft data containing large measurement errors can lead to disputable policy messages, in spite of the use of state-of-the-art methodology in its construction.[1] This Handbook has nothing to say about specific theoretical frameworks: our opinion is that the peer community is ultimately the legitimate forum to judge the soundness of the framework and fitness for purpose of the derived composite. Our aim is much less ambitious, namely to propose a set of statistical approaches and common practices which can assure the technical quality of a composite. Whichever framework is used, transparency must be the guiding principle of the entire exercise.

During the process of revision of this handbook we received many useful suggestions about arguments or issues to add (or to treat in more detail). These will be the subject of future work. In particular the following aspects should receive more attention in future versions of this handbook:

- Time dimension and longitudinal datasets

- Criteria for deciding whether an indicator is appropriate

- More on normalization methods and on their relationship with measurement issues.

- Relationship between the practice of CI and the traditional measurement theory developed in psychometrics and in particular the relationship between effect and cause indicators and the statistical tools proposed in the various chapters.

- More detailed discussion and application of structural equation modelling and Bayesian analysis for composite indicator development.

HANDBOOK ON CONSTRUCTING COMPOSITE INDICATORS: METHODOLOGY AND USER GUIDE – ISBN 978-92-64-04345-9 – © OECD 2008

PART I. CONSTRUCTING A COMPOSITE INDICATOR

1. STEPS FOR CONSTRUCTING A COMPOSITE INDICATOR

This Handbook presents its recommendations following an "ideal sequence" of ten steps, from the development of a theoretical framework to the presentation and dissemination of a composite indicator. Each step is extremely important, but coherence in the whole process is equally vital. Choices made in one step can have important implications for others: therefore, the composite indicator builder has not only to make the most appropriate methodological choices in each step, but also to identify whether they fit together well.

Composite indicator developers have to face a justifiable degree of scepticism from statisticians, economists and other groups of users. This scepticism is partially due to the lack of transparency of some existing indicators, especially as far as methodologies and basic data are concerned. To avoid these risks, the Handbook puts special emphasis on documentation and metadata. In particular, the Handbook recommends the preparation of relevant documentation at the end of each phase, both to ensure the coherence of the whole process and to prepare in advance the methodological notes that will be disseminated together with the numeric results.

Part 1 of the Handbook provides an overview of the individual steps in the construction of composite indicators and discusses the quality framework for composite indicators.

Table 1 provides a stylised 'checklist' to be followed in the construction of a composite indicator, which is discussed in more detail in the next sections. Detailed information about the methodological tools to be used in each step is presented in the Part II of the Handbook.

Table 1. Checklist for building a composite indicator

Step	Why it is needed
1. Theoretical framework Provides the basis for the selection and combination of variables into a meaningful composite indicator under a fitness-for-purpose principle (involvement of experts and stakeholders is envisaged at this step).	• To get a clear understanding and definition of the multidimensional phenomenon to be measured. • To structure the various sub-groups of the phenomenon (if needed). • To compile a list of selection criteria for the underlying variables, *e.g.*, input, output, process.
2. Data selection Should be based on the analytical soundness, measurability, country coverage, and relevance of the indicators to the phenomenon being measured and relationship to each other. The use of proxy variables should be considered when data are scarce (involvement of experts and stakeholders is envisaged at this step).	• To check the quality of the available indicators. • To discuss the strengths and weaknesses of each selected indicator. • To create a summary table on data characteristics, *e.g.*, availability (across country, time), source, type (hard, soft or input, output, process).
3. Imputation of missing data Is needed in order to provide a complete dataset (*e.g.* by means of single or multiple imputation).	• To estimate missing values. • To provide a measure of the reliability of each imputed value, so as to assess the impact of the imputation on the composite indicator results. • To discuss the presence of outliers in the dataset.
4. Multivariate analysis Should be used to study the overall structure of the dataset, assess its suitability, and guide subsequent methodological choices (*e.g.*, weighting, aggregation).	• To check the underlying structure of the data along the two main dimensions, namely individual indicators and countries (by means of suitable multivariate methods, *e.g.*, principal components analysis, cluster analysis). • To identify groups of indicators or groups of countries that are statistically "similar" and provide an interpretation of the results. • To compare the statistically-determined structure of the data set to the theoretical framework and discuss possible differences.
5. Normalisation Should be carried out to render the variables comparable.	• To select suitable normalisation procedure(s) that respect both the theoretical framework and the data properties. • To discuss the presence of outliers in the dataset as they may become unintended benchmarks. • To make scale adjustments, if necessary. • To transform highly skewed indicators, if necessary.

HANDBOOK ON CONSTRUCTING COMPOSITE INDICATORS: METHODOLOGY AND USER GUIDE – ISBN 978-92-64-04345-9 – © OECD 2008

Step	Why it is needed
6. Weighting and aggregation Should be done along the lines of the underlying theoretical framework.	• To select appropriate weighting and aggregation procedure(s) that respect both the theoretical framework and the data properties. • To discuss whether correlation issues among indicators should be accounted for. • To discuss whether compensability among indicators should be allowed.
7. Uncertainty and sensitivity analysis Should be undertaken to assess the robustness of the composite indicator in terms of e.g., the mechanism for including or excluding an indicator, the normalisation scheme, the imputation of missing data, the choice of weights, the aggregation method.	• To consider a multi-modelling approach to build the composite indicator, and if available, alternative conceptual scenarios for the selection of the underlying indicators. • To identify all possible sources of uncertainty in the development of the composite indicator and accompany the composite scores and ranks with uncertainty bounds. • To conduct sensitivity analysis of the inference (assumptions) and determine what sources of uncertainty are more influential in the scores and/or ranks.
8. Back to the data Is needed to reveal the main drivers for an overall good or bad performance. Transparency is primordial to good analysis and policymaking.	• To profile country performance at the indicator level so as to reveal what is driving the composite indicator results. • To check for correlation and causality (if possible). • to identify if the composite indicator results are overly dominated by few indicators and to explain the relative importance of the sub-components of the composite indicator.
9. Links to other indicators Should be made to correlate the composite indicator (or its dimensions) with existing (simple or composite) indicators as well as to identify linkages through regressions.	• To correlate the composite indicator with other relevant measures, taking into consideration the results of sensitivity analysis. • To develop data-driven narratives based on the results.
10. Visualisation of the results Should receive proper attention, given that the visualisation can influence (or help to enhance) interpretability	• To identify a coherent set of presentational tools for the targeted audience. • To select the visualisation technique which communicates the most information. • To present the composite indicator results in a clear and accurate manner.

1.1. Developing a theoretical framework

What is badly defined is likely to be badly measured

A sound theoretical framework is the starting point in constructing composite indicators. The framework should clearly define the phenomenon to be measured and its sub-components, selecting individual indicators and weights that reflect their relative importance and the dimensions of the overall composite. This process should ideally be based on what is desirable to measure and not on which indicators are available.

For example, gross domestic product (GDP) measures the total value of goods and services produced in a given country, where the weights are estimated based on economic theory and reflect the relative price of goods and services. The theoretical and statistical frameworks to measure GDP have been developed over the last 50 years and a revision of the 1993 System of National Accounts is currently being undertaken by the major international organisations. However, not all multi-dimensional concepts have such solid theoretical and empirical underpinnings. Composite indicators in newly emerging policy areas, *e.g.* competitiveness, sustainable development, e-business readiness, etc., might be very subjective, since the economic research in these fields is still being developed. Transparency is thus essential in constructing credible indicators. This entails:

- <u>Defining the concept</u>. The definition should give the reader a clear sense of what is being measured by the composite indicator. It should refer to the theoretical framework, linking various sub-groups and the underlying indicators. For example, the Growth Competitiveness Index (GCI) developed by the World Economic Forum is founded on the idea "that the process of economic growth can be analysed within three important broad categories: the macroeconomic environment, the quality of public institutions, and technology." The GCI has, therefore, a clear link between the framework (whatever this is) and the structure of the composite indicator. Some complex concepts, however, are difficult to define and measure precisely or may be subject to controversy among stakeholders. Ultimately, the users of composite indicators should assess their quality and relevance.

- <u>Determining sub-groups</u>. Multi-dimensional concepts can be divided into several sub-groups. These sub-groups need not be (statistically) independent of each other, and existing linkages should be described theoretically or empirically to the greatest extent possible. The Technology Achievement Index, for example, is conceptually divided into four groups of technological capacity: creation of technology, diffusion of recent innovations, diffusion of old innovations and human skills. Such a nested structure improves the user's understanding of the driving forces behind the composite indicator. It may also make it easier to determine the relative weights across different factors. This step, as well as the next, should involve experts and stakeholders as much as possible, in order to take into account multiple viewpoints and to increase the robustness of the conceptual framework and set of indicators.

- <u>Identifying the selection criteria</u> for the underlying indicators. The selection criteria should work as a guide to whether an indicator should be included or not in the overall composite index. It should be as precise as possible and should describe the phenomenon being measured, *i.e.* input, output or process. Too often composite indicators include both input and output measures. For example, an Innovation Index could combine R&D expenditures (inputs) and the number of new products and services (outputs) in order to measure the scope of innovative activity in a given country. However, only the latter set of output indicators should be included (or expressed in terms of output per unit of input) if the index is intended to measure innovation performance.

 HANDBOOK ON CONSTRUCTING COMPOSITE INDICATORS: METHODOLOGY AND USER GUIDE – ISBN 978-92-64-04345-9 - © OECD 2008

1.2. Selecting variables

A composite indicator is above all the sum of its parts

The strengths and weaknesses of composite indicators largely derive from the quality of the underlying variables. Ideally, variables should be selected on the basis of their relevance, analytical soundness, timeliness, accessibility, *etc.* Criteria for assuring the quality of the basic data set for composite indicators are discussed in detail in Section 2: "Quality Framework for Composite Indicators". While the choice of indicators must be guided by the theoretical framework for the composite, the data selection process can be quite subjective as there may be no single definitive set of indicators. A lack of relevant data may also limit the developer's ability to build sound composite indicators. Given a scarcity of internationally comparable quantitative (hard) data, composite indicators often include qualitative (soft) data from surveys or policy reviews.

Proxy measures can be used when the desired data are unavailable or when cross-country comparability is limited. For example, data on the number of employees that use computers might not be available. Instead, the number of employees who have access to computers could be used as a proxy. As in the case of soft data, caution must be taken in the utilisation of proxy indicators. To the extent that data permit, the accuracy of proxy measures should be checked through correlation and sensitivity analysis. The builder should also pay close attention to whether the indicator in question is dependent on GDP or other size-related factors. To have an objective comparison across small and large countries, scaling of variables by an appropriate size measure, *e.g.* population, income, trade volume, and populated land area, etc. is required. Finally, the type of variables selected – input, output or process indicators – must match the definition of the intended composite indicator.

The quality and accuracy of composite indicators should evolve in parallel with improvements in data collection and indicator development. The current trend towards constructing composite indicators of country performance in a range of policy areas may provide further impetus to improving data collection, identifying new data sources and enhancing the international comparability of statistics. On the other hand we do not marry the idea that using what is available is necessarily enough. Poor data will produce poor results in a "garbage-in, garbage-out logic. From a pragmatic point of view, however, compromises need to be done when constructing a composite. What we deem essential is the transparency of these compromises.

1.3. Imputation of missing data

The idea of imputation could be both seductive and dangerous

Missing data often hinder the development of robust composite indicators. Data can be missing in a random or non-random fashion. The missing patterns could be:

Missing completely at random (MCAR). Missing values do not depend on the variable of interest or on any other observed variable in the data set. For example, the missing values in variable income would be of the MCAR type if (i) people who do not report their income have, on average, the same income as people who do report income; and if (ii) each of the other variables in the data set would have to be the same, on average, for the people who did not report their income and the people who did report their income.

Missing at random (MAR). Missing values do not depend on the variable of interest, but are conditional on other variables in the data set. For example, the missing values in income would be MAR if the probability of missing data on income depends on marital status but, within each category of marital status, the probability of missing income is unrelated to the value of income. Missing by design, *e.g.* if survey question 1 is answered yes, then survey question 2 is not to be answered, are also MAR as missingness depends on the covariates.

Not missing at random (NMAR). Missing values depend on the values themselves. For example, high income households are less likely to report their income.

Unfortunately, there is no statistical test for NMAR and often no basis on which to judge whether data are missing at random or systematically, while most of the methods that impute missing values require a missing at random mechanism, *i.e.* MCAR or MAR. When there are reasons to assume a non-random missing pattern (NMAR), the pattern must be explicitly modelled and included in the analysis. This could be very difficult and could imply *ad hoc* assumptions that are likely to influence the result of the entire exercise.

There are three general methods for dealing with missing data: (i) case deletion, (ii) single imputation or (iii) multiple imputation. The first, also called complete case analysis, simply omits the missing records from the analysis. However, this approach ignores possible systematic differences between complete and incomplete samples and produces unbiased estimates only if deleted records are a random sub-sample of the original sample (MCAR assumption). Furthermore, standard errors will generally be larger in a reduced sample, given that less information is used. As a rule of thumb, if a variable has more than 5% missing values, cases are not deleted (Little & Rubin, 2002).

The other two approaches consider the missing data as part of the analysis and try to impute values through either single imputation, *e.g.* mean/median/mode substitution, regression imputation, hot-and cold-deck imputation, expectation-maximisation imputation, or multiple imputation, *e.g.* Markov Chain Monte Carlo algorithm. Data imputation could lead to the minimisation of bias and the use of 'expensive to collect' data that would otherwise be discarded by case deletion. However, it can also allow data to influence the type of imputation. In the words of Dempster & Rubin (1983):

> The idea of imputation is both seductive and dangerous. It is seductive because it can lull the user into the pleasurable state of believing that the data are complete after all, and it is dangerous because it lumps together situations where the problem is sufficiently minor that it can be legitimately handled in this way and situations where standard estimators applied to real and imputed data have substantial bias.

The uncertainty in the imputed data should be reflected by variance estimates. This makes it possible to take into account the effects of imputation in the course of the analysis. However, single imputation is known to underestimate the variance, because it partially reflects the imputation uncertainty. The multiple imputation method, which provides several values for each missing value, can more effectively represent the uncertainty due to imputation.

No imputation model is free of assumptions and the imputation results should hence be thoroughly checked for their statistical properties, such as distributional characteristics, as well as heuristically for their meaningfulness, *e.g.* whether negative imputed values are possible.

By the end of Step 3 the constructor should have:

- A complete data set without missing values.

- A measure of the reliability of each imputed value so as to explore the impact of imputation on the composite indicator.

- Discussed the presence of outliers in the dataset

- Documented and explained the selected imputation procedures and the results.

1.4. Multivariate analysis

Analysing the underlying structure of the data is still an art

Over the last few decades, there has been an increase in the number of composite indicators being developed by various national and international agencies. Unfortunately, individual indicators are sometimes selected in an arbitrary manner with little attention paid to the interrelationships between them. This can lead to indices which overwhelm, confuse and mislead decision-makers and the general public. Some analysts characterise this environment as "indicator rich but information poor". The underlying nature of the data needs to be carefully analysed before the construction of a composite indicator. This preliminary step is helpful in assessing the suitability of the data set and will provide an understanding of the implications of the methodological choices, *e.g.* weighting and aggregation, during the construction phase of the composite indicator. Information can be grouped and analysed along at least two dimensions of the data set: individual indicators and countries.

- **Grouping information on individual indicators**. The analyst must first decide whether the nested structure of the composite indicator is well defined (see Step 1) and whether the set of available individual indicators is sufficient or appropriate to describe the phenomenon (see Step 2). This decision can be based on expert opinion and the statistical structure of the data set. Different analytical approaches, such as principal components analysis, can be used to explore whether the dimensions of the phenomenon are statistically well-balanced in the composite indicator. If not, a revision of the individual indicators might be necessary.

The goal of principal components analysis (PCA) is to reveal how different variables change in relation to each other and how they are associated. This is achieved by transforming correlated variables into a new set of uncorrelated variables using a covariance matrix or its standardised form – the correlation matrix. Factor analysis (FA) is similar to PCA, but is based on a particular statistical model. An alternative way to investigate the degree of correlation among a set of variables is to use the Cronbach coefficient alpha (c-alpha), which is the most common estimate of internal consistency of items in a model or survey. These multivariate analysis techniques are useful for gaining insight into the structure of the data set of the composite. However, it is important to avoid carrying out multivariate analysis if the sample is small compared to the number of indicators, since results will not have known statistical properties.

- **Grouping information on countries**. Cluster analysis is another tool for classifying large amounts of information into manageable sets. It has been applied to a wide variety of research problems and fields, from medicine to psychiatry and archaeology. Cluster analysis is also used in the development of composite indicators to group information on countries based on their similarity on different individual indicators. Cluster analysis serves as: (i) a purely statistical method of aggregation of the indicators, ii) a diagnostic tool for exploring the impact of the methodological choices made during the construction phase of the composite indicator, (iii) a method of disseminating information on the composite indicator without losing that on the dimensions of the individual indicators, and (iv) a method for selecting groups of countries for the imputation of missing data with a view to decreasing the variance of the imputed values.

When the number of variables is large or when is it believed that some of them do not contribute to identifying the clustering structure in the data set, continuous and discrete models can be applied sequentially. Researchers frequently carry out a PCA and then apply a clustering algorithm on the object scores on the first few components, called "tandem analysis". However, caution is required, as PCA or FA may identify dimensions that do not necessarily help to reveal the clustering structure in the data and may actually mask the taxonomic information (Table 2).

Table 2.   Strengths and weaknesses of multivariate analysis

	Strengths	Weaknesses
Principal Components/ Factor Analysis	<ul><li>Can summarise a set of individual indicators while preserving the maximum possible proportion of the total variation in the original data set.</li><li>Largest factor loadings are assigned to the individual indicators that have the largest variation across countries, a desirable property for cross-country comparisons, as individual indicators that are similar across countries are of little interest and cannot possibly explain differences in performance.</li></ul>	<ul><li>Correlations do not necessarily represent the real influence of the individual indicators on the phenomenon being measured.</li><li>Sensitive to modifications in the basic data: data revisions and updates, *e.g.* new countries.</li><li>Sensitive to the presence of outliers, which may introduce a spurious variability in the data.</li><li>Sensitive to small-sample problems, which are particularly relevant when the focus is on a limited set of countries.</li><li>Minimisation of the contribution of individual indicators which do not move with other individual indicators.</li></ul>

HANDBOOK ON CONSTRUCTING COMPOSITE INDICATORS: METHODOLOGY AND USER GUIDE – ISBN 978-92-64-04345-9 - © OECD 2008

	Strengths	Weaknesses
Cronbach Coefficient Alpha	▪ Measures the internal consistency in the set of individual indicators, *i.e.* how well they describe a uni-dimensional construct. Thus it is useful to cluster similar objects.	▪ Correlations do not necessarily represent the real influence of the individual indicators on the phenomenon expressed by the composite indicator. ▪ Meaningful only when the composite indicator is computed as a 'scale' (*i.e.* as the sum of the individual indicators).
Cluster Analysis	▪ Offers a different way to group countries; gives some insight into the structure of the data set.	▪ Purely a descriptive tool; may not be transparent if the methodological choices made during the analysis are not motivated and clearly explained.

Various alternative methods combining cluster analysis and the search for a low-dimensional representation have been proposed, focusing on multi-dimensional scaling or unfolding analysis. Factorial k-means analysis combines k-means cluster analysis with aspects of FA and PCA. A discrete clustering model together with a continuous factorial model are fitted simultaneously to two-way data to identify the best partition of the objects, described by the best orthogonal linear combinations of the variables (factors) according to the least-squares criterion. This has a wide range of applications since it achieves a double objective: data reduction and synthesis, simultaneously in the direction of objects and variables. Originally applied to short-term macroeconomic data, factorial k-means analysis has a fast alternating least-squares algorithm that extends its application to large data sets. This methodology can be recommended as an alternative to the widely-used tandem analysis.

By the end of Step 4 the constructor should have:

- Checked the underlying structure of the data along various dimensions, *i.e.* individual indicators, countries.

- Applied the suitable multivariate methodology, *e.g.* PCA, FA, cluster analysis.

- Identified sub-groups of indicators or groups of countries that are statistically "similar".

- Analysed the structure of the data set and compared this to the theoretical framework.

- Documented the results of the multivariate analysis and the interpretation of the components and factors.

1.5. Normalisation of data

Avoid adding up apples and oranges

Normalisation is required prior to any data aggregation as the indicators in a data set often have different measurement units. A number of normalisation methods exist (Table 3) (Freudenberg, 2003; Jacobs *et al.*, 2004):

1. *Ranking* is the simplest normalisation technique. This method is not affected by outliers and allows the performance of countries to be followed over time in terms of relative positions (rankings). Country performance in absolute terms however cannot be evaluated as information on levels is lost. Some examples that use ranking include: the Information and Communications Technology Index (Fagerberg, 2001) and the Medicare Study on Healthcare Performance across the United States (Jencks *et al.*, 2003).

2. *Standardisation* (or z-scores) converts indicators to a common scale with a mean of zero and standard deviation of one. Indicators with extreme values thus have a greater effect on the composite indicator. This might not be desirable if the intention is to reward exceptional behaviour, *i.e.*, if an extremely good result on a few indicators is thought to be better than a lot of average scores. This effect can be corrected in the aggregation methodology, *e.g.* by excluding the best and worst individual indicator scores from inclusion in the index or by assigning differential weights based on the "desirability" of the individual indicator scores.

3. Min-Max normalises indicators to have an identical range [0, 1] by subtracting the minimum value and dividing by the range of the indicator values.[2] However, extreme values/or outliers could distort the transformed indicator. On the other hand, Min-Max normalisation could widen the range of indicators lying within a small interval, increasing the effect on the composite indicator more than the z-score transformation.

4. Distance to a reference measures the relative position of a given indicator vis-à-vis a reference point. This could be a target to be reached in a given time frame. For example, the Kyoto Protocol has established an 8% reduction target for CO_2 emissions by 2010 for European Union members. The reference could also be an external benchmark country. For example, the United States and Japan are often used as benchmarks for the composite indicators built in the framework of the EU Lisbon agenda. Alternatively, the reference country could be the average country of the group and would be assigned a value of 1, while other countries would receive scores depending on their distance from the average. Hence, standardised indicators that are higher than 1 indicate countries with above-average performance. The reference country could also be the group leader, in which the leading country receives 1 and the others are given percentage points away from the leader. This approach, however, is based on extreme values which could be unreliable outliers.

5. Categorical scale assigns a score for each indicator. Categories can be numerical, such as one, two or three stars, or qualitative, such as 'fully achieved', 'partly achieved' or 'not achieved'. Often, the scores are based on the percentiles of the distribution of the indicator across countries. For example, the top 5% receive a score of 100, the units between the 85th and 95th percentiles receive 80 points, the values between the 65th and the 85th percentiles receive 60 points, all the way to 0 points, thereby rewarding the best performing countries and penalising the worst. Since the same percentile transformation is used for different years, any change in the definition of the indicator over time will not affect the transformed variable. However, it is difficult to follow increases over time. Categorical scales exclude large amounts of information about the variance of the transformed indicators. Besides, when there is little variation within the original scores, the percentile bands force the categorisation on the data, irrespective of the underlying distribution. A possible solution is to adjust the percentile brackets across the individual indicators in order to obtain transformed categorical variables with almost normal distributions.

6. Indicators above or below the mean are transformed such that values around the mean receive 0, whereas those above/below a certain threshold receive 1 and -1 respectively, *e.g.* the Summary Innovation Index (EC, 2001a). This normalisation method is simple and is not affected by outliers. However, the arbitrariness of the threshold level and the omission of absolute level information are often criticised. For example, if the value of a given indicator for country A is 3 times (300%) above the mean, and the value for country B is 25% above the mean, both countries would be counted as 'above average' with a threshold of 20% around the mean.

HANDBOOK ON CONSTRUCTING COMPOSITE INDICATORS: METHODOLOGY AND USER GUIDE – ISBN 978-92-64-04345-9 – © OECD 2008

7. Methods for cyclical indicators. The results of business tendency surveys are usually combined into composite indicators to reduce the risk of false signals, and to better forecast cycles in economic activities (Nilsson, 2000). See, for example, the OECD composite leading indicators, and the EU economic sentiment indicators (EC, 2004a). This method implicitly gives less weight to the more irregular series in the cyclical movement of the composite indicator, unless some prior *ad hoc* smoothing is performed.

8. The latter is a special case of balance of opinions, in which managers of firms from different sectors and of varying sizes are asked to express their opinion on their firm's performance.

9. Percentage of annual differences over consecutive years represents the percentage growth with respect to the previous year instead of the absolute level. The transformation can be used only when the indicators are available for a number of years, *e.g.* Internal Market Index (EC, 2001b; Tarantola *et al.*, 2002; Tarantola *et al.*, 2004).

Table 3. Normalisation methods

Method	Equation
1. Ranking	$I_{qc}^{t} = Rank(x_{qc}^{t})$
2. Standardisation (or z-scores)	$I_{qc}^{t} = \dfrac{x_{qc}^{t} - x_{qc=\bar{c}}^{t}}{\sigma_{qc=\bar{c}}^{t}}$
3. Min-Max	$I_{qc}^{t} = \dfrac{x_{qc}^{t} - \min_{c}(x_{q}^{t_0})}{\max_{c}(x_{q}^{t_0}) - \min_{c}(x_{q}^{t_0})}$.
4. Distance to a reference country	$I_{qc}^{t} = \dfrac{x_{qc}^{t}}{x_{qc=\bar{c}}^{t_0}}$ or $I_{qc}^{t} = \dfrac{x_{qc}^{t} - x_{qc=\bar{c}}^{t_0}}{x_{qc=\bar{c}}^{t_0}}$
5. Categorical scales	Example: $$I_{qc}^{t} = \begin{cases} 0 & \text{if } x_{qc}^{t} < P^{15} \\ 20 & \text{if } P^{15} \leq x_{qc}^{t} < P^{25} \\ 40 & \text{if } P^{25} \leq x_{qc}^{t} < P^{65} \\ 60 & \text{if } P^{65} \leq x_{qc}^{t} < P^{85} \\ 80 & \text{if } P^{85} \leq x_{qc}^{t} < P^{95} \\ 100 & \text{if } P^{95} \leq x_{qc}^{t} \end{cases}$$
6. Indicators above or below the mean	$$I_{qc}^{t} = \begin{cases} 1 & \text{if } w > (1+p) \\ 0 & \text{if } (1-p) \leq w \leq (1+p) \\ -1 & \text{if } w < (1-p) \end{cases}$$ where $w = x_{qc}^{t} \big/ x_{qc=\bar{c}}^{t_0}$
7. Cyclical indicators (OECD)	$I_{qc}^{t} = \dfrac{x_{qc}^{t} - E_{t}\left(x_{qc}^{t}\right)}{E_{t}\left(\left\lvert x_{qc}^{t} - E_{t}\left(x_{qc}^{t}\right)\right\rvert\right)}$
8. Balance of opinions (EC)	$I_{qc}^{t} = \dfrac{100}{N_{e}} \sum_{e}^{N_{e}} \text{sgn}_{e}\left(x_{qc}^{t} - x_{qc}^{t-1}\right)$
9. Percentage of annual differences over consecutive years	$I_{qc}^{t} = \dfrac{x_{qc}^{t} - x_{qc}^{t-1}}{x_{qc}^{t}}$

Note: x_{qc}^{t} is the value of indicator q for country c at time t. $\bar{c}$ is the reference country. The operator *sgn* gives the sign of the argument (*i.e.* +1 if the argument is positive, -1 if the argument is negative). N_{e} is the total number of experts surveyed. P^{i} is the i-th percentile of the distribution of the indicator x_{qc}^{t} and p an arbitrary threshold around the mean.

The selection of a suitable method, however, is not trivial and deserves special attention to eventual scale adjustments (Ebert & Welsh, 2004) or transformation or highly skewed indicators. The normalisation method should take into account the data properties, as well as the objectives of the composite indicator. Robustness tests might be needed to assess their impact on the outcomes.

HANDBOOK ON CONSTRUCTING COMPOSITE INDICATORS: METHODOLOGY AND USER GUIDE – ISBN 978-92-64-04345-9 - © OECD 2008

By the end of Step 5 the constructor should have:
• Selected the appropriate normalisation procedure(s) with reference to the theoretical framework and to the properties of the data.
• Made scale adjustments, if necessary.
• Transformed highly skewed indicators, if necessary.
• Documented and explained the selected normalisation procedure and the results.

1.6. Weighting and aggregation

The relative importance of the indicators is a source of contention

When used in a benchmarking framework, weights can have a significant effect on the overall composite indicator and the country rankings. A number of weighting techniques exist (Table 4). Some are derived from statistical models, such as factor analysis, data envelopment analysis and unobserved components models (UCM), or from participatory methods like budget allocation processes (BAP), analytic hierarchy processes (AHP) and conjoint analysis (CA). Unobserved component and conjoint analysis approaches are explained in the "Toolbox for Constructors". Regardless of which method is used, weights are essentially value judgements. While some analysts might choose weights based only on statistical methods, others might reward (or punish) components that are deemed more (or less) influential, depending on expert opinion, to better reflect policy priorities or theoretical factors.

Most composite indicators rely on equal weighting (EW), *i.e.* all variables are given the same weight. This essentially implies that all variables are "worth" the same in the composite, but it could also disguise the absence of a statistical or an empirical basis, *e.g.* when there is insufficient knowledge of causal relationships or a lack of consensus on the alternative. In any case, equal weighting does not mean "no weights", but implicitly implies that the weights are equal. Moreover, if variables are grouped into dimensions and those are further aggregated into the composite, then applying equal weighting to the variables may imply an unequal weighting of the dimension (the dimensions grouping the larger number of variables will have higher weight). This could result in an unbalanced structure in the composite index.

Table 4. Compatibility between aggregation and weighting methods

Weighting methods	Aggregation methods		
	Linear[4]	Geometric[4]	Multi-criteria
EW	Yes	Yes	Yes
PCA/FA	Yes	Yes	Yes
BOD	Yes[1]	No[2]	No[2]
UCM	Yes	No[2]	No[2]
BAP	Yes	Yes	Yes
AHP	Yes	Yes	No[3]
CA	Yes	Yes	No[3]

1. Normalized with the Min-Max method.

2. BOD requires additive aggregation, similar arguments apply to UCM.

3. At least with the multi-criteria methods requiring weights as importance coefficients.

4. With both linear and geometric aggregations weights are trade-offs and not "importance" coefficients.

Weights may also be chosen to reflect the statistical quality of the data. Higher weights could be assigned to statistically reliable data with broad coverage. However, this method could be biased towards the readily available indicators, penalising the information that is statistically more problematic to identify and measure.

When using equal weights, it may happen that – by combining variables with a high degree of correlation – an element of double counting may be introduced into the index: if two collinear indicators are included in the composite index with a weight of w_1 and w_2, the unique dimension that the two indicators measure would have weight ($w_1 + w_2$) in the composite. The response has often been to test indicators for statistical correlation – for example using the Pearson correlation coefficient (Manly, 1994; see Box 7) – and to choose only indicators which exhibit a low degree of correlation or to adjust weights correspondingly, e.g. giving less weight to correlated indicators. Furthermore, minimizing the number of variables in the index may be desirable on other grounds, such as transparency and parsimony.

Note that there will almost always be some positive correlation between different measures of the same aggregate. Thus, a rule of thumb should be introduced to define a threshold beyond which the correlation is a symptom of double counting. On the other hand, relating correlation analysis to weighting could be dangerous when motivated by apparent redundancy. For example, in the CI of e-Business Readiness the indicator I_1 "Percentage of firms using Internet" and indicator I_2 "Percentage of enterprises that have a website" display a correlation of 0.88 in 2003: given the high correlation, is it permissible to give less weight to the pair (I_1, I_2) or should the two indicators be considered to measure different aspects of innovation and adoption of communication technologies and therefore bear equal weight in the construction of the composite? If weights should ideally reflect the contribution of each indicator to the composite, double counting should not only be determined by statistical analysis but also by the analysis of the indicator itself vis-à-vis the rest of indicators and the phenomenon they all aim to capture.

The existing literature offers a quite rich menu of alternative weighting methods all having pros and cons. Statistical models such as principal components analysis (PCA) or factor analysis (FA) could be used to group individual indicators according to their degree of correlation. Weights, however, cannot be estimated with these methods if no correlation exists between indicators. Other statistical methods, such as the "benefit of the doubt" (BOD) approach, are extremely parsimonious about weighting assumptions as they allow the data to decide on the weights and are sensitive to national priorities. However, with BOD weights are country specific and have a number of estimation problems.

Alternatively, participatory methods that incorporate various stakeholders – experts, citizens and politicians – can be used to assign weights. This approach is feasible when there is a well-defined basis for a national policy (Munda, 2005a, 2007). For international comparisons, such references are often not available, or deliver contradictory results. In the budget allocation approach, experts are given a "budget" of N points, to be distributed over a number of individual indicators, "paying" more for those indicators whose importance they want to stress (Jesinghaus, in Moldan et al., 1997). The budget allocation is optimal for a maximum of 10-12 indicators. If too many indicators are involved, this method can induce serious cognitive stress in the experts who are asked to allocate the budget. Public opinion polls have been extensively used over the years as they are easy and inexpensive to carry out (Parker, 1991).

Aggregation methods also vary. While the linear aggregation method is useful when all individual indicators have the same measurement unit, provided that some mathematical properties are respected. Geometric aggregations are better suited if the modeller wants some degree of non compensability between individual indicators or dimensions. Furthermore, linear aggregations reward base-indicators proportionally to the weights, while geometric aggregations reward those countries with higher scores.

In both linear and geometric aggregations, weights express trade-offs between indicators. A deficit in one dimension can thus be offset (compensated) by a surplus in another. This implies an inconsistency between how weights are conceived (usually measuring the importance of the associated variable) and the actual meaning when geometric or linear aggregations are used. In a linear aggregation, the compensability is constant, while with geometric aggregations compensability is lower for the composite indicators with low values. In terms of policy, if compensability is admitted (as in the case of pure economic indicators), a country with low scores on one indicator will need a much higher score on the others to improve its situation when geometric aggregation is used. Thus, in benchmarking exercises, countries with low scores prefer a linear rather than a geometric aggregation. On the other hand, the marginal utility from an increase in low absolute score would be much higher than in a high absolute score under geometric aggregation. Consequently, a country would have a greater incentive to address those sectors/activities/alternatives with low scores if the aggregation were geometric rather than linear, as this would give it a better chance of improving its position in the ranking (Munda & Nardo, 2005).

To ensure that weights remain a measure of importance, other aggregation methods should be used, in particular methods that do not allow compensability. Moreover, if different goals are equally legitimate and important, a non-compensatory logic might be necessary. This is usually the case when highly different dimensions are aggregated in the composite, as in the case of environmental indices that include physical, social and economic data. If the analyst decides that an increase in economic performance cannot compensate for a loss in social cohesion or a worsening in environmental sustainability, then neither the linear nor the geometric aggregation is suitable. A non-compensatory multi-criteria approach (MCA) could assure non-compensability by finding a compromise between two or more legitimate goals. In its basic form this approach does not reward outliers, as it retains only ordinal information, *i.e.* those countries having a greater advantage (disadvantage) in individual indicators. This method, however, could be computationally costly when the number of countries is high, as the number of permutations to calculate increases exponentially (Munda & Nardo, 2007).

With regard to the time element, keeping weights unchanged across time might be justified if the researcher is willing to analyse the evolution of a certain number of variables, as in the case of the evolution of the EC Internal Market Index from 1992 to 2002. Weights do not change with MCA, being associated to the intrinsic value of the indicators used to explain the phenomenon. If, instead, the objective of the analysis is that of defining best practice or of setting priorities, then weights should necessarily change over time.

The absence of an "objective" way to determine weights and aggregation methods does not necessarily lead to rejection of the validity of composite indicators, as long as the entire process is transparent. The modeller's objectives must be clearly stated at the outset, and the chosen model must be tested to see to what extent it fulfils the modeller's goal.

1.7. Robustness and sensitivity

Sensitivity analysis can be used to assess the robustness of composite indicators

Several judgements have to be made when constructing composite indicators, *e.g.* on the selection of indicators, data normalisation, weights and aggregation methods, etc. The robustness of the composite indicators and the underlying policy messages may thus be contested. A combination of uncertainty and sensitivity analysis can help gauge the robustness of the composite indicator and improve transparency.

Uncertainty analysis focuses on how uncertainty in the input factors propagates through the structure of the composite indicator and affects the composite indicator values. Sensitivity analysis assesses the contribution of the individual source of uncertainty to the output variance. While uncertainty analysis is used more often than sensitivity analysis and is almost always treated separately, the iterative use of uncertainty and sensitivity analysis during the development of a composite indicator could improve its structure (Saisana *et al.*, 2005a; Tarantola *et al.*, 2000; Gall, 2007). Ideally, all potential sources of uncertainty should be addressed: selection of individual indicators, data quality, normalisation, weighting, aggregation method, *etc*. The approach taken to assess uncertainties could include the following steps:

1. Inclusion and exclusion of individual indicators.
2. Modelling data error based on the available information on variance estimation.
3. Using alternative editing schemes, *e.g.* single or multiple imputation.
4. Using alternative data normalisation schemes, such as Mni-Max, standardisation, use of rankings.
5. Using different weighting schemes, *e.g.* methods from the participatory family (budget allocation, analytic hierarchy process) and endogenous weighting (benefit of the doubt).
6. Using different aggregation systems, *e.g.* linear, geometric mean of un-scaled variables, and multi-criteria ordering.
7. Using different plausible values for the weights.

The consideration of the uncertainty inherent in the development of a composite indicator is mentioned in very few studies. The Human Development Index produced annually since 1990 by the United Nations Development Programme has encouraged improvement of the indicators used in its formulation: *"No index can be better than the data it uses. But this is an argument for improving the data, not abandoning the index."* (UN, 1992). The results of the robustness analysis are generally reported as country rankings with their related uncertainty bounds, which are due to the uncertainties at play. This makes it possible to communicate to the user the plausible range of the composite indicator values for each country. The sensitivity analysis results are generally shown in terms of the sensitivity measure for each input source of uncertainty. These sensitivity measures represent how much the uncertainty in the composite indicator for a country would be reduced if that particular input source of uncertainty were removed. The results of a sensitivity analysis are often also shown as scatter plots with the values of the composite indicator for a country on the vertical axis and each input source of uncertainty on the horizontal axis. Scatter plots help to reveal patterns in the input-output relationships.

Is the assessment of robustness enough for guaranteeing a sensible composite? Certainly not. We already claimed that a sound theoretical framework is the primary ingredient. Nevertheless the statistical analysis could (and should) help in thinking about the framework used. This is a sort of "backward thinking" that should enable the modeller to answer questions like: "does the theoretical derived model provide a good fit to the data? What the lack of fit tells about the conceptual definition of the composite of the indicators chosen for it? What concept would the available indicators good measure of? Is that concept useful? Proving an answer to these questions assures the robustness and coherence of the index given that, in our experience, getting the theoretical model correct is the main challenge of a composite.

By the end of Step 7 the constructor should have:

- Identified the sources of uncertainty in the development of the composite indicator.

- Assessed the impact of the uncertainties/assumptions on the final result.

- Conducted sensitivity analysis of the inference, *e.g.* to show what sources of uncertainty are more influential in determining the relative ranking of two entities.

- Documented and explained the sensitivity analyses and the results.

1.8. Back to the details

De-constructing composite indicators can help extend the analysis

Composite indicators provide a starting point for analysis. While they can be used as summary indicators to guide policy and data work, they can also be decomposed such that the contribution of sub-components and individual indicators can be identified and the analysis of country performance extended.

For example, the TAI index has four sub-components, which contribute differently to the aggregated composite indicator and country rankings (Figure 1). This shows that a country like Finland is very strong in human skills and diffusion of recent innovations, while Japan is strong in technology creation but weaker in human skills. The decomposition of the composite indicator can thus shed light on the overall performance of a given country. Tools like path analysis, Bayesian networks and structural equation modelling could help to further illuminate the relationship between the composite and its components.

To profile national innovation performance, each sub-component of the index has been further disaggregated. The individual indicators are then used to show strengths and weaknesses. There is no optimal way of presenting individual indicators and country profiles can be presented variously. The following discusses three examples: (i) leaders and laggards, (ii) spider diagrams and (iii) traffic light presentations.

Figure 1. Example of bar chart decomposition presentation

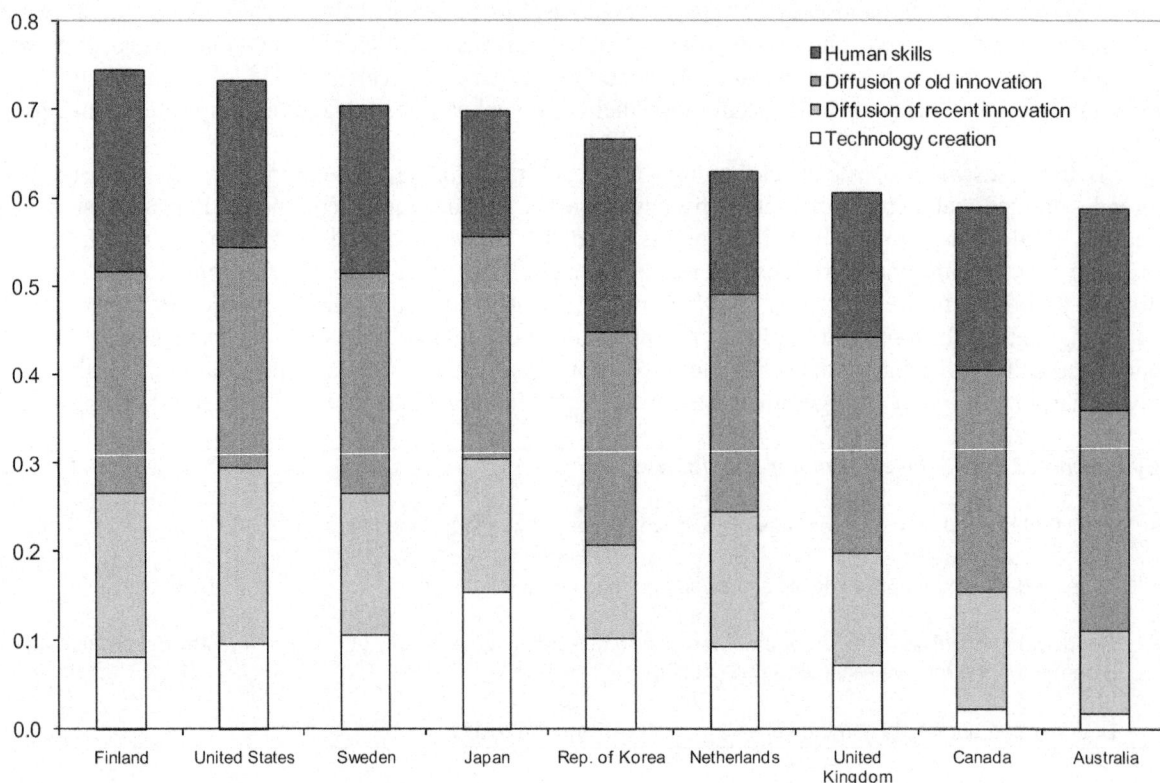

Note: Contribution of components to overall Technology Achievement Index (TAI) composite indicator. The figure is constructed by showing the standardised value of the sub-components multiplied by their individual weights. The sum of these four components equals the overall TAI index.

In the first example, performance on each indicator can be compared to the leader, the laggard and the average performance (Figure 2). Finland's top ranking is primarily based on having the highest values for the indicators relating to the *Internet* and *university*, while the country's only weakness relates to the *patents* indicator.

HANDBOOK ON CONSTRUCTING COMPOSITE INDICATORS: METHODOLOGY AND USER GUIDE – ISBN 978-92-64-04345-9 – © OECD 2008

Figure 2. Example of leader/laggard decomposition presentation

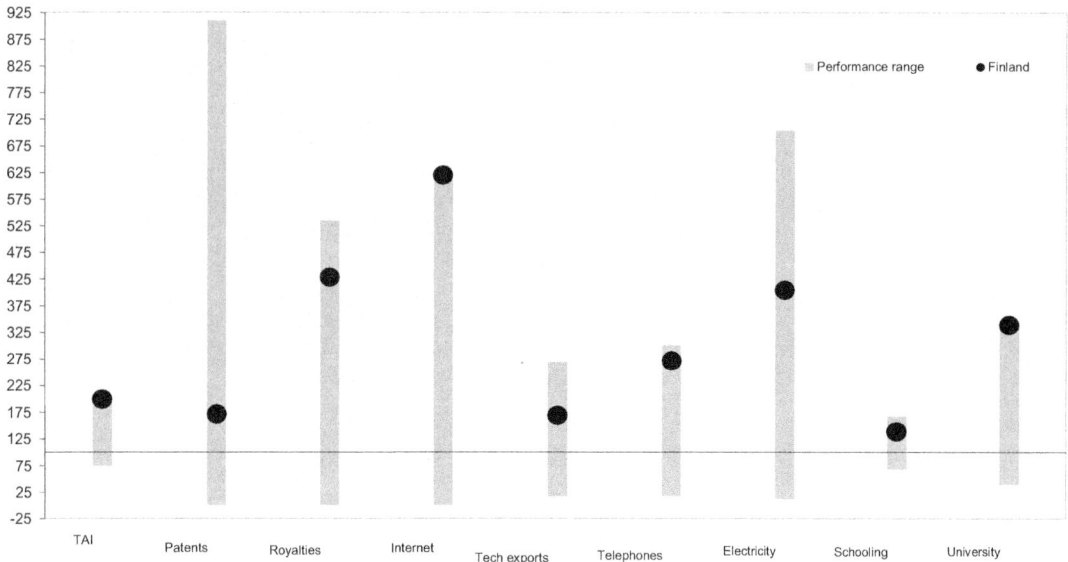

Note: Technology Achievement Index (TAI). Finland (the dot) is used as an example. The figure is based on the standardised indicators (using distance to the mean). The grey area shows the range of values for that particular indicator. The average of all countries is illustrated by the 100-line.

Figure 3. Example of spider diagram decomposition presentation

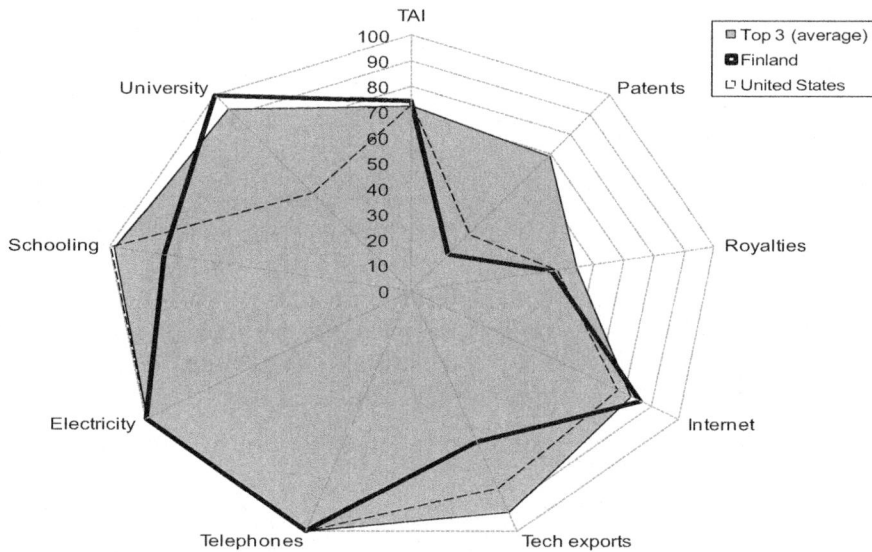

Note: Technology Achievement Index (TAI). Finland is compared to the top three TAI performers and to the United States. The best performing country for each indicator takes the value 100, and the worst, 0.

Figure 4. Example of colour decomposition presentation

	score	Well below average (under 20)	Below average (20-40)	Average (40-60)	Above average (60-80)	Well above average (over 80)
Finland						
TAI	74				X	
Patents	19	X				
Royalties	46			X		
Internet	86					X
Tech exports	63				X	
Telephones	100					X
Electricity	100					X
Schooling	82					X
University	100					X
Japan						
TAI	70				X	
Patents	100					X
Royalties	24		X			
Internet	21		X			
Tech exports	100					X
Telephones	100					X
Electricity	100					X
Schooling	78				X	
University	36		X			

Note: Technology Achievement Index (TAI). There are several ways to assign colours. In the chosen format five shades of grey are used but the number of shades (or colours) can be reduced or increased as appropriate.

Another way of illustrating country performance is to use spider diagrams or radar charts (Figure 3). Here Finland is compared to the three best countries on each indicator and to one other country, here the United States.

Finally, one can use a colour decomposition presentation, where each indicator takes the colour white, light grey, grey, dark grey, or black according to the relative performance of the country. This approach is useful when many indicators are used in the composite. For example, Figure 4 shows that Finland has one indicator in white (*patents*) where performance is relatively low, one indicator in grey (*royalties*), one indicator in dark grey (*tech exports*) and five indicators in black where performance is the highest. Upon these considerations it is clear why the overall TAI performance of Finland is in the dark grey zone where scores are above the average (range 60-80).

By the end of Step 8 the constructor should have:

- Decomposed the composite indicator into its individual parts and tested for correlation and causality (if possible).

- Profiled country performance at the indicator level to reveal what is driving the composite indicator results, and in particular whether the composite indicator is overly dominated by a small number of indicators.

- Documented and explained the relative importance of the sub-components of the composite indicator.

HANDBOOK ON CONSTRUCTING COMPOSITE INDICATORS: METHODOLOGY AND USER GUIDE – ISBN 978-92-64-04345-9 - © OECD 2008

1.9. Links to other variables

Composite indicators can be linked to other variables and measures

Composite indicators often measure concepts that are linked to well-known and measurable phenomena, *e.g.* productivity growth, entry of new firms. These links can be used to test the explanatory power of a composite. Simple cross-plots are often the best way to illustrate such links. An indicator measuring the environment for business start-ups, for example, could be linked to entry rates of new firms, where good performance on the composite indicator of business environment would be expected to yield higher entry rates.

For example, the Technology Achievement Index helps to assess the position of a country relative to others concerning technology achievements. Higher technology achievement should lead to higher wealth, that is, countries with a high TAI would be expected to have high GDP per capita. Correlating TAI with GDP per capita shows this link (Figure 5). Most countries are close to the trend line. Only Norway and Korea are clear outliers. Norway is an outlier due to revenues from oil reserves, while Korea has long prioritised technology development as an industrial strategy to catch up with high-income countries.

Figure 5. Link between TAI and GDP per capita, 2000

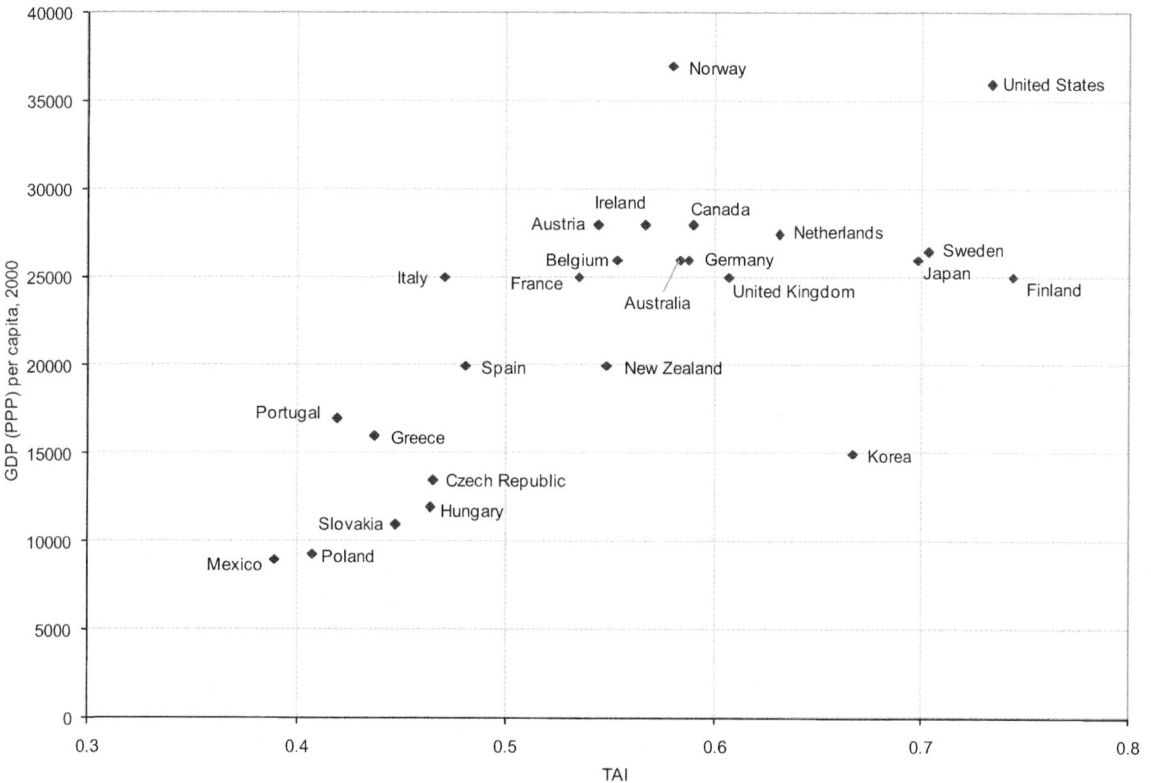

Note: The correlation is significantly different from zero at the 1% level and r^2 between GDP (PPP, $) and TAI (unitless) equals 0.47. Only OECD countries are included in the correlation, as correlation with very heterogeneous groups tends to be misleading.

One remark is worthwhile at this point. Correlation analysis should not be mistaken with causality analysis. Correlation simply indicates that the variation in the two data sets is similar. A change in the indicator does not necessarily lead to a change in the composite indicator and vice versa. Countries with high GDP might invest more in technology or more technology might lead to higher GDP. The causality remains unclear in the correlation analysis. More detailed econometric analyses can be used to determine causality, *e.g.* the Granger causality test. However, Granger causality tests require time series for all variables, which are often not available.

The impact of the weights (or normalisation method, or other) on the degree of correlation between a composite indicator and another variable of interest can be evaluated in a Monte Carlo framework. At each simulation, a weight can, for example, be allowed to vary between 0 and 1 and the simulated weights for all the indicators are then divided by the overall sum of the weights (unity sum property). This simulation is repeated 10 000 times and the composite indicator scores for each country (or unit of reference in general) are calculated 10 000 times. The correlation coefficient can thus be calculated for each simulation and the highest, median and lowest possible correlation determined. Alternatively, the correlation between the composite indicator and the measurable phenomenon can be maximised or minimised by choosing a proper set of weights.

It should be noted that composite indicators often include some of the indicators with which they are being correlated, leading to double counting. For example, most composite indicators of sustainable development include some measure of GDP as a sub-component. In such cases, the GDP measure should be removed from the composite indicator before running any correlation.

By the end of Step 9 the constructor should have:

- Correlated the composite indicator with related measurable phenomena,

- Tested the links with variations of the composite indicator as determined through sensitivity analysis.

- Developed data-driven narratives on the results

- Documented and explained the correlations and the results.

---

1. 10. Presentation and dissemination

A well-designed graph can speak louder than words

The way composite indicators are presented is not a trivial issue. Composite indicators must be able to communicate a story to decision-makers and other end-users quickly and accurately. Tables, albeit providing the complete information, can sometimes obscure sensitive issues immediately visible with a graphical representation. Therefore presenter needs to decide, in each situation, whether to include a table a graphic or both. Our examples show three situations where indicator information is communicated graphically. There are plenty of other possibilities. In all situations graphics need to be designed carefully for clarity and aesthetics. In all situations we need to have words, numbers and graphics working together (see Trufte, 2001).

A tabular format is the simplest presentation, in which the composite indicator is presented for each country as a table of values. Usually countries are displayed in descending rank order. Rankings can be used to track changes in country performance over time as, for example, the Growth Competitiveness

Index, which shows the rankings of countries for two consecutive years (Figure 6). While tables are a comprehensive approach to displaying results, they may be too detailed and not visually appealing. However, they can be adapted to show targeted information for sets of countries grouped by geographic location, GDP, etc.

Composite indicators can be expressed via a simple bar chart (Figure 7). The countries are on the vertical axis and the values of the composite on the horizontal. The top bar indicates the average performance of all countries and enables the reader to identify how a country is performing *vis-à-vis* the average. The underlying individual indicators can also be displayed on a bar chart. The use of colours can make the graph more visually appealing and highlight the countries performing well or not so well, growing or not growing, etc.[3] The top bar can be thought of as a target to be reached by countries.

Figure 6. Example of tabular presentation of composite indicator

GROWTH COMPETITIVENESS INDEX RANKINGS

Country	Growth Competitiveness ranking 2003	Growth Competitiveness ranking 2003 among GCR 2002 countries	Growth Competitiveness ranking 2002*
Finland	1	1	1
United States	2	2	2
Sweden	3	3	3
Denmark	4	4	4
Taiwan	5	5	6
Singapore	6	6	7
Switzerland	7	7	5
Iceland	8	8	12
Norway	9	9	8
Australia	10	10	10
Japan	11	11	16
Netherlands	12	12	13
Germany	13	13	14
New Zealand	14	14	15
United Kingdom	15	15	11
Canada	16	16	9
Austria	17	17	18
Korea	18	18	25
Malta	19	—	—
Israel	20	19	17
Luxembourg	21	—	—
Estonia	22	20	27

Source: WEF, 2004   www.weforum.org/gcr

Figure 7. Example of bar chart presentation of composite indicator

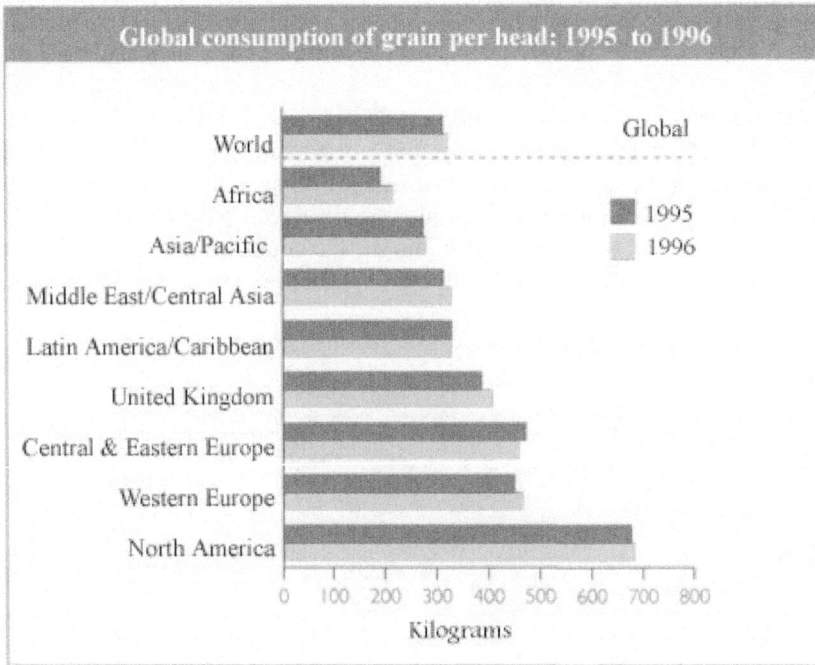

Global consumption of grain per head: 1995 to 1996

Source: (U.K Government, 2004)

Figure 8. Example of line chart presentation of composite indicator

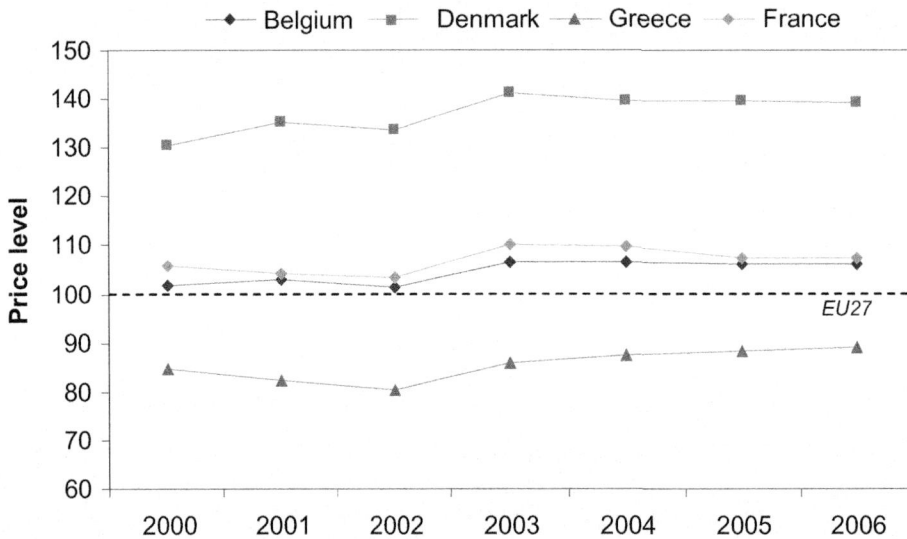

Note: EU price level index. Comparative price levels of final consumption by private households including indirect taxes (EU-27=100). JRC elaboration, data source: Eurostat, 2007. http:// ec.europa.eu/eurostat

HANDBOOK ON CONSTRUCTING COMPOSITE INDICATORS: METHODOLOGY AND USER GUIDE – ISBN 978-92-64-04345-9 – © OECD 2008

Figure 9. Example of trend diagram composite indicator

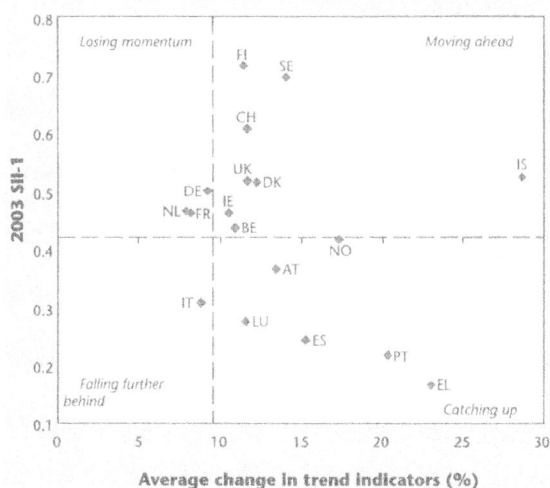

Note: 2003 SII-1 stands for 2003 EU Summary Innovation Index

Source: The European Innovation Scoreboard 2003, at
ftp://ftp.cordis.europa.eu/pub/focus/docs/innovation_scoreboard_2003_en.pdf For the definition of SII-1 see ibid., p. 9.

Line charts can be used to illustrate the changes of a composite (or its dimensions/components) across time. The values for different countries (or different indicators) are shown by different colours and or symbols. The indicators can be displayed using, for example, a) absolute levels, b) absolute growth rates, *e.g.* in percentage points with respect to the previous year or a number of past years, c) indexed levels and d) indexed growth rates. When indexed, the values of the indicator are linearly transformed so that their indexed value for a given year is 100 (or another integer). The price level index shows values such that EU27=100 for each year, with more expensive countries having values greater than 100 and less expensive countries below 100 (Figure 8).

Trends in country performance as revealed through a composite indicator can be presented through trend diagrams. When a composite indicator is available for a set of countries for at least two different time points, changes or growth rates can be depicted. The EU Summary Innovation Index is used to track relative performance of European countries on innovation indicators (Figure 9). Country trends are reported on the X-axis and levels are given on the Y-axis (although levels in the abscissa and % changes in the y-axis constitute the usual practice). In this picture, the horizontal axis gives the EU average value and the vertical axis shows the EU trend. The two axes divide the area into four quadrants. Countries in the upper quadrant are "moving ahead", because both their value and their trend are above the EU average. Countries in the bottom left quadrant are "falling further behind" because they are below the EU average for both variables.

By the end of Step 10 the constructor should have:

- Identified a coherent set of presentational tools for the target audience.

- Selected the visualisation technique which communicates the most information.

- Visualised the results of the composite indicator in a clear and accurate manner.

---

2. A QUALITY FRAMEWORK FOR COMPOSITE INDICATORS

2.1. Quality profile for composite indicators

The development of a quality framework for composite indicators is not an easy task. In fact, the overall quality of the composite indicator depends on several aspects, related both to the quality of elementary data used to build the indicator and the soundness of the procedures used in its construction. Quality is usually defined as "fitness for use" in terms of user needs. As far as statistics are concerned, this definition is broader than has been used in the past when quality was equated with accuracy. It is now generally recognised that there are other important dimensions. Even if data are accurate, they cannot be said to be of good quality if they are produced too late to be useful, cannot be easily accessed, or appear to conflict with other data. Thus, quality is a multi-faceted concept. The most important quality characteristics depend on user perspectives, needs and priorities, which vary across user-groups.

Several organisations (*e.g.*, Eurostat, International Monetary Fund, Statistics Canada, Statistics Sweden) have been working towards the identification of various dimensions of quality for statistical products. Particularly important are the frameworks developed by Eurostat and the International Monetary Fund (IMF). With the adoption of the European Statistics Code of Practice in 2005, the Eurostat quality framework is now quite similar to the IMF's "Data Quality Framework (DQAF)", in the sense that both frameworks provide a comprehensive approach to quality, through coverage of governance, statistical processes and observable features of the outputs. The IMF developed the DQAF to assess the overall quality of statistics produced by its member countries, addressing a broad range of questions which are captured through (i) the prerequisites of quality and (ii) five quality dimensions.

With regard to the prerequisites of quality, the DQAF assesses how the quality of statistics is affected by the legal and institutional environment and the available resources, and also whether there is an awareness of quality in the management of statistical activities. An evaluation of the way in which national statistical offices (or systems) perform their tasks is carried out by means of a detailed questionnaire to identify the degree of scientific independence of statistical agencies, the autonomy given to statistical agencies, etc.

The five quality dimensions used by the IMF are the following:

1. *Assurance of integrity*: What are the features that support firm adherence to objectivity in the production of statistics, so as to maintain users' confidence?

2. *Methodological soundness*: How do the current practices relate to the internationally agreed methodological practices for specific statistical activities?

3. *Accuracy and reliability*: Are the source data, statistical techniques, *etc.*, adequate to portray the reality to be captured?

4. *Serviceability*: How are users' needs met in terms of timeliness of the statistical products, their frequency, consistency, and their revision cycle?

5. *Accessibility*: Are effective data and metadata easily available to data users and is there assistance to users?

HANDBOOK ON CONSTRUCTING COMPOSITE INDICATORS: METHODOLOGY AND USER GUIDE – ISBN 978-92-64-04345-9 – © OECD 2008

Given the institutional set-up of the European Statistical System, the main aim of the Eurostat quality approach is to ensure that certain standards are met in various aspects of statistical production processes carried out by national statistical agencies and by Eurostat itself. In addition, it largely aims to use quantifiable measures, such as measurement errors or days (or months) of publication delay after the reference period.

The European Statistics Code of Practice (Principles 11-15) focuses on statistical outputs as viewed by users. Six quality dimensions are considered:

1. *Relevance* refers to the degree to which statistics meet current and potential needs of the users;

2. *Accuracy* refers to the closeness of computations or estimates to the exact or true values;

3. *Timeliness* and *Punctuality*. "Timeliness" refers to the length of time between the availability of the information and the event or phenomenon it describes. "Punctuality" refers to the time lag between the target delivery date and the actual date of the release of the data;

4. *Accessibility* and *Clarity*. "Accessibility" refers to the physical conditions in which users can access statistics: distribution channels, ordering procedures, time required for delivery, pricing policy, marketing conditions (copyright, etc.), availability of micro or macro data, media (paper, CD-ROM, Internet, etc). "Clarity" refers to the statistics' information environment: appropriate metadata provided with the statistics (textual information, explanations, documentation, etc); graphs, maps, and other illustrations; availability of information on the statistics' quality (possible limitation in use);

5. *Comparability* refers to the measurement of the impact of differences in applied statistical concepts and measurement tools and procedures when statistics are compared between geographical areas, non-geographical domains or over time;

6. *Coherence* refers to the adequacy of the data to be reliably combined in different ways and for various uses.

In 2003 the OECD published the first version of its "Quality Framework and Guidelines for OECD Statistics" (OECD, 2003). It relies heavily on the results achieved by the international statistical community, adapting them to the OECD context. In fact, for an international organisation, the quality of statistics disseminated depends on two aspects: (i) the quality of national statistics received, and (ii) the quality of internal processes for collection, processing, analysis and dissemination of data and metadata. From this point of view, there are some similarities between what the OECD has done in the development of its own quality framework and the characteristics of composite indicators, whose overall quality depends on two aspects: (i) the quality of basic data, and (ii) the quality of procedures used to build and disseminate the composite indicator.

Both elements are equally important: the application of the most advanced approaches to the development of composite indicators based on inaccurate or incoherent data would not produce good quality results, but the quality of a composite indicator will be largely determined by the appropriateness of the indicators used. If they do not fit with the theoretical concept being measured, then the quality of the composite indicator will be weak, regardless of the quality of the basic indicators. Finally, composite indicators disseminated without appropriate metadata could easily be misinterpreted. Therefore the quality framework for composite indicators must consider all these aspects. In the following section each is considered separately

2.2. Quality dimensions for basic data

The selection of basic data should maximise the overall quality of the final result. In particular, in selecting the data the following dimensions (drawing on the IMF, Eurostat and OECD) are to be considered:

Relevance

The relevance of data is a qualitative assessment of the value contributed by these data. Value is characterised by the degree to which statistics meet current and potential needs of the users. It depends upon both the coverage of the required topics and the use of appropriate concepts.

> In the context of composite indicators, relevance has to be evaluated considering the overall purpose of the indicator. Careful evaluation and selection of basic data have to be carried out to ensure that the right range of domains is covered in a balanced way. Given the actual availability of data, "proxy" series are often used, but in this case some evidence of their relationships with "target" series should be produced whenever possible.

Accuracy

The accuracy of basic data is the degree to which they correctly estimate or describe the quantities or characteristics that they are designed to measure. Accuracy refers to the closeness between the values provided and the (unknown) true values. Accuracy has many attributes, and in practical terms it has no single aggregate or overall measure. Of necessity, these attributes are typically measured or described in terms of the error, or the potential significance of error, introduced through individual major sources of error.

In the case of sample survey-based estimates, the major sources of error include coverage, sampling, non-response, response, processing, and problems in dissemination. For derived estimates, such as for national accounts or balance of payments, sources of error arise from the surveys and censuses that provide source data; from the fact that source data do not fully meet the requirements of the accounts in terms of coverage, timing, and valuation and that the techniques used to compensate can only partially succeed; from seasonal adjustment; and from separation of price and quantity in the preparation of volume measures.

An aspect of accuracy is the closeness of the initially released value(s) to the subsequent value(s) of estimates. In light of the policy and media attention given to first estimates, a key point of interest is how close a preliminary value is to subsequent estimates. In this context it useful to consider the sources of revision, which include (i) replacement of preliminary source data with later data, (ii) replacement of judgemental projections with source data, (iii) changes in definitions or estimating procedures, and (iv) updating of the base year for constant-price estimates. Smaller and fewer revisions is an aim; however, the absence of revisions does not necessarily mean that the data are accurate.

In the context of composite indicators, accuracy of basic data is extremely important. Here the issue of credibility of the source becomes crucial. The credibility of data products refers to confidence that users place in those products based simply on their image of the data producer, i.e., the brand image. One important aspect is trust in the objectivity of the data. This implies that the data are perceived to be produced professionally in accordance with appropriate statistical standards and policies and that practices are transparent (for example, data are not manipulated, nor their release timed in response to political pressure). Other things being equal, data produced by "official sources" (e.g. national statistical offices or other public bodies working under national statistical regulations or codes of conduct) should be preferred to other sources.

Timeliness

The timeliness of data products reflects the length of time between their availability and the event or phenomenon they describe, but considered in the context of the time period that permits the information to be of value and to be acted upon. The concept applies equally to short-term or structural data; the only difference is the timeframe. Closely related to the dimension of timeliness, the punctuality of data products is also very important, both for national and international data providers. Punctuality implies the existence of a publication schedule and reflects the degree to which data are released in accordance with it.

In the context of composite indicators, timeliness is especially important to minimise the need for the estimation of missing data or for revisions of previously published data. As individual basic data sources establish their optimal trade-off between accuracy and timeliness, taking into account institutional, organisational and resource constraints, data covering different domains are often released at different points of time. Therefore special attention must be paid to the overall coherence of the vintages of data used to build composite indicators (see also coherence).

Accessibility

The accessibility of data products reflects how readily the data can be located and accessed from original sources, i.e. the conditions in which users can access statistics (such as distribution channels, pricing policy, copyright, etc.). The range of different users leads to considerations such as multiple dissemination formats and selective presentation of metadata. Thus, accessibility includes the suitability of the form in which the data are available, the media of dissemination, and the availability of metadata and user support services. It also includes the affordability of the data to users in relation to its value to them and whether the user has a reasonable opportunity to know that the data are available and how to access them.

In the context of composite indicators, accessibility of basic data can affect the overall cost of production and updating of the indicator over time. It can also influence the credibility of the composite indicator if poor accessibility of basic data makes it difficult for third parties to replicate the results of the composite indicators. In this respect, given improvements in electronic access to databases released by various sources, the issue of coherence across data sets can become relevant. Therefore, the selection of the source should not always give preference to the most accessible source, but should also take other quality dimensions into account.

Interpretability

The interpretability of data products reflects the ease with which the user may understand and properly use and analyse the data. The adequacy of the definitions of concepts, target populations, variables and terminology underlying the data and of the information describing the limitations of the data, if any, largely determines the degree of interpretability. The range of different users leads to considerations such as the presentation of metadata in layers of increasing detail. Definitional and procedural metadata assist in interpretability; thus, the coherence of these metadata is an aspect of interpretability.

In the context of composite indicators, the wide range of data used to build them and the difficulties due to the aggregation procedure require the full interpretability of basic data. The availability of definitions and classifications used to produce basic data is essential to assess the comparability of data over time and across countries (see coherence): for example, series breaks need to be assessed when composite indicators are built to compare performances over time. Therefore the availability of adequate metadata is an important element in the assessment of the overall quality of basic data.

Coherence

The coherence of data products reflects the degree to which they are logically connected and mutually consistent, *i.e.* the adequacy of the data to be reliably combined in different ways and for various uses. Coherence implies that the same term should not be used without explanation for different concepts or data items; that different terms should not be used for the same concept or data item without explanation; and that variations in methodology that might affect data values should not be made without explanation. Coherence in its loosest sense implies the data are "at least reconcilable". For example, if two data series purporting to cover the same phenomena differ, the differences in time of recording, valuation, and coverage should be identified so that the series can be reconciled.

In the context of composite indicators, two aspects of coherence are especially important: coherence over time and across countries. *Coherence over time* implies that the data are based on common concepts, definitions and methodology over time, or that any differences are explained and can be allowed for. Incoherence over time refers to breaks in a series resulting from changes in concepts, definitions, or methodology. *Coherence across countries* implies that from country to country the data are based on common concepts, definitions, classifications and methodology, or that any differences are explained and can be allowed for.

2.3. Quality dimensions for procedures to build and disseminate composite indicators

Each phase of the composite indicator building process is important and has to be carried out with quality concerns in mind. For example, the design of the theoretical framework can affect the relevance of the indicator; the multivariate analysis is important to increase its reliability; the imputation of missing data, as well as the normalisation and the aggregation, can affect its accuracy, etc. In the following matrix, the most important links between each phase of the building process and quality dimensions are identified, using the seven dimensions of the OECD Quality Framework (Table 5).

The proper definition of the *theoretical framework* affects not only the relevance of the composite indicator, but also its credibility and interpretability. The relevance of a composite indicator is usually evaluated on the basis of analytical and policy needs, but also takes into account its theoretical foundation. From this point of view, several composite indicators are quite weak and such weakness is often offered as a criticism of the general idea of composite indicators.

The *imputation of missing data* affects the accuracy of the composite indicator and its credibility. Furthermore, too much use of imputation techniques can undermine the overall quality of the indicator and its relevance, even if it can improve the dimension of timeliness. The *normalisation* phase is crucial both for the accuracy and the coherence of final results. An inappropriate normalisation procedure can give rise to unreliable or biased results. On the other hand, the interpretability of the composite indicator relies heavily on the correctness of the approach followed in the normalisation phase.

The quality of basic data chosen to build the composite indicator strongly affects its accuracy and credibility. Timeliness can also be greatly influenced by the *choice of appropriate data*. The use of *multivariate analysis* to identify the data structure can increase both the accuracy and the interpretability of final results. This step is also very important to identify redundancies among selected phenomena and to evaluate possible gaps in basic data.

One of the key issues in the construction of composite indicators is the choice of the *weighting and aggregation* model. Almost all quality dimensions are affected by this choice, especially accuracy, coherence and interpretability. This is also one of the most criticised characteristics of composite indicators: therefore, the indicator developer has to pay special attention to avoid internal contradictions and mistakes when dealing with weighting and aggregating individual indicators.

To minimise the risks of producing meaningless composite indicators, *sensitivity* and *robustness analysis* are required. Analysis of this type can improve the accuracy, credibility and interpretability of the final results. Given public and media interest in country rankings, sensitivity checks can help distinguish between significant and insignificant differences, thereby minimising the risk of misinterpretation and misuse.

A *comparison* between the composite indicator and other well known and "classical" measures of relevant phenomena can be very useful to evaluate the capacity of the former to produce meaningful and relevant results. Therefore, relevance and interpretability of the results can be strongly reinforced by such comparison. In addition, the credibility of the indicator can benefit from its capacity to produce results which are highly correlated with the reference data.

The *presentation* of composite indicators and their visualisation affects both relevance and interpretability of the results. Given the complexity of composite indicators, neither the general public (media, citizens, etc.) nor policy-makers generally read methodological notes and "caveats". Therefore, their comprehension of the results will be largely based on the "messages" transmitted through summary tables or charts.

As highlighted in this Handbook, composite indicators provide a starting point for *analysis*, which has then to be deepened by going back to the detail. Therefore, this analytical phase can affect the relevance of the indicator and also its interpretability. Moreover, if the way in which the indicator is built or disseminated does not allow users and analysts to go into the details, the overall credibility of the exercise can be impaired.

Finally, the *dissemination* phase is crucial to assure the relevance of the indicator, its credibility, accessibility and interpretability. Too often statisticians do not pay enough attention to this fundamental phase, thus limiting the audience for their products and their overall impact. The OECD has recently developed the "Data and Metadata Reporting and Presentation Handbook" (OECD, 2007), which describes practices useful to improve the dissemination of statistical products.

Table 5. **Quality dimensions of composite indicators**

CONSTRUCTION PHASE	QUALITY DIMENSIONS						
	Relevance	Accuracy	Credibility	Timeliness	Accessibility	Interpretability	Coherence
Theoretical framework	✓		✓			✓	
Data selection		✓	✓	✓			
Imputation of missing data	✓	✓	✓	✓			
Multivariate analysis		✓				✓	✓
Normalisation		✓				✓	✓
Weighting and aggregation	✓	✓	✓			✓	✓
Back to the data	✓		✓			✓	
Robustness and sensitivity		✓	✓			✓	
Links to other variables	✓		✓			✓	✓
Visualisation	✓					✓	
Dissemination	✓		✓		✓	✓	

PART 2. A TOOLBOX FOR CONSTRUCTORS

A number of statistical methods are discussed in detail below to provide constructors with the necessary tools for building sound composite indicators, focusing on the practical implementation of the steps 3 to 8 outlined above. The problem of missing data is discussed first. The need for multivariate analysis prior to the aggregation of the individual indicators is stressed. The techniques used to standardise indicators of disparate natures into a common unit are also presented. Different methodologies for weighting and aggregating indicators into a composite are explored, as well as the need to test the robustness of the composite indicator using uncertainty and sensitivity analysis. The example of the Technology Achievement Index (TAI) (see Appendix) is used as a baseline case to illustrate differences across various methods and to highlight potential pitfalls.

For the sake of clarity, some basic definitions are given at the outset. These definitions have been adapted to the context of composite indicators, drawing on concepts from multi-criteria decision theory and complex system theory (see Munda & Nardo, 2007).

Dimension: is the highest hierarchical level of analysis and indicates the scope of objectives, individual indicators and variables. For example, a sustainability composite indicator can include economic, social, environmental and institutional dimensions.

Objective: indicates the desired direction of change. For example, within the economic dimension GDP has to be maximised; within the social dimension social exclusion has to be minimised; within the environmental dimension CO_2 emissions have to be minimised. This is not always obvious: international mobility of researchers for example, could be minimized when the hierarchical level is the country and the scope of the analysis is, for example, measuring *brain drain*. But this could also be maximized when the hierarchical level is constituted by OECD countries and *peer learning* is under analysis.

Individual indicator: is the basis for evaluation in relation to a given objective (any objective may imply a number of different individual indicators). It is a function that associates each single country with a variable indicating its desirability according to expected consequences related to the same objective, *e.g.* GDP, saving rate and inflation rate within the objective "growth maximisation".

Variable: is a constructed measure stemming from a process that represents, at a given point in space and time, a shared perception of a real-world state of affairs consistent with a given individual indicator. For example, in comparing two countries within the economic dimension, one objective could be "maximisation of economic growth"; the individual indicator might be R&D performance, the indicator score or variable could be "number of patents per million of inhabitants". Another example: an objective connected with the social dimension might be "maximisation of residential attractiveness". A possible individual indicator could then be "residential density". The variable providing the individual indicator score might be the ratio of persons per hectare.

A **composite indicator** or synthetic index is an aggregate of all dimensions, objectives, individual indicators and variables used. This implies that what formally defines a composite indicator is the set of properties underlying its aggregation convention.[4]

Given a set of Q individual indicators for country c at time t: $X_c^t = \{ x_{q,c}^t \}$, $q=1,2,...,Q$, and a finite set:

$C = \{ c_i \}$, $i=1, 2,..., M$ of countries, let us assume that the variable (*i.e.* the individual indicator score) of each country c_i with respect to an individual indicator $x_{q,c}^t$ is based on an ordinal, interval or ratio scale of measurement (Box 3). For simplicity of explanation, we assume that a higher value of a variable is preferred to a lower one (*i.e.* the higher, the better), that is:

$$\begin{cases} c_j Pc_k \Leftrightarrow x_q^t(c_j) > x_q^t(c_k) \\ c_j Ic_k \Leftrightarrow x_q^t(c_j) = x_q^t(c_k) \end{cases}$$

where P and I indicate a preference and an indifference relation respectively, both fulfilling the transitive property.[5]

Let us also assume the existence of a set of indicator weights (calculated according to the weighting method r $W_r = \{ w_{r,q} \}$, $q=1,2,...,Q$, with $\sum_q w_{r,q} = 1$, derived as importance coefficients.[6] The mathematical problem is then how to use this available information to rank in a complete pre-order (*i.e.* without any incomparability relation) all the countries from the best to the worst. In doing so the following operational properties are desirable:

- The sources of uncertainty and imprecise assessment should be reduced as much as possible.

- The manipulation rules should be as objective and simple as possible, that is, all *ad hoc* parameters should be avoided.

An additional property could be the guarantee that weights are used with the meaning of "importance of the associated individual indicator". Arrow's impossibility theorem (Arrow, 1963) clearly shows that no perfect aggregation convention can exist (see the section on aggregation and weighting). It is therefore essential to check not only which properties are respected by a given ranking procedure, but also whether any essential property for the problem being tackled has been lost.

Box 3. Measurement scales[7]

Let us start by clarifying what a measurement scale is. The process of grouping individual observations into qualitative classes is measurement at its most primitive level. Sometimes this is called categorical or *nominal scaling* (e.g. classification according to gender, marital status, profession, etc.). The set of equivalence classes itself is called a nominal scale. The word measurement is usually reserved for the situation in which a number is assigned to each observation; this number reflects a magnitude of some quantitative property (how to assign this number constitutes the so-called *representation problem*).

There are at least three kinds of numerical measurement that can be distinguished (Roberts, 1979; Vansnick, 1990): these are called *ordinal scale* (e.g. restaurant ratings, preference for seaside resorts, etc.), *interval scale* (e.g. temperature) and *ratio scale* (e.g. weight, height, age, etc.). Often, information measured on a nominal or ordinal scale is called qualitative information, while that measured on an interval or ratio scale is called quantitative. Imagine a set of objects O, and suppose that there is some property that all objects in the set possess, such as value, weight, length, intelligence or motivation. Furthermore, let us suppose that each object o has a certain amount or degree of that property. In principle it is possible to assign a number $t(o)$, to any object $o \in O$, standing for the amount that o actually "has" of that characteristic. Ideally, to measure an object o, we would like to determine this number $t(o)$ directly. However, this is not always possible; therefore it is necessary to find a procedure for pairing each object with another number, $m(o)$, which can be called its *numerical measurement*. The measurement procedure used constitutes a function rule $m : O \to R$, instructing how to give an object o its $m(o)$ value in a systematic way. Measurement operations or procedures differ in the information that the numerical measurements themselves provide about the true magnitudes.

Let us suppose that there is a measurement rule for assigning a number $m(o)$ to each object $o \in O$, and suppose that the following statements are true for any pair of objects o_1 and $o_2 \in O$,

$$\begin{cases} m(o_1) \neq m(o_2) \ only \ if \quad t(o_1) \neq t(o_2) \\ m(o_1) > m(o_2) \ only \ if \quad t(o_1) > t(o_2) \end{cases} \qquad \text{(a)}$$

In other words, by this rule it is possible to say that if two measurements are unequal, and if one measurement is larger than another, then one magnitude exceeds another. Any measurement procedure for which equation (a) applies is an example of *ordinal scaling*, or measurement at the ordinal level.

A fundamental point in measurement theory is that of the *uniqueness of scale*, *i.e.* which admissable transformations of scale allow for the truth or falsity of the statement involving numerical scales to remain unchanged (*problem of meaningfulness*). In the case of an ordinal scale, it is unique up to a strictly monotone increasing transformation (with infinite degrees of liberty). Other measurement procedures associate objects $o \in O$ with a real number $m(o)$, where much stronger statements can be made about the true magnitudes from the numerical measurements. Suppose that the statement of equation (b) is true:

$$\begin{cases} m(o_1) \neq m(o_2) \ only \ if \quad t(o_1) \neq t(o_2) \\ m(o_1) > m(o_2) \ only \ if \quad t(o_1) > t(o_2) \\ t(o) = x \ iff \ m(o) = ax + b, where \ a \in R^+ \end{cases} \qquad \text{(b)}$$

where *iff* stands for "if and only if". That is, the numerical measurement $m(o)$ is some affine function of the true magnitude x. When equation (b) applies, the measurement operation is called *interval scaling*, or measurement at the *interval-scale level*. An interval scale is unique up to a positive affine transformation (with two degrees of freedom).

When measurement is at the interval scale level, any of the ordinary operations of arithmetic can be applied to the differences between numerical measurements, and the results can be interpreted as statements about *magnitudes* of the underlying property. The important part is the interpretation of a numerical result as a *quantitative statement* about the property shown by the objects. This is not possible for ordinal-scale numbers but can be done for differences between interval-scale numbers. Interval scaling is the best that can be done in most scientific work, and even this level of measurement is all too rare in social sciences. However, especially in the physical sciences, it is sometimes possible to find measurement operations making the statement of equation (c) true:

$$\begin{cases} m(o_1) \neq m(o_2) \ only \ if \ \ t(o_1) \neq t(o_2) \\ m(o_1) > m(o_2) \ only \ if \ \ t(o_1) > t(o_2) \\ t(o) = x \ \ iff \ \ m(o) = ax, where \ a \in R^+ \end{cases}$$

(c)

When the measurement operation defines a function such that the statement contained in equation (c) is true, then measurement is said to be at the *ratio-scale level*. For such scales, ratios of numerical measurements are unique and can be interpreted directly as ratios of magnitudes of objects. A ratio scale is unique up to a linear transformation; in this case, the ratio between differences is unique (with only one degree of liberty).

Of course, the fewer the admissible transformations of a scale, the more meaningful the statements involving that scale. From this point of view, it is better to have a ratio scale than an interval scale, and it is better to have an interval scale than an ordinal scale.

The table below presents in a comparative manner the main characteristics of the measurement scales.

Type of Scale	Characteristics			
	Allows classification	Allows ordering	Equal intervals	Unique origin
Nominal	Yes	No	No	No
Ordinal	Yes	Yes	No	No
Interval	Yes	Yes	Yes	No
Ratio	Yes	Yes	Yes	Yes

HANDBOOK ON CONSTRUCTING COMPOSITE INDICATORS: METHODOLOGY AND USER GUIDE – ISBN 978-92-64-04345-9 - © OECD 2008

STEP 3. IMPUTATION OF MISSING DATA

The literature on the analysis of missing data is extensive and in rapid development. This section covers the main methods. More comprehensive surveys can be found in Little & Rubin (2002), Little (1997) and Little & Schenker (1994).

3.1. Single imputation

Imputations are means or draws from a predictive distribution of missing values. The predictive distribution must be generated by employing the observed data either through implicit or explicit modelling:

Implicit modelling. The focus is on an algorithm, with implicit underlying assumptions which need to be verified in terms of whether they are reasonable and fit for the issue under consideration. The danger of this type of modelling of missing data is the tendency to consider the resulting data set as complete, forgetting that an imputation has been carried out. Implicit modelling includes:

- **Hot deck imputation.** Filling in blanks cells with individual data, drawn from "similar" responding units. For example, missing values for individual income may be replaced with the income of another respondent with similar characteristics, *e.g.* age, sex, race, place of residence, family relationships, job, etc.

- **Substitution.** Replacing non-responding units with unselected units in the sample. For example, if a household cannot be contacted, then a previously non-selected household in the same housing block is selected.

- **Cold deck imputation.** Replacing the missing value with a value from an external source, *e.g.* from a previous realisation of the same survey.

Explicit modelling. The predictive distribution is based on a formal statistical model where the assumptions are made explicitly, as in the following:

- **Unconditional mean/median/mode imputation.** The sample mean (median, mode) of the recorded values for the given individual indicator replaces the missing values.

- **Regression imputation**. Missing values are substituted by the predicted values obtained from regression. The dependent variable of the regression is the individual indicator hosting the missing value, and the regressor(s) is (are) the individual indicator(s), showing a strong relationship with the dependent variable, *i.e.* usually a high degree of correlation.

- **Expectation Maximisation (EM) imputation.** This model focuses on the interdependence between model parameters and the missing values. The missing values are substituted by estimates obtained through an iterative process. First, the missing values are predicted based on initial estimates of the model parameter values. These predictions are then used to update the parameter values, and the process is repeated. The sequence of parameters converges to maximum-likelihood estimates, and the time to convergence depends on the proportion of missing data and the flatness of the likelihood function.

If simplicity is its main appeal, an important limitation of the single imputation method is its systematic underestimation of the variance of the estimates (with some exceptions for the EM method, where the bias depends on the algorithm used to estimate the variance). Therefore, this method does not fully assess the implications of imputation or the robustness of the composite index derived from the imputed data set.

3.2. Unconditional mean imputation

Let X_q be the random variable associated with the individual indicator q, with $q=1,...,Q$, and $x_{q,c}$ the observed value of X_q for country c, with $c=1,..,M$. Let m_q be the number of recorded or non-missing values on X_q, and $M\text{-}m_q$ the number of missing values. The unconditional mean is then given by:

$$\bar{x}_q = \frac{1}{m_q} \sum_{recorded} x_{q,c} \tag{1}$$

Similarly, the median[8] and the mode[9] of the distribution could be calculated on the available sample and to substitute missing values.[10] By "filling in" blank spaces with the sample mean, the imputed value becomes a biased estimator of the population mean, even in the case of MCAR mechanisms, and the sample variance underestimates true variance, thus underestimating the uncertainty in the composite due to the imputation.

3.3. Regression imputation

Suppose a set of $h\text{-}1<Q$ fully observed individual indicators $(x_1,...,x_{h-1})$ and an individual indicator x_h observed for r countries, but missing for the remaining $M\text{-}r$ countries. Regression imputation computes the regression of x_h on $(x_1,...,x_{h-1})$ using r complete observations, and imputes the missing values as a prediction from the regression:[11]

$$\hat{x}_{ih} = \hat{\beta}_0 + \sum_{j=1}^{h-1} \hat{\beta}_j x_{ij} \quad i=1,..,M-r \tag{2}$$

In general, the strategy to define the 'best' regression is a two-step procedure. First, all different subsets of predictors are adopted in a multiple regression manner. Then the best subset(s) is determined using the following criteria:[12]

- the value of the explanation rate R^2;

- the value of the residual mean square RMS;

- the value of Mallows' C_k;

- stepwise regression.

A variation of the regression approach is the stochastic regression approach, which imputes a conditional draw instead of the conditional mean:

$$\hat{x}_{ih} = \hat{\beta}_0 + \sum_{j=1}^{h-1} \hat{\beta}_j x_{ij} + \varepsilon_i \quad i = 1,..,M-r \tag{3}$$

where, ε_i is a random variable $N(0,\hat{\sigma}^2)$ and $\hat{\sigma}^2$ is the residual variance from the regression of x_h on $(x_1,...,x_{h-1})$, based on the r complete cases.

A key problem in both approaches is again the underestimation of the standard errors, although stochastic regression lessens the distortions. Hence, the inference based on the entire data set, including the imputed data, does not fully count for imputation uncertainty. The result is that *p-values* of tests are too small and confidence intervals too narrow. Replication methods and multiple imputation could correct the loss of precision of simple imputation.

In the case that the variable with missing observations is categorical, regression imputation is still possible but adjustment is required, using, for example, rounding of the predictions or a logistic, ordinal or multinomial logistic regression model. For nominal variables, frequency statistics such as the mode or hot- and cold-deck imputation methods might be more appropriate.

3.4. Expected maximisation imputation

Suppose that X denotes the matrix of data. In the likelihood-based estimation, the data is assumed to be generated by a model, described by a probability or density function $f(X|\theta)$, where θ is the unknown parameter vector lying in the parameter space Ω_θ (e.g. the real line for means, the positive real line for variances and the interval $[0,1]$ for probabilities). The probability function captures the relationship between the dataset and the parameter of the model, and describes the probability of observing a data set for a given $\theta \in \Omega_\theta$. Since θ is unknown, while the dataset is known, it makes sense to reverse the argument, and look for the probability, or the likelihood, of observing a certain θ, given X. Therefore, given X, the likelihood function $L(\theta|X)$ is any function of $\theta \in \Omega_\theta$ proportional to $f(X|\theta)$:

$$L(\theta|X) = k(X)f(X|\theta) \tag{4}$$

where $k(X) > 0$ is a function of X and not of θ. The log-likelihood is then the natural logarithm of the likelihood function. For M independent and identically distributed observations $X = (x_1,...,x_M)^T$ from a normal population with mean μ and variance σ^2, the joint density is

$$f(X|\mu,\sigma^2) = (2\pi\sigma^2)^{-M/2} \exp\left(-\frac{1}{2}\sum_{c=1}^{M} \frac{(x_c-\mu)^2}{\sigma^2}\right) \tag{5}$$

For a given sample X the log-likelihood is (ignoring additive constants of function $f(\cdot)$) a function of (μ, σ^2):

$$l(\mu, \sigma^2 \mid X) = \ln[L(\mu, \sigma^2 \mid X)] = \ln[k(X)f(X \mid \mu, \sigma^2)]$$
$$= \ln k(X) - \frac{M}{2}\ln\sigma^2 - \frac{1}{2}\sum_{c=1}^{M}\frac{(x_c - \mu)^2}{\sigma^2} \qquad (6)$$

Maximising the likelihood function corresponds to the question of which value of $\theta \in \Omega_\theta$ is best supported by a given sampling realisation X. This implies solving the likelihood equation:

$$D_l(\theta \mid X_{obs}) \equiv \frac{\partial \ln L(\theta \mid X_{obs})}{\partial \theta} = 0 \qquad (7)$$

When a closed-form solution of equation (7) cannot be found, iterative methods can be applied. The Expected maximisation (EM) algorithm is one of these iterative methods.[13] The issue is that X contains both observable and missing values, *i.e.* $X = (X_{obs}, X_{mis})$. Thus both the unknown parameters and the unknown observations of the model have to be found.

Assuming that missing data are MAR or MCAR[14], the EM consists of two components: the expectation (E) and maximisation (M) steps. Each step is completed once within each algorithm cycle. Cycles are repeated until a suitable convergence criterion is satisfied. The procedure is as follows. First (M), the parameter vector θ is estimated by applying maximum likelihood as if there were no missing data, and second (E), the expected values of the missing variables are calculated, given the estimate of θ obtained in the M-step. This procedure is repeated until convergence (absence of changes in estimates and in the variance-covariance matrix). Effectively, this process maximises the expectation of the complete data log-likelihood in each cycle, conditional on the observed data and parameter vector. To start the process, however, an initial estimate of the missing data is needed. This is obtained by running the first M-step on the non-missing observations only and then predicting the missing variables by using the estimate on θ.

The advantage of the EM is its broadness. It can be used for a broad range of problems, *e.g.* variance component estimation or factor analysis. An EM algorithm is also often easy to construct conceptually and practically. Besides, each step has a statistical interpretation and convergence is reliable. The main drawback, however, is that convergence may be very slow when a large proportion of information is missing (if there were no missing information, convergence would be immediate). The user should also be careful that the maximum found is indeed a global maximum and not local. To test this, different initial starting values for θ can be used.

3.5. Multiple imputation

Multiple imputation (MI) is a general approach that does not require a specification of parameterised likelihood for all data (Figure 10). The imputation of missing data is performed with a random process that reflects uncertainty. Imputation is done N times, to create N "complete" datasets. The parameters of interest are estimated on each data set, together with their standard errors. Average (mean or median) estimates are combined using the N sets and between-and within-imputation variance is calculated.

HANDBOOK ON CONSTRUCTING COMPOSITE INDICATORS: METHODOLOGY AND USER GUIDE – ISBN 978-92-64-04345-9 – © OECD 2008

Figure 10. Logic of multiple imputation

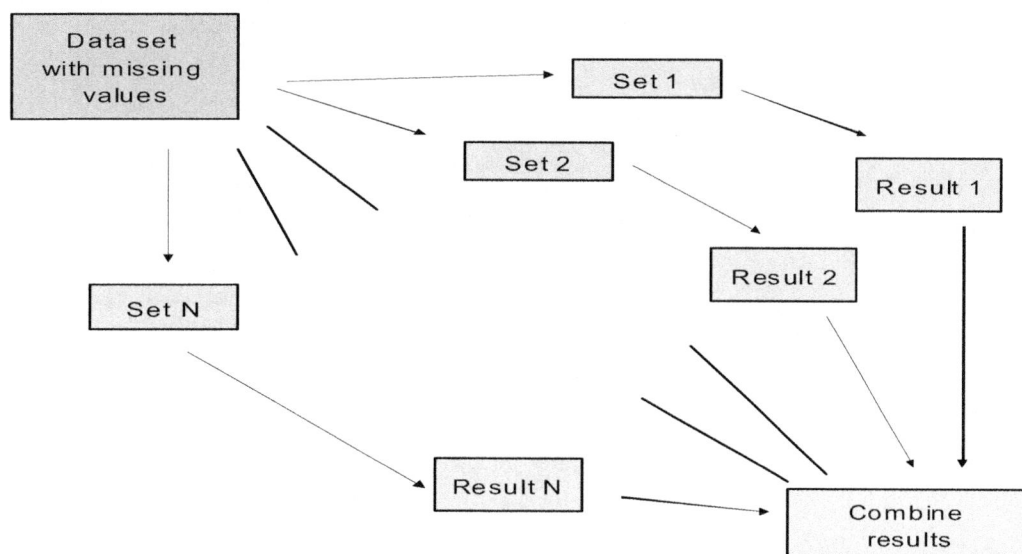

Any "proper" imputation method can be used in multiple imputation. For example, regression imputation could be used repeatedly, drawing N values of the regression parameters using the variance matrix of estimated coefficients. However, one of the most general models is the *Markov Chain Monte Carlo* (MCMC) method. MCMC is a sequence of random variables in which the distribution of the actual element depends on the value of the previous one. It assumes that data are drawn from a multivariate normal distribution and requires MAR or MCAR assumptions.

The theory of MCMC is most easily understood using Bayesian methodology (Figure 11). The observed data are denoted Xobs, and the complete data set, X=(Xobs, Xmis), where X_{mis} is to be filled in via multiple imputation. If the distribution of X_{mis}, with parameter vector θ, were known, then X_{mis} could be imputed by drawing from the conditional distribution $f(X_{mis}|X_{obs}, \theta)$. However, since θ is unknown, it shall be estimated from the data, yielding $\hat{\theta}$, and using the distribution $f(X_{mis}|X_{obs}\hat{\theta})$. Since $\hat{\theta}$ is itself a random variable, we must also take its variability into account in drawing imputations.

The missing-data generating process may also depend on additional parameters φ, but if φ and θ are independent, the process is called ignorable and the analyst may concentrate on modelling the missing data given the observed data and θ. If the two processes are not independent, then a non-ignorable missing-data generating process pertains, which cannot be solved adequately without making assumptions on the functional form of the interdependency.

Figure 11.   Markov Chain Monte Carlo imputation method

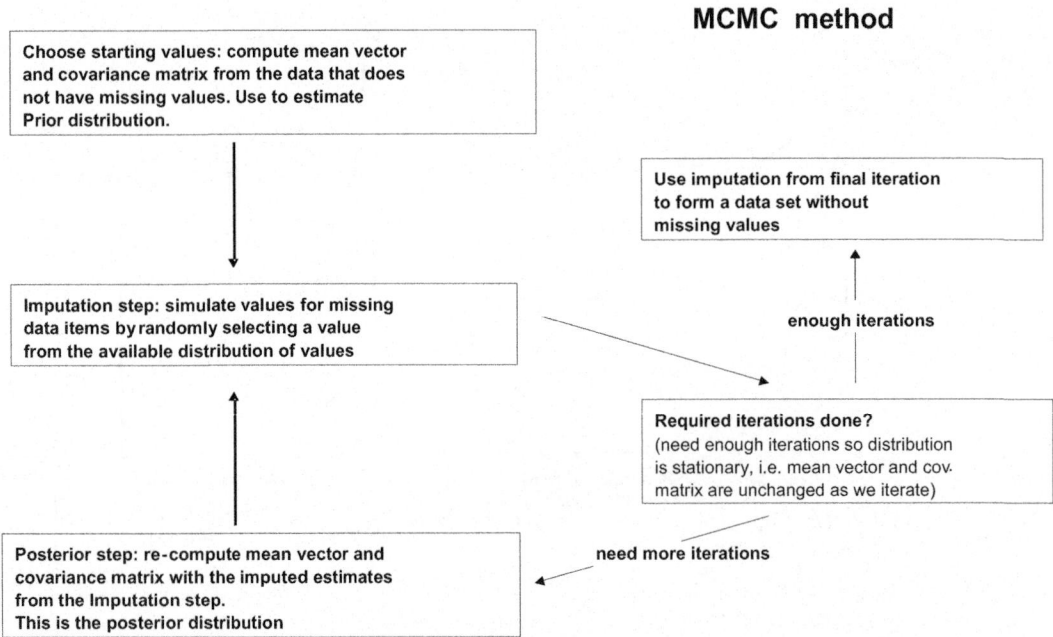

Source: Rearranged from Chantala & Suchindran (2003)

In Bayesian terms, θ is a random variable, the distribution of which depends on the data. The first step in its estimation is to obtain the posterior distribution of θ from the data. Usually this posterior is approximated by a normal distribution. After formulating the posterior distribution of θ, the following imputation algorithm can be used:

- Draw θ^* from the posterior distribution of θ, $f(\theta|Y, X_{obs})$, where Y denotes exogenous variables that may influence θ.

- Draw X_{mis} from $f(X_{mis}|Y, X_{obs}, \theta^*)$

- Use the completed data X and the model to estimate the parameter of interest (*e.g.* the mean) β^* and its variance $V(\beta^*)$ (within-imputation variance).

These steps are repeated independently N times, resulting in β_n^*, $V(\beta_n^*)$, $n=1,...,N$. Finally, the N imputations are combined. A possible *combination* is the mean of all individual estimates (but the median can also be used):

$$\beta^* = \frac{1}{N}\sum_{n=1}^{N}\beta_n^* \tag{8}$$

HANDBOOK ON CONSTRUCTING COMPOSITE INDICATORS: METHODOLOGY AND USER GUIDE – ISBN 978-92-64-04345-9 – © OECD 2008

This *combination* will be the value that fills in the blank space in the data set. The total variance is obtained as a weighted sum of the *within-imputation* variance and the *between-imputation* variance:

$$V^* = \overline{V} + \frac{N+1}{N}B \tag{9}$$

where the mean of the *within-imputation* variances is

$$\overline{V} = \frac{1}{N}\sum_{n=1}^{N}V\left(\beta_n^*\right) \tag{10}$$

and the *between-imputation* variance is given by

$$B = \frac{1}{N-1}\sum_{n=1}^{N}\left(\beta_n^* - \beta^*\right)\left(\beta_n^* - \beta^*\right)' \tag{11}$$

Confidence intervals are obtained by taking the overall estimate plus or minus a multiple of standard error, where that number is a quantile of Student's t-distribution with degrees of freedom:

$$df = (N-1)\left(1+\frac{1}{r}\right)^2 \tag{12}$$

where r is the *between-to-within* ratio.

$$r = \left(1+\frac{1}{N}\right)\frac{B}{\overline{V}} \tag{13}$$

Based on these variances, approximate 95% confidence intervals can be calculated.

The *Multiple Imputation* method imputes several values (N) for each missing value (from the predictive distribution of the missing data), to represent the uncertainty about which values to impute. The N versions of completed data sets are analysed by standard complete data methods and the results combined using simple rules to yield single combined estimates (*e.g.* MSE, regression coefficients), standard errors and p-values, which formally incorporate missing data uncertainty. The pooling of the results of the analyses performed on the multiple imputed data sets implies that the resulting point estimates are averaged over the N completed sample points, and the resulting standard errors and p-values are adjusted according to the variance of the corresponding N completed sample point estimates. Thus, the "*between-imputation variance*" provides a measure of the extra inferential uncertainty due to missing data which is not reflected in single imputation).

Box 4. Rules of thumb in choosing the imputation method

The main question a modeler has to face when dealing with imputation is which method he/she has to use to fill in empty data spaces. To the best of our knowledge there is no definitive answer to this question but a number of rules of thumb (and lot of common sense). The choice principally depends on the dataset available (*e.g.* data expressed on a continuous scale or ordinal data where methods like MCMC cannot be used), the number of missing data as compared to the dimension of the dataset (few missing data in a large dataset do not probably require sophisticated imputation methods), and the identity of the country and the indicator for which the data is missing.

Therefore there is not "a" method we advise to use but the method should be fitted to the characteristics of the missing information.

A useful (but time consuming) exercise is the application of the "in sample/out of sample" logic in order to find the suitable imputation method. This consists in taking the complete part of the dataset, eliminate some of the data (for the same countries and in the same proportion of the complete dataset), use several imputation methods and evaluate the performance of each of them. The goodness of imputation can be checked using several instruments: the correlation coefficient (R) and its square, the coefficient of determination (R^2)

$$ R^2 = \left[\frac{1}{N} \frac{\sum_{i=1}^{N} \left[(P_i - \overline{P})(O_i - \overline{O}) \right]}{\sigma_P \sigma_O} \right]^2 $$

With N the number of imputations, O_i the observed data point (the one that has been excluded to do the imputation), P_i the imputed data point and $\overline{O}(\overline{P})$ the average of the observed (imputed) data, $\sigma_O(\sigma_P)$ the standard deviation of the observed (imputed) data. As noticed by Willmott et al. (1985) the value of R^2 could be unrelated to the sizes of the difference between the predicted and the observed values. To solve the problem Willmott (1982) developed an index of agreement:

$$ d = 1 - \left[\frac{\sum_{i=1}^{N} (P_i - O_i)^k}{\sum_{i=1}^{N} \left[(|P_i - \overline{O}| + |O_i - \overline{O}|)^k \right]} \right]^2 \qquad \text{with k equal to 1 or 2.} $$

Another measure of the average error of the model is the root mean square error and the mean absolute error:

$$ RMSE = \left(\frac{1}{N} \sum_{i=1}^{N} (P_i - O_i)^2 \right)^{1/2} $$

$$ MAE = \frac{1}{N} \sum_{i=1}^{N} |P_i - O_i| $$

Finally a complementary measure of accuracy of imputation is the use of bootstrapping methods to generate samples of imputed values. For each sample the performance analysis is performed. Standard errors are then calculated as a standard deviation of the performance analysis.

HANDBOOK ON CONSTRUCTING COMPOSITE INDICATORS: METHODOLOGY AND USER GUIDE – ISBN 978-92-64-04345-9 - © OECD 2008

STEP 4. MULTIVARIATE ANALYSIS

Multivariate data analysis techniques which have found use in the construction or analysis of composite indicators are described in this section. For further details refer to, *e.g.*, Hair *et al.*, (2006). The majority of methods in this section are thought for data expressed in an interval or ratio scale, although some of the methods have been used with ordinal data (for example principal components and factor analysis, see Vermunt & Magidson 2005).

4.1. Principal components analysis

The objective is to explain the variance of the observed data through a few linear combinations of the original data. [15] Even though there are Q variables, $x_1, x_2, ... x_Q$, much of the data's variation can often be accounted for by a small number of variables – principal components, or linear relations of the original data, $Z_1, Z_2, ... Z_Q$, that are uncorrelated. At this point there are still Q principal components, *i.e.*, as many as there are variables. The next step is to select the first, *e.g.*, P<Q principal components that preserve a "high" amount of the cumulative variance of the original data.

$$Z_1 = a_{11}x_1 + a_{12}x_2 + ... + a_{1Q}x_Q$$
$$Z_2 = a_{21}x_1 + a_{22}x_2 + ... + a_{2Q}x_Q \qquad (14)$$
$$...$$
$$Z_Q = a_{Q1}x_1 + a_{Q2}x_2 + ... + a_{QQ}x_Q$$

A lack of correlation in the principal components is a useful property. It indicates that the principal components are measuring different "statistical dimensions" in the data. When the objective of the analysis is to present a huge data set using a few variables, some degree of economy can be achieved by applying Principal Components Analysis (PCA) if the variation in the Q original x variables can be accounted for by a small number of Z variables. It must be stressed that PCA cannot always reduce a large number of original variables to a small number of transformed variables. Indeed, if the original variables are uncorrelated, then the analysis is of no value. On the other hand, a significant reduction can be obtained when the original variables are highly correlated – positively or negatively.

The weights a_{ij} (also called component or factor loadings) applied to the variables x_j in equation (14) are chosen so that the principal components Z_i satisfy the following conditions:

(i)   they are uncorrelated (orthogonal);

(ii) the first principal component accounts for the maximum possible proportion of the variance of the set of x s, the second principal component accounts for the maximum of the remaining variance, and so on until the last of the principal components absorbs all the remaining variance not accounted for by the preceding components, and [16]

$$a_{i1}^2 + a_{i2}^2 + ... + a_{iQ}^2 = 1, i = 1, 2, ..., Q$$

where a_{ij} are the factor loadings, $x_1, x_2, \ldots x_Q$ are the variables (indicators), and Q the number of variables.

PCA involves finding the *eigenvalues* λ_j, $j=1,\ldots,Q$, of the sample covariance matrix CM,

$$CM = \begin{bmatrix} cm_{11}\ cm_{12}\ \ldots cm_{1Q} \\ cm_{21}\ cm_{22}\ \ldots cm_{2Q} \\ \ldots \\ cm_{Q1}\ cm_{Q2}\ \ldots cm_{QQ} \end{bmatrix} \tag{15}$$

where the diagonal element cm_{ii} is the variance of x_i and cm_{ij} is the covariance of variables x_i and x_j. The eigenvalues of the matrix CM are the variances of the principal components and can be found by solving the characteristic equation $\left| CM - \lambda I \right| = 0$, where I is the identity matrix with the same order as CM and λ is the vector of eigenvalues. This is possible, however, only if Q is small. If there are too many variables, solving for λ is non-trivial and other methods exist (see *e.g.* Gentle *et al.*, 2004; Golub & van der Vorst, 2000).[17] There are Q eigenvalues, some of which may be negligible. Negative eigenvalues are not possible for a covariance matrix. An important property of the eigenvalues is that they add up to the sum of the diagonal elements of CM. That is, the sum of the variances of the principal components is equal to the sum of the variances of the original variables:

$$\lambda_1 + \lambda_2 + \ldots + \lambda_Q = cm_{11} + cm_{22} + \ldots + cm_{QQ} \tag{16}$$

In order to prevent one variable having an undue influence on the principal components, it is common to standardise the variables $- x\,s -$ to have zero means and unit variances at the start of the analysis. The co-variance matrix CM then takes the form of the correlation matrix (Table 6). In the TAI example, the highest correlation is found between the individual indicators *electricity* and *Internet*, with a coefficient of 0.84.

Table 6. Correlation matrix for individual TAI indicators

	PATENTS	ROYALTIES	INTERNET	EXPORTS	TELEPHONE	ELECTRICITY	SCHOOLING	UNIVERSITY
PATENTS	1.00	0.13	-0.09	**0.45**	0.28	0.03	0.22	0.08
ROYALTIES		1.00	**0.46**	0.25	**0.56**	0.32	0.30	0.06
INTERNET			1.00	**-0.45**	**0.56**	**0.84**	**0.63**	0.27
EXPORTS				1.00	0.00	-0.36	-0.35	-0.03
TELEPHONE					1.00	**0.64**	0.30	0.33
ELECTRICITY						1.00	**0.65**	0.26
SCHOOLING							1.00	0.08
UNIVERSITY								1.00

Note: n=23. Marked correlations are statistically significant at p < 0.05.

HANDBOOK ON CONSTRUCTING COMPOSITE INDICATORS: METHODOLOGY AND USER GUIDE – ISBN 978-92-64-04345-9 – © OECD 2008

Table 7 gives the eigenvalues of the correlation matrix of the eight individual indicators (standardised values) that compose TAI. Note that the sum of the eigenvalues is equal to the number of individual indicators ($Q = 8$). Figure 12 (left graph) is a graphical presentation of the eigenvalues in descending order. Given that the correlation matrix rather than the covariance matrix is used in the PCA, all eight individual indicators are assigned equal weights in forming the principal components (Chatfield & Collins, 1980). The first principal component explains the maximum variance in all the individual indicators (eigenvalue of 3.3). The second principal component explains the maximum amount of the remaining variance, with a variance of 1.7. The third and fourth principal components have an eigenvalue close to 1. The last four principal components explain the remaining 12.8% of the variance in the data set.

Table 7.   Eigenvalues of individual TAI indicators

PC	Eigenvalue	% of variance	Cumulative %
1	3.3	41.9	41.9
2	1.7	21.8	63.7
3	1.0	12.3	76.0
4	0.9	11.1	87.2
5	0.5	6.0	93.2
6	0.3	3.7	96.9
7	0.2	2.2	99.1
8	0.1	0.9	100.0

A drawback of the conventional PCA is that it does not allow for inference on the properties of the general population. Traditionally, drawing such inferences requires certain distributional assumptions to be made regarding the population characteristics, which PCA techniques are not based on. There are several assumptions made in the application of PCA/FA which are discussed in Box 5.

These assumptions are referred to in almost all textbooks, yet are often neglected in the development of composite indicators.

Furthermore, in a traditional PCA framework there is no estimation of the statistical precision of the results, which is essential for relatively small sample sizes, as in the present example of the TAI. The bootstrap method has therefore been utilised in conjunction with PCA to make inferences about the population (Efron & Tibshirani, 1991, 1993). Bootstrap refers to the process of randomly re-sampling the original data set to generate new data sets. Estimates of the relevant statistics are made for each bootstrap sample. A very large number of bootstrap samples will give satisfactory results but the computation may be cumbersome. Various values have been suggested, ranging from 25 (Efron & Tibshirani, 1991) to as high as 1000 (Efron, 1987).

Box 5. Assumptions in principal component analysis

Sufficient number of cases. The question of how many cases (or countries) are necessary to perform PCA/FA has no scientific answer and methodologists' opinions differ. Alternative arbitrary rules of thumb in descending order of popularity include the following:

Rule of 10. There should be at least 10 cases for each variable.

3:1 ratio. The cases-to-variables ratio should be no lower than 3.

5:1 ratio. The cases-to-variables ratio should be no lower than 5 (Bryant & Yarnold, 1995; Nunnaly, 1978, Gorsuch, 1983).

Rule of 100: The number of cases should be the larger of "5 × number of variables" and 100 (Hatcher, 1994).

Rule of 150: Hutcheson & Sofroniou (1999) recommend at least 150 - 300 cases (closer to 150 when there are a few highly correlated variables).

Rule of 200. There should be at least 200 cases, regardless of the cases-to-variables ratio (Gorsuch, 1983).

Significance rule. There should be 51 more cases than the number of variables, to support chi-square testing (Lawley & Maxwell, 1971)

These rules are not mutually exclusive. Bryant & Yarnold (1995), for instance, endorse both the cases-to-variables ratio and the Rule of 200. In the TAI example, there are 23:8 cases-to-variables, therefore the first and (to a large extent) the second rule are satisfied.

No bias in selecting individual indicators. The exclusion of relevant individual indicators and the inclusion of irrelevant individual indicators in the correlation matrix being factored will affect, often substantially, the factors which are uncovered. Although social scientists may be attracted to factor analysis as a way of exploring data whose structure is unknown, knowing the factorial structure in advance helps select the individual indicators to be included and yields the best analysis of factors. This dilemma creates a chicken-and-egg problem. Note that this is not just a matter of including all relevant individual indicators. Also, if individual indicators are deleted arbitrarily in order to obtain a "cleaner" factorial solution, erroneous conclusions about the factor structure will result (Kim & Mueller, 1978).

No outliers. As with most techniques, the presence of outliers can affect interpretations arising from PCA/FA. Mahalanobis distance may be used to identify cases, which are multivariate outliers and remove them prior to the analysis. Alternatively, a dummy variable, set to 1, can be created for cases with high Mahalanobis distance, then regressed on all other variables. If this regression is non-significant (or simply has a low R-squared for large samples), then the outliers are judged to be at random and there is less danger in retaining them. The ratio of the regression coefficients indicates which variables are most associated with the outlier cases.

Assumption of interval data. Kim & Mueller (1978) note that ordinal data may be used if it is thought that the assignment of ordinal categories to the data will not seriously distort the underlying metric scaling. Likewise, the use of dichotomous data is allowed if the underlying metric correlation between the variables is thought to be moderate (.7) or lower. The result of using ordinal data is that the factors may be much harder to interpret. Note that categorical variables with similar splits will necessarily tend to correlate with each other, regardless of their content (see Gorsuch, 1983). This is particularly apt to occur when dichotomies are used. The correlation will reflect similarity of "difficulty" for items in a testing context; hence such correlated variables are called *difficulty factors*. The researcher should examine the factor loadings of categorical variables with care, in order to assess whether common loading reflects a difficulty factor or a substantive correlation.

Linearity. Principal component factor analysis (PFA), which is the most common variant of FA, is a linear procedure. As with multiple linear regression, non-linear transformation of selected variables may be a pre-processing step, but is not common. The smaller the sample size, the more important it is to screen data for linearity.

HANDBOOK ON CONSTRUCTING COMPOSITE INDICATORS: METHODOLOGY AND USER GUIDE – ISBN 978-92-64-04345-9 – © OECD 2008

Multivariate normality of data is required for related significance tests. PCA and PFA have no distributional assumptions. Note, however, that a variant of factor analysis, maximum likelihood factor analysis, does assume multivariate normality. The smaller the sample size, the more important it is to screen data for normality. Moreover, as factor analysis is based on correlation (or sometimes covariance), both correlation and covariance will be attenuated when variables come from different underlying distributions (*e.g.*, a normal vs. a bimodal variable will correlate less than 1.0 even when both series are perfectly co-ordered).

Underlying dimensions shared by clusters of individual indicators are assumed. If this assumption is not met, the "garbage in, garbage out" principle applies. Factor analysis cannot create valid dimensions (factors) if none exist in the input data. In such cases, factors generated by the factor analysis algorithm will not be comprehensible. Likewise, the inclusion of multiple definitionally-similar individual indicators representing essentially the same data will lead to tautological results.

Strong intercorrelations are not mathematically required, but applying factor analysis to a correlation matrix with only low intercorrelations will require nearly as many factors as there are original variables, thereby defeating the data reduction purposes of factor analysis. On the other hand, too high intercorrelations may indicate a multi-collinearity problem and collinear terms should be combined or otherwise eliminated prior to factor analysis. Notice also that PCA and Factor analysis (as well as Cronbach's alpha) assume **uncorrelated measurement errors.**

(a) The Kaiser-Meyer-Olkin (KMO) measure of sampling adequacy is a statistic for comparing the magnitudes of the observed correlation coefficients to the magnitudes of the partial correlation coefficients. The concept is that the partial correlations should not be very large if distinct factors are expected to emerge from factor analysis (Hutcheson & Sofroniou, 1999). A KMO statistic is computed for each individual indicator, and their sum is the KMO overall statistic. KMO varies from 0 to 1.0. A KMO overall should be .60 or higher to proceed with factor analysis (Kaiser & Rice, 1974), though realistically it should exceed 0.80 if the results of the principal components analysis are to be reliable. If not, it is advisable to drop the individual indicators with the lowest individual KMO statistic values, until KMO overall rises above .60.

(b) Variance-inflation factor (VIF) is simply the reciprocal of tolerance. A VIF value greater than 4.0 is an arbitrary but common cut-off criterion for suggesting that there is a multi-collinearity problem. Some researchers use the more lenient cut-off VIF value of 5.0.

(c) The Bartlett's test of sphericity is used to test the null hypothesis that the individual indicators in a correlation matrix are uncorrelated, *i.e.* that the correlation matrix is an identity matrix. The statistic is based on a chi-squared transformation of the determinant of the correlation matrix. However, as Bartlett's test is highly sensitive to sample size (Knapp & Swoyer, 1967), Tabachnick & Fidell (1989) suggest implementing it with the KMO measure.

An important issue, however, is whether the TAI data set for the 23 countries can be viewed as a "random" sample of the entire population, as required by the bootstrap procedures (Efron, 1987; Efron & Tibshirani, 1993). Several points can be made regarding the issues of randomness and representativeness of the data. First, it is often difficult to obtain complete information for a data set in the social sciences, as controlled experiments are not always possible, unlike in natural sciences. As Efron and Tibshirani (1993) state that, 'in practice the selection process is seldom this neat […], but the conceptual framework of random sampling is still useful for understanding statistical inferences.' Second, the countries included in the restricted set show no apparent pattern as to whether or not they are predominately developed or developing countries. In addition, the countries are of varying sizes and span all the major continents of the world, ensuring a wide representation of the global state of technological development. Consequently, the restricted set could be considered representative of the total population. A third point on data quality is that a certain amount of measurement error is likely to pertain. While such measurement error can only be controlled at the data collection stage, rather than at the analytical stage, it is argued that the data represent the best estimates currently available (UN, 2001).

Figure 12 (right graph) demonstrates graphically the relationship between the eigenvalues from the deterministic PCA, their bootstrapped confidence intervals (5th and 95th percentiles) and the ranked principal components. These confidence intervals make it possible to generalise the conclusions concerning the small set of the individual indicators (23 countries) to the entire population (*e.g.* of 72 countries or even more generally), rather than confining the conclusions only to the sample set under analysis. Bootstrapping was performed for 1 000 sample sets of size 23 (random sampling with replacement). It is shown that the values of the eigenvalues drop sharply at the beginning and then gradually approach zero after a certain point.

Figure 12. Eigenvalues for individual TAI numbers

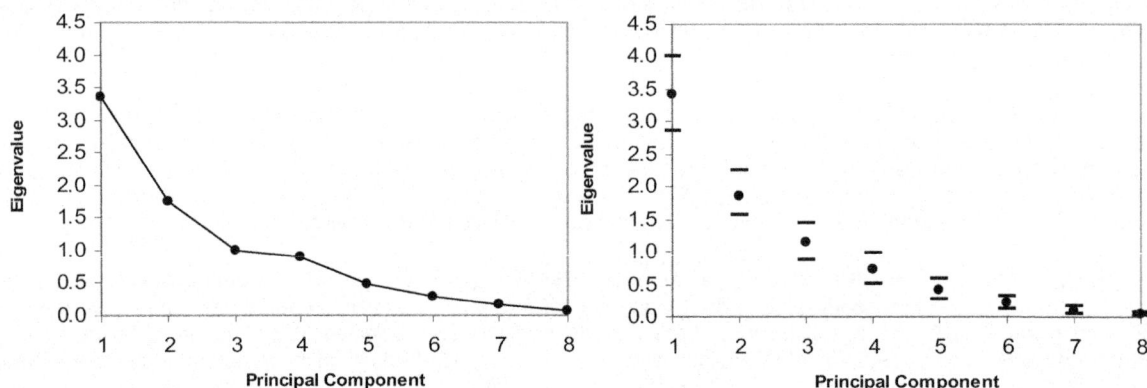

Note: (left graph) Scree plot: Eigenvalues from traditional Principal Components Analysis

(right graph) Bootstrapped eigenvalues based on 1000 samples randomly selected with replacement

The correlation coefficients between the principal components Z and the variables x are called *component loadings*, $r(Z_j, x_i)$. In the case of uncorrelated variables x, the loadings are equal to the weights a_{ij} given in equation (14). Analogously to Pearson's r, the squared loading is the percentage of variance in that variable explained by the principal component. The *component scores* are the scores of each case (each country in our example) on each principal component. The component score for a given case for a principal component is calculated by taking the case's standardised value on each variable, multiplying by the corresponding loading of the variable for the given principal component factor, and summing these products.

Table 8 presents the component loadings for the individual TAI indicators. High and moderate loadings (>0.50) indicate how the individual indicators are related to the principal components. It can be seen that with the exception of *patents* and *royalties*, all the other individual indicators are entirely accounted for by one principal component alone and that the high and moderate loadings are all found in the first four principal components. An undesirable property of these components is that two individual indicators are related strongly to two principal components.

HANDBOOK ON CONSTRUCTING COMPOSITE INDICATORS: METHODOLOGY AND USER GUIDE – ISBN 978-92-64-04345-9 – © OECD 2008

Table 8. Component loadings for individual TAI indicators

	Principal components							
	1	2	3	4	5	6	7	8
PATENTS	-0.11	**-0.75**	0.13	**0.60**	-0.10	-0.12	-0.17	0.05
ROYALTIES	**-0.56**	-0.48	0.22	**-0.54**	0.27	-0.17	-0.04	0.10
INTERNET	**-0.92**	0.21	0.02	-0.10	0.04	0.11	-0.27	-0.13
EXPORTS	0.35	**-0.85**	0.01	-0.13	0.11	0.35	0.06	-0.08
TELEPHONES	**-0.76**	-0.39	-0.16	-0.16	-0.41	-0.16	0.16	-0.09
ELECTRICITY	**-0.91**	0.13	0.01	0.07	-0.19	0.30	0.04	0.16
SCHOOLING	**-0.74**	0.11	0.37	0.39	0.33	-0.02	0.20	-0.07
UNIVERSITY	-0.36	-0.12	**-0.87**	0.15	0.26	-0.03	0.02	0.02

Note: Extraction method: PCA. Loadings greater than 0.5 (absolute values) are highlighted, n=23 countries.

The question of how many principal components should be retained in the analysis without losing too much information and of how the interpretation of the components might be improved are addressed in the following section on Factor Analysis.

4.2. Factor analysis

Factor analysis (FA) is similar to PCA. It aims to describe a set of Q variables $x_1, x_2,..., x_Q$ in terms of a smaller number of m factors and to highlight the relationship between these variables. However, while PCA is based simply on linear data combinations, FA is based on a rather special model. Contrary to the PCA, the FA model assumes that the data is based on the underlying factors of the model, and that the data variance can be decomposed into that accounted for by common and unique factors. The model is given by:

$$x_1 = \alpha_{11}F_1 + \alpha_{12}F_2 +...+ \alpha_{1m}F_m + e_1$$
$$x_2 = \alpha_{21}F_1 + \alpha_{22}F_2 +...+ \alpha_{2m}F_m + e_2 \qquad (17)$$
$$...$$
$$x_Q = \alpha_{Q1}F_1 + \alpha_{Q2}F_2 +...+ \alpha_{Qm}F_m + e_Q$$

where x_i $(i=1,...,Q)$ represents the original variables but standardized with zero mean and unit variance; $\alpha_{i1}, \alpha_{i2}, ..., \alpha_{im}$ are the factor loadings related to the variable X_i; $F_1, F_2,...,F_m$ are m uncorrelated common factors, each with zero mean and unit variance; and e_i are the Q specific factors supposed independently and identically distributed with zero mean. There are several approaches to dealing with the model given in equation (17), e.g. communalities, maximum likelihood factors, centroid method, principal axis method, etc. The most common is the use of PCA to extract the first m principal components and to consider them as factors, neglecting those remaining. Principal components factor analysis is most preferred in the development of composite indicators, e.g. in the Product Market Regulation Index (Nicoletti et al., 2000), as it has the virtue of simplicity and allows for the construction of weights representing the information content of individual indicators. Note, however, that different extraction methods supply different values for the factors and thus for the weights, influencing the score of the composite and the corresponding country ranking.

On the issue of how factors should be retained in the analysis without losing too much information, methodologists are divided. The decision on when to stop extracting factors depends basically on when there is only very little "random" variability left, and is rather arbitrary. However, various guidelines ("stopping rules") have been developed, roughly in the order of frequency of their use in social science (Dunteman, 1989: 22-3) (Box 6).

Box 6. A sample of "stopping rules"

Kaiser criterion. Drop all factors with eigenvalues below 1.0. The simplest justification for this is that it makes no sense to add a factor that explains less variance than is contained in one individual indicator. According to this rule, three factors should be retained in the analysis of the TAI example, although the fourth factor follows closely with an eigenvalue of 0.90.

Scree plot. This method, proposed by Cattell, plots the successive eigenvalues, which drop sharply and then level off. It suggests retaining all eigenvalues in the sharp descent before the first one on the line where they start to level off. This approach would result in retaining three factors in the TAI example (Figure 12, left graph).

Variance explained criteria. Some researchers simply use the rule of keeping enough factors to account for 90% (sometimes 80%) of the variation. The first four factors account for 87.2% of the total variance.

Joliffe criterion. Drop all factors with eigenvalues under 0.70. This rule may result in twice as many factors as the Kaiser criterion produces and is less often used. In the present case study, this criterion would have led to the selection of four factors.

Comprehensibility. Though not a strictly mathematical criterion, there is much to be said for limiting the number of factors to those whose dimension of meaning is readily comprehensible. Often this means the first two or three.

A method for deciding on the number of factors to retain combines the bootstrapped eigenvalues and eigenvectors (Jackson, 1993). Based on a combination of the Kaiser criterion and the bootstrapped eigenvalues, the first four factors should be considered in the TAI example. In light of the above analysis, the first four principal components, as identified by the bootstrap eigenvalue approach combined with the Kaiser criterion, are retained. This choice implies a greater willingness to overstate the significance of the fourth component and is in line with the idea that there are four main categories of technology achievement indicators.

After choosing the number of factors to keep, it is standard practice to perform rotation so as to enhance the interpretability of the results. The sum of eigenvalues is not affected by rotation, but changing the axes will alter the eigenvalues of particular factors and will change the factor loadings. Various rotational strategies have been proposed. The goal of all of these strategies is to obtain a clear pattern of loadings. However, different rotations imply different loadings, and thus different meanings of principal components – a problem some cite as a drawback to the method. The most common rotation method is the "varimax rotation".

Table 9 presents the factor loadings for the first factors in the TAI example. Note that the eigenvalues have been affected by the rotation. The variance accounted for by the rotated components is spread more evenly than for the unrotated. The first four factors now account for 87% of the total variance and are not sorted into descending order according to how much of the original data set's variance is explained. The first factor has high positive coefficients (loadings) with *Internet* (0.79), *electricity* (0.82) and *schooling* (0.88). Factor 2 is mainly dominated by *patents* and *exports*, while *university* is exclusively loaded on Factor 3. Finally, Factor 4 is formed by *royalties* and *telephones*. Yet, despite the rotation of factors, the individual indicator *exports* has sizeable loadings in both Factor 1 (negative loading) and Factor 2 (positive loading). A meaningful interpretation of the factors is not straightforward. Furthermore, the statistical treatment of the eight individual indicators results in different groups (factors) to the conceptual ones (see Table A.1 in Appendix). The factor loading shown in Table 9 will be used later in the section on "Weighting and aggregation" to construct weights for the TAI composite indicator.

Table 9. Rotated factor loadings for individual TAI indicators (method 1)

	Factor 1	Factor 2	Factor 3	Factor 4	Communality
PATENTS	0.07	**0.97**	0.06	0.06	0.95
ROYALTIES	0.13	0.07	-0.07	**0.93**	0.89
INTERNET	**0.79**	-0.21	0.21	0.42	0.89
EXPORTS	-0.64	**0.56**	-0.04	0.36	0.86
TELEPHONES	0.37	0.17	0.38	**0.68**	0.77
ELECTRICITY	**0.82**	-0.04	0.25	0.35	0.85
SCHOOLING	**0.88**	0.23	-0.09	0.09	0.85
UNIVERSITY	0.08	0.04	**0.96**	0.04	0.93
Explained variance	2.64	1.39	1.19	1.76	
Cumulative (%)	33	50	65	87	

Note: Extraction method: principal components, varimax normalised rotation. Positive loadings greater than 0.5 are highlighted.

Another method of extracting factors that deals with the non-correlation of the specific factors would have given different results. Table 10 presents the rotated factor loadings of the four factors for the TAI case study (extraction method: principal factors maximum likelihood). For instance, *electricity* and *schooling* are no longer loaded on F1: *electricity* is loaded on F4 and *schooling* on F2. 76% of the total variance is explained by the four rotated common factors. In contrast, the total variance explained by the four rotated principal components was much higher in the previous analysis (87%). The commonalties for seven individual indicators are greater than 0.64, with the exception of *university*, for which the communality is only 0.15, which indicates that *university* does not move with the other individual indicators in the data set, and therefore is not well-represented by the four common factors. This conclusion does not depend on the factor analysis method, as it has been confirmed by different methods (centroid method, principal axis method).

Table 10. Rotated factor loadings for individual TAI indicators (method 2)

	Factor 1	Factor 2	Factor 3	Factor 4	Communality
PATENTS	0.01	0.11	**0.88**	0.13	0.80
ROYALTIES	**0.96**	0.14	0.09	0.18	0.99
INTERNET	0.31	**0.56**	-0.29	**0.60**	0.86
EXPORTS	0.29	-0.45	**0.58**	-0.14	0.65
TELEPHONES	0.41	0.13	0.18	**0.73**	0.75
ELECTRICITY	0.13	0.57	-0.13	**0.73**	0.89
SCHOOLING	0.14	**0.95**	0.10	0.14	0.95
UNIVERSITY	-0.01	0.03	0.03	0.39	0.15
Explained Variance	1.31	1.80	1.27	1.67	
Cumulative (%)	16	39	55	76	

Note: Extraction method: principal factors maximum likelihood, varimax normalised rotation.

Summarizing the steps of the PCA/FA exploratory analysis method:

1. Calculate the covariance/correlation matrix: if the correlation between individual indicators is small, it is unlikely that they share common factors.
2. Identify the number of factors necessary to represent the data and the method for calculating them.
3. Rotate factors to enhance their interpretability (by maximising loading of individual indicators on individual factors).

4.3. Cronbach Coefficient Alpha

The Cronbach Coefficient Alpha (henceforth c-alpha) (Cronbach, 1951) is the most common estimate of internal consistency of items in a model or survey – Reliability/Item Analysis (*e.g.* Boscarino *et al.*, 2004; Raykov, 1998; Cortina, 1993; Feldt *et al.*, 1987; Green *et al.*, 1977; Hattie, 1985; Miller, 1995). It assesses how well a set of items (in our terminology individual indicators) measures a single uni-dimensional object (*e.g.* attitude, phenomenon, etc.).

Cronbach's Coefficient Alpha can be defined as:

$$\alpha_c = \left(\frac{Q}{Q-1}\right)\frac{\sum_{i \neq j} \text{cov}(x_i, x_j)}{\text{var}(x_o)} = \left(\frac{Q}{Q-1}\right)\left(1 - \frac{\sum_j \text{var}(x_j)}{\text{var}(x_o)}\right) \quad c = 1,..,M; i,j = 1,..,Q \tag{18}$$

where M indicates the number of countries considered, Q the number of individual indicators available, and $x_o = \sum_{q=1}^{Q} x_j$ is the sum of all individual indicators. C-alpha measures the portion of total variability of the sample of individual indicators due to the correlation of indicators. It increases with the number of individual indicators and with the covariance of each pair. If no correlation exists and individual indicators are independent, then C-alpha is equal to zero, while if individual indicators are perfectly correlated, C-alpha is equal to one.

C-alpha is not a statistical test, but a coefficient of reliability based on the correlation between individual indicators. That is, if the correlation is high, then there is evidence that the individual indicators are measuring the same underlying construct. Therefore a high c-alpha, or equivalently a high "reliability", indicates that the individual indicators measure the latent phenomenon well. Although widely interpreted as such, strictly speaking c-alpha is *not a measure of uni-dimensionality*. A set of individual indicators can have a high alpha and still be multi-dimensional. This happens when there are separate clusters of individual indicators (separate dimensions) which intercorrelate highly, even though the clusters themselves are not highly correlated. A question is how large the c-alpha must be. Nunnally (1978) suggests 0.7 as an acceptable reliability threshold. Yet some authors use .75 or .80 as a cut-off value, while others are as lenient as to go to 0.6. In general this varies by discipline.

If the variances of the individual indicators vary widely, as in our test case, a standard practice is to standardise the individual indicators to a standard deviation of 1 before computing the coefficient alpha. In our notation this would mean substituting x_i with I_i. The c-alpha is .70 for the data set of the 23 countries, which is equal to Nunnally's cut-off value. An interesting exercise is to determine how the c-alpha varies with the deletion of each individual indicator at a time. This helps to reveal the existence of clusters of individual indicators, thus it is useful to determine the nested structure of the composite. If the reliability coefficient increases after deleting an individual indicator from the scale, one can assume that the individual indicator is not correlated highly with other individual indicators in the scale.

Table 11 presents the values for the Cronbach coefficient alpha and the correlation with the total after deleting one individual indicator at a time. *Telephones* has the highest variable-total correlation and if deleted the coefficient alpha would be as low as 0.60. If *exports* were to be deleted from the set, then the value of the standardised coefficient alpha would increase from the current .70 to .77. Note that the same individual indicator has the lowest variable-total correlation value (-.108). This indicates that *exports* are not measuring the same construct as the rest of the individual indicators. Note also that the factor analysis in the previous section had indicated *university* as the individual indicator that shared the least amount of common variance with the other individual indicators. Although both factor analysis and the Cronbach coefficient alpha are based on correlations among individual indicators, their conceptual framework is different.

Table 11. Cronbach coefficient alpha results for individual TAI indicators

Deleted individual indicator	Correlation with total	Cronbach coefficient alpha
PATENTS	0.261	0.704
ROYALTIES	0.527	0.645
INTERNET	0.566	0.636
EXPORTS	-0.108	0.774
TELEPHONES	0.701	0.603
ELECTRICITY	0.614	0.624
SCHOOLING	0.451	0.662
UNIVERSITY	0.249	0.706

Note: Cronbach coefficient alpha results for the 23 countries after deleting one individual indicator (standardised values) at a time.

4.4. Cluster analysis

Cluster analysis (CLA) is a collection of algorithms to classify objects such as countries, species, and individuals (Anderberg, 1973; Massart & Kaufman, 1983). The classification aims to reduce the dimensionality of a data set by exploiting the similarities/dissimilarities between cases. CLA techniques can be hierarchical if the classification has an increasing number of nested classes, *e.g. tree clustering*; or non-hierarchical when the number of clusters is decided *ex ante*, *e.g. k-means clustering*. However, care should be taken that classes are meaningful and not arbitrary or artificial.

Homogeneous and distinct groups could be delineated according to assessment of distances or, as in the case of Ward's method, an F-test (Davis, 1986). A distance measure is an appraisal of the degree of similarity or dissimilarity between cases in the set. A small distance is equivalent to a strong similarity. It can be based on a single dimension or on multiple dimensions, for example, countries in the TAI example can be evaluated according to the TAI composite indicator or according to all individual indicators. Some of the most common distance measures are listed in Table 12, including Euclidean and non-Euclidean distances.[18]

The next step is to choose the clustering algorithm, *i.e.* the rules which govern how distances are measured between clusters. There are many methods for this. The selection criteria could differ and hence different classifications may be obtained for the same data, even using the same distance measure. The most common linkage rules are (Spath, 1980):

- **Single linkage** (nearest neighbour). The distance between two clusters is determined by the distance between the two closest elements in the different clusters. This rule produces clusters chained together by single objects.

- **Complete linkage** (farthest neighbour). The distance between two clusters is determined by the greatest distance between any two objects belonging to different clusters. This method usually performs well when objects naturally form distinct groups.

- **Unweighted pair-group average**. The distance between two clusters is calculated as the average distance between all pairs of objects in the two clusters. This method usually performs well when objects naturally form distinct groups. A variation of this method uses the centroid of a cluster – the distance is the average point in the multi-dimensional space defined by the dimensions.

- **Weighted pair-group average**. Similar to the unweighted pair-group average (centroid included), except that the size of the cluster, *i.e.* the number of objects contained, is used as a weight for the average distance. This method is useful when cluster sizes are very different.

- **Ward's method** (Ward, 1963). Cluster membership is determined by calculating the variance of elements, *i.e.* the sum of the squared deviations from the mean of the cluster. An element will belong to the cluster if it produces the smallest possible increase in the variance.

HANDBOOK ON CONSTRUCTING COMPOSITE INDICATORS: METHODOLOGY AND USER GUIDE – ISBN 978-92-64-04345-9 - © OECD 2008

Table 12. Distance measures $D(x, y)$ for individual TAI indicators between two objects x and y over N_d dimensions

Euclidean	$$D(x, y) = \left(\frac{\sum_{i=1}^{N_d} (x_i - y_i)^2}{N_d} \right)^{1/2}$$	This is the geometric distance in a multi-dimensional space and is usually computed from raw data (prior to any normalisation). This measure is not affected by the addition of new objects such as outliers. However, it is highly affected by the difference in scale, *e.g.*, whether the same object is measured in centimetres or in metres the $D(x,y)$
Squared Euclidean	$$D(x, y) = \frac{\sum_{i=1}^{N_d} (x_i - y_i)^2}{N_d}$$	This measure places progressively greater weight on objects that are further apart. Usually this is computed from raw data and shares the same advantages and disadvantages of the Euclidean distance.
City-block[19] (Manhattan)	$$D(x, y) = \frac{\sum_{i=1}^{N_d} |x_i - y_i|}{N_d}$$	This distance is the average of distances across dimensions and it yields similar results to the Euclidean distance. In this measure the effect of outliers is less pronounced, since it is not squared.
Chebychev	$$D(x, y) = Max|x_i - y_i|$$	This measure is mostly used when it is desired to define objects as "different" if they are different in any one of the dimensions.
Power	$$D(x, y) = \left(\frac{\sum_{i=1}^{N_d} (x_i - y_i)^p}{N_d} \right)^{1/r}$$	This distance measure is useful when it is desired to increase or decrease the progressive weight placed on one dimension for which the respective objects are very different. The parameters r and p are user-defined, such that p controls the progressive weights placed on differences between individual dimensions, and r controls the progressive weight placed on larger differences between objects. Note that for p=r=2 corresponds to the Euclidean distance.
Percent disagreement	$$D(x, y) = \frac{number\ of\ x_i \neq y_i}{N_d}$$	This measure is useful if the data are categorical in nature.

Figure 13 shows the country clusters based on the individual Technology Achievement Index indicators using tree clustering (hierarchical) with single linkage and squared Euclidean distances. Similarity between countries belonging to the same cluster decreases as the linkage distance increases. One of the biggest problems with CLA is identifying the optimum number of clusters. As the amalgamation process continues, increasingly dissimilar clusters must be fused, *i.e.* the classification becomes increasingly artificial. Deciding on the optimum number of clusters is largely subjective, although looking at the plot of linkage distance across fusion steps may help (Milligan & Cooper, 1985).

Figure 13. Country clusters for individual TAI indicators

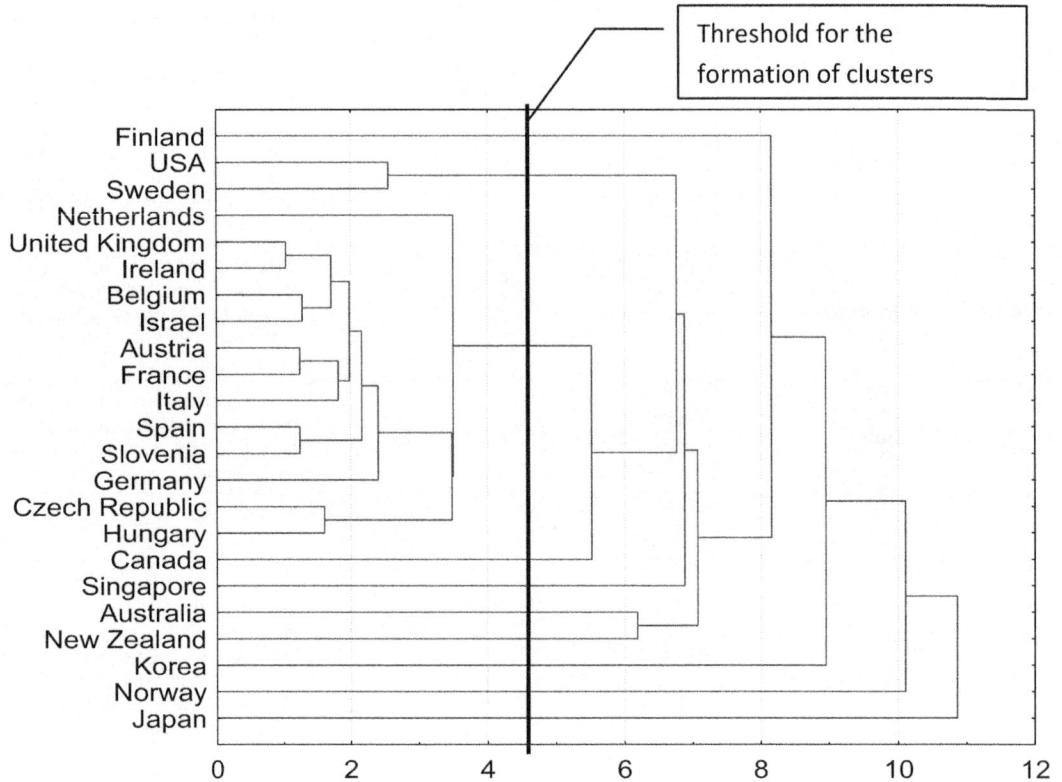

Note: Standardised data. Type: Hierarchical, single linkage, squared Euclidean distances.

Sudden jumps in the level of similarity (abscissa) could indicate that dissimilar groups or outliers are fused. Such a plot is presented in Figure 14, where the greatest dissimilarity among the 23 countries in the TAI example is found at a linkage distance close to 4.0, which indicates that the data are best represented by ten clusters: Finland; Sweden and the USA; the group of countries located between the Netherlands and Hungary; Canada; Singapore; Australia; New Zealand; Korea; Norway; and Japan. Note that the most dissimilar are Korea, Norway and Japan, which are aggregated only at the very end of the analysis. Besides, this result does not fully correspond to the division into laggard, average and leading countries resulting from the standard aggregation methods. Japan, in fact, would be in the group of leading countries, together with Finland, Sweden, USA, while Hungary, the Czech Republic, Slovenia and Italy would be the laggards, at a great distance from the Netherlands, the USA or Sweden (see Table 38 in the 'Performance of the different aggregation methods').

HANDBOOK ON CONSTRUCTING COMPOSITE INDICATORS: METHODOLOGY AND USER GUIDE – ISBN 978-92-64-04345-9 – © OECD 2008

A non-hierarchical method of clustering, different from the *joining* or *tree* clustering shown below, is k-means clustering (Hartigan, 1975). This method is useful when the aim is to divide the sample into k clusters of the greatest possible distinction. The parameter k is decided by the analyst; for example, it may be decided to cluster the 23 countries in the TAI example into three groups, *e.g.* leaders, potential leaders, and dynamic adopters. The k-means algorithm will supply three clusters, as distinct as possible, by analysing the variance of each cluster. This algorithm can be applied with continuous variables, yet it can be also modified to accommodate other types of variables. The algorithm starts with k random clusters and moves the objects in and out of the clusters with the aim of (i) minimising the variance of elements within the clusters, and (ii) maximising the variance of the elements outside the clusters.

A line graph of the means across clusters is displayed in Figure 15. This plot could be very useful in summarising the differences in the means between clusters. It is shown, for example, that the main difference between the *leaders* and the *potential leaders* (Table 13) is between *royalties* and *exports*. At the same time, the *dynamic adopters* are lagging behind the *potential leaders* due to their lower performance on *Internet*, *electricity* and *schooling*. They are, however, performing better on *exports* Two of the individual indicators, *patents* and *university*, are not useful in distinguishing between these three groups, as the cluster means are very close.

Figure 14.   Linkage distance vs fusion step in TAI's hierarchical cluster

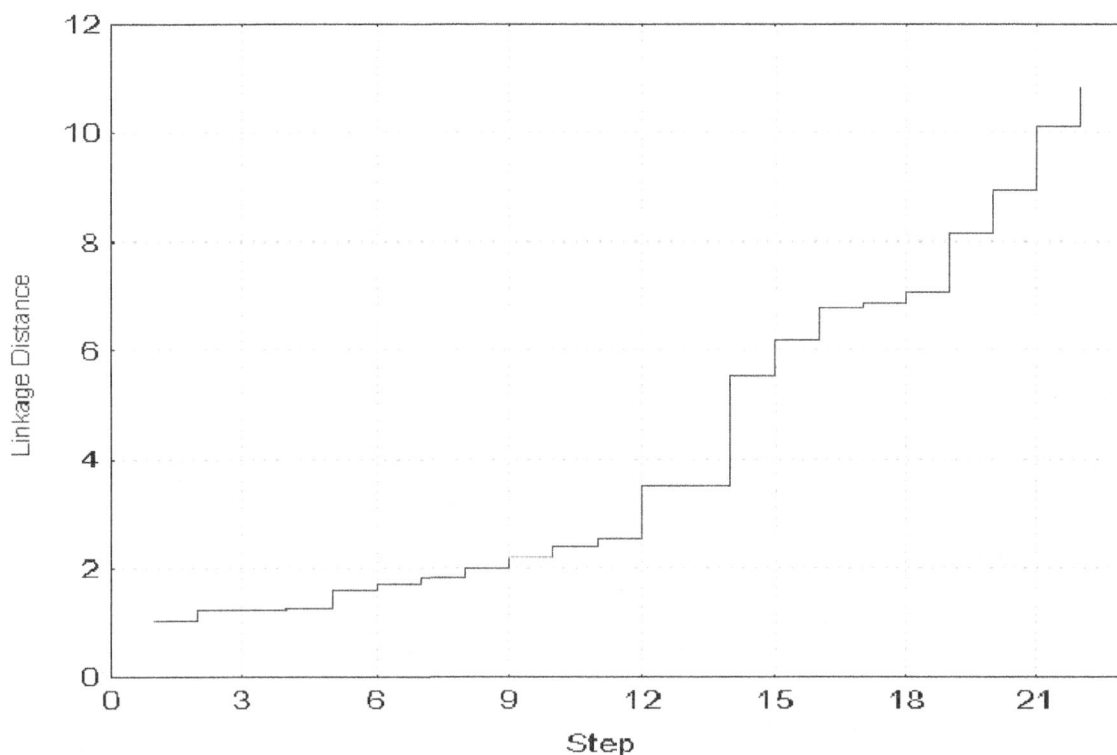

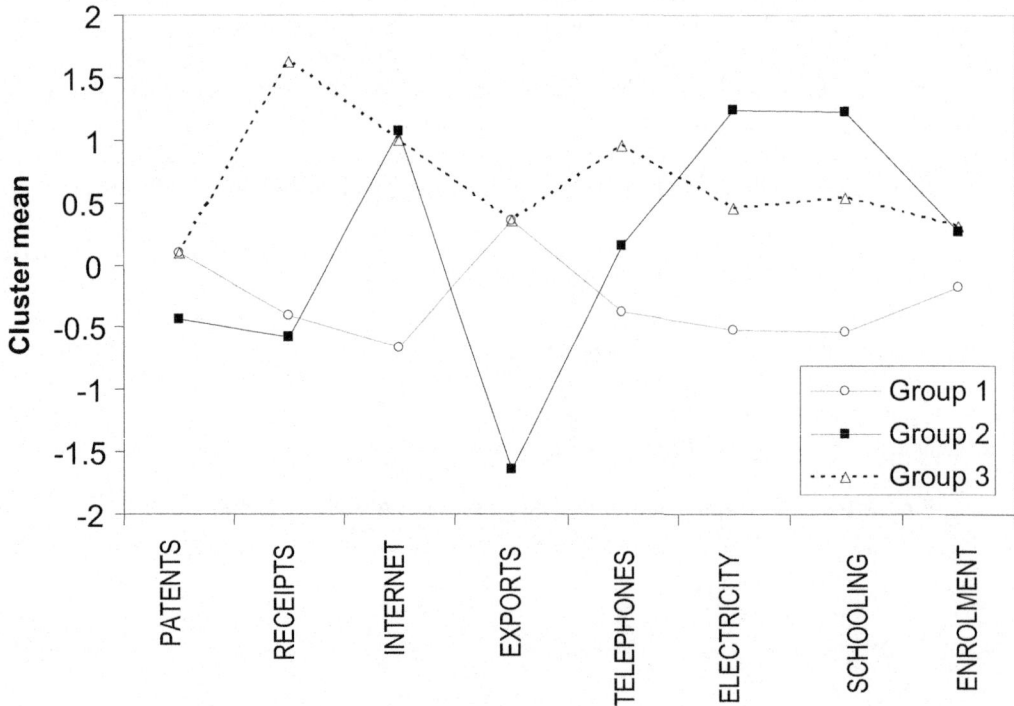

Figure 15.   Means plot for TAI clusters

Note: Type: k-means clustering (standardised data).

Table 13. K-means for clustering TAI countries

Group1 (leaders)	Group 2 (potential leaders)	Group 3 (dynamic adopters)	
Finland	Australia	Austria	Italy
Netherlands	Canada	Belgium	Japan
Sweden	New Zealand	Czech Rep.	Korea
USA	Norway	France	Singapore
		Germany	Slovenia
		Hungary	Spain
		Ireland	UK
		Israel	

Finally, expectation maximisation (EM) clustering extends the simple k-means clustering in two ways. First, instead of clustering the objects by maximising the differences in means for continuous variables, EM clusters membership on the basis of probability distributions – each observation will belong to each cluster with a certain probability. EM estimates mean and standard deviation of each cluster so as to maximise the overall likelihood of the data, given the final clusters (Binder, 1978). Second, unlike k-means, EM can be applied to both continuous and categorical data.

HANDBOOK ON CONSTRUCTING COMPOSITE INDICATORS: METHODOLOGY AND USER GUIDE – ISBN 978-92-64-04345-9 – © OECD 2008

Ordinary significance tests are not valid for testing differences between clusters, as clusters are formed to be as distinct as possible. Thus the assumption of usual tests – parametric or non-parametric – is violated (see Hartigan, 1975). As a final remark, a warning: CLA will always produce a grouping; this means that clusters may or may not prove useful for classifying objects, depending upon the objectives of the analysis. For example, zip-code areas could be grouped into categories based on age, gender, education and income to discriminate between wine-drinking behaviours, but this would only be useful information if the aim of the CLA was to establish a good location for a new wine store. Furthermore, CLA methods are not clearly established – there are many options, all giving very different results (Everitt, 1979).

Various alternative methods combining cluster analysis and the search for a low-dimensional representation have been proposed and focus on multi-dimensional scaling or unfolding analysis (*e.g.* Heiser, 1993; De Soete & Heiser, 1993). A method that combines k-means cluster analysis with aspects of Factor Analysis and PCA is offered by Vichi & Kiers (2001). A discrete clustering model and a continuous factorial model are fitted simultaneously to two-way data with the aim of identifying the best partition of the objects, described by the best orthogonal linear combinations of the variables (factors) according to the least-squares criterion.

This methodology, known as factorial k-means analysis, has a wide range of applications, since it achieves a double objective: data reduction and synthesis simultaneously in the direction of objects and variables. Originally applied to short-term macroeconomic data, factorial k-means analysis has a fast alternating least-squares algorithm that extends its application to large data sets, *i.e.*, multivariate data sets with >2 variables. The methodology can therefore be recommended as an alternative to the widely used tandem analysis that sequentially performs PCA and CLA.

4.5. Other methods for multivariate analysis

Other methods can be used for multivariate analysis of the data set. The characteristics of some of these methods are sketched below, citing textbooks where the reader may find additional information and references. Box 7 contains additional information about correlation measures, from the most widely used (Pearson correlation coefficient or Spearman rank correlation) to the least common measures based on sophisticated statistical concepts. Again, this is not an exhaustive list but rather a snapshot of the existing literature aiming to encourage further exploration.

Correspondence Analysis is a descriptive/exploratory technique to analyse discrete variables with many categories and to group relevant information (or relevant relationships between rows and columns of the table) by reducing the dimensionality of the data set. Correspondence analysis is a non-parametric technique which makes no distributional assumptions, unlike factor analysis. This technique finds scores for the rows and columns on a small number of dimensions which account for the greatest proportion of the χ^2 for association between the rows and columns, just as principal components account for maximum variance. Correspondence analysis therefore uses a definition of chi-square distance rather than Euclidean distance between points. This is a special case of canonical correlation, in which one set of entities (categories rather than variables as in conventional canonical correlation) is related to another set. Correspondence analysis starts with tabular data, *e.g.* a multi-dimensional time series describing the variable "number of doctorates" in 12 scientific disciplines (categories) given in the USA between 1960 and 1975 (Greenacre, 1984). Case values cannot be negative. The variable(s) must be discrete: nominal, ordinal, or continuous variables segmented into ranges (in this case information may be lost, thus affecting the interpretation of the results). The correspondence analysis of this data would show, for example, whether anthropology and engineering degrees are at a distance from each other (based on the number of doctorates for the eight years of the sample). This is visualized on the correspondence map, which plots points (categories, *i.e.* values of the discrete variable) along the computed factor axes. However, while conventional factor analysis determines which variables cluster together (parametric approach), correspondence analysis determines which category values are close together (non-parametric approach). Correspondence analysis can be used with many discrete variables. However, it handles only two or three variables well – beyond this interpretability might be problematic. Furthermore, a certain number of categories is needed, given that with only two or three categories, the dimensions computed in correspondence analysis usually are not more informative than the original small table itself. Note that correspondence analysis is an exploratory, not a confirmatory technique, thus appropriate variables and value categories must be specified a priori. The classical textbooks for this technique are Greenacre (1984, 1993)

Canonical correlation analysis (CCA) can be used to investigate the relationship between two groups of variables. Suppose, for example, that the question is to investigate the relationship between reading ability, measured by variables X_1 and X_2, and arithmetic ability, measured by Y_1 and Y_2. Canonical correlation looks for a linear combination of X_1 and X_2 (*e.g* $U = \alpha_1 X_1 + \alpha_2 X_2$) and a linear combination of Y_1 and Y_2 (*e.g.* $V = \beta_1 Y_1 + \beta_2 Y_2$) chosen so that the correlation between U and V (the canonical variables) is maximized. Note that CCA groups variables such that correlation between groups is maximized, whereas Principal Component Analysis (PCA) groups variables maximizing the variance (and thus the difference between groups). As in PCA, CCA implies the extraction of the eigenvalues and eigenvectors of the data matrix. In particular in the example above, we will have two canonical correlations corresponding to the square root of the eigenvalues $\lambda_1 > \lambda_2$. An approximate test for the relationship between (X_1, X_2) and (Y_1, Y_2) is the Bartlett test[20], involving the calculation of the statistic:

$$ B = -\{n - \frac{1}{2}(p + q + 1)\}\sum_{i=1}^{r} \log_e (1 - \lambda_i) $$

where n is the sample size, p the number of X variables, q the number of Y variables and $r = \min(p, q)$. The statistic B is distributed as a χ_{pq}. The null hypothesis of the test is that at least one of the r canonical correlations is significant. Obviously, the possibility of detecting canonical correlation robustly decreases with the sample size. For small sample sizes (n around 50) only strong canonical correlations will be detected, whereas larger samples ($n>200$) make it possible to identify weaker canonical correlations as well (*e.g.* 0.3). More information on Johnson & Wichern (2002).

A way to classify variables (or cases) into the values of a dichotomous dependent variable is given by **Discriminant Function Analysis** (DFA), for example, to classify males and females according to different body measurements. When the dependent variable has more than two categories then it is a case of multiple Discriminant Analysis (or also Discriminant Factor Analysis or Canonical Discriminant Analysis), *e.g.* to discriminate countries on the basis of employment patterns in nine industries (predictors). The classification into groups will be done by estimating a set of discriminant functions (also called canonical roots), where the eigenvalues (one for each discriminant function) reflect the ratio of importance of the dimensions which classify cases of the dependent variable. Pairwise group comparison (for more than two groups) will be done through an F-test of significance of the (Mahalanobis) distance between group means. Computationally, DFA is similar to the analysis of variance. Note that the number of desired groups must be decided in advance. This is the main difference to Cluster Analysis, in which groups are not predetermined. There are also conceptual similarities with Principal Components and Factor Analysis, but while PCA maximises the variance in all the variables accounted for by a factor, DFA maximises the differences between values of the dependent. DFA is based on a number of assumptions, including: (i) DFA results being highly sensitive to variables added or subtracted and to outliers; (ii) low correlation of the predictors, (iii) linearity and additivity; and (iv) adequate sample size (a recommended four or five times as many cases as predictors). More details can be found in McLachlan (2004).

Box 7. Measures of association

Pearson's correlation coefficient

Suppose there are n measurements of two random variables X and Y normally distributed: x_i, y_i where $i=1,...,n$. The Pearson correlation coefficient (also called Pearson product-moment correlation coefficient or sample correlation coefficient) is the following:

$$r_{xy} = \frac{\sum_i (x_i - \bar{x})(y_i - \bar{y})}{(n-1)s_x s_y}$$

where $\bar{x}, \bar{y}$ (s_x, s_y) are the sample means (standard deviations) of x_i, y_i, $i=1,...,n$. The square of the sample correlation coefficient is known as the coefficient of determination and is the fraction of the variance in y_i that is accounted for by a linear fit of x_i to y_i.

Spearman's rank correlation coefficient ρ

$$\rho = 1 - \frac{6 \sum_i d_i^2}{n(n^2 - 1)}$$

where d_i is the difference between each rank of corresponding values of x and y. Spearman's rank correlation is equivalent to Pearson correlation on ranks but does not require the assumption of normality of X and Y. Nor does it require variables measured on an interval scale or a linear association between variables. For a sufficiently large sample size (> 20), the variable $t = \frac{\rho}{\sqrt{(1-\rho^2)/(n-2)}}$ has a Student's t-distribution under the null hypothesis (absence of correlation) and can be used to test the presence of statistically significant rank correlations.

Kendall τ rank correlation coefficient

Kendall τ measures the degree of correspondence between two rankings (and the statistical significance of this association).

$$\tau = \frac{4P}{n(n-1)} - 1$$

where P is the sum of "concordant pairs" in the two rankings. More precisely, P is the sum, over all the items, of items ranked after the given item by both rankings. Consider the following example.

Person	A	B	C	D	E	F	G	H
Rank by height	1	2	3	4	5	6	7	8
Rank by weight	3	4	1	2	5	7	8	6

The first entry in the second row (rank by weight) is 3. This means that there are five higher ranks to the left of "3"; the contribution of the first entry to P is then 5. The second entry is "4" and its contribution to P is 4 (because it has four higher ranks to the left)....*etc.* With this reasoning, P=5+4+5+4+3+1+0+0=22 and τ =0.57. Therefore, if the two rankings are equal, τ =1; if they are completely opposite, τ =-1. If the rankings are completely independent, τ =0.

Correlation ratio

The correlation ratio is a measure of the relationship between the statistical dispersion within categories and the dispersion across the entire population. Suppose that y_{xi} indicates the observation y_i within the category x, and n_x, the number of observations in category x. Let $\bar{y}_x = \frac{1}{n_x} \sum_i y_{xi}$, and $\bar{y} = \sum_x n_x \bar{y}_x / \sum_x n_x$, the sample mean of y within category x and across the whole population respectively. Then the correlation ratio η is defined so as to satisfy:

$$\eta^2 = \frac{\sum_x n_x (\bar{y}_x - \bar{y})^2}{\sum_{xi} (y_{xi} - \bar{y})^2}$$

Mutual information

A general concept of association is given by *mutual information*. Given two random variables X and Y, mutual information $I(X;Y)$ can be defined as:

$$I(X;Y) = \sum_{y \in Y} \sum_{x \in X} p(x,y) \log_2 \frac{p(x,y)}{p(x)p(y)}$$

where $p(x,y)$ is the joint probability distribution of X and Y and $p(x)$, $p(y)$ are the marginal probability density functions of X and Y, respectively. Note that the logarithm has base 2. Mutual information measures the mutual dependency of two variables or, in other terms, by how much knowledge of one variable will reduce the uncertainty in (or increase the information about) the other. If two variables X and Y are independent, then $p(x,y) = p(x) \, p(y)$ and *I(X;Y)=0*. Moreover, $I(X;Y) \geq 0$. For further details see Papoulis, *Probability, Random Variables and Stochastic Processes* (1991, 3rd edition, NY: McGraw-Hill). The generalization of mutual information to more than two variables is called **total correlation** (or multivariate constraint or multi-information) (see Watanabe, 1960).

An even more general concept of association is given by the **copula**. A copula, in statistics, is a function summarizing all the information on the nature of the dependencies in a set of random variables. Technically it is a multivariate distribution function defined on the n-dimensional unit cube (see Nelsen, 1999).

HANDBOOK ON CONSTRUCTING COMPOSITE INDICATORS: METHODOLOGY AND USER GUIDE – ISBN 978-92-64-04345-9 - © OECD 2008

STEP 5. NORMALISATION

The objective is to identify the most suitable normalisation procedures to apply to the problem at hand, taking into account their properties with respect to the measurement units in which the indicators are expressed, and their robustness against possible outliers in the data (Ebert & Welsch, 2004). Different normalisation methods will produce different results for the composite indicator. Therefore, overall robustness tests should be carried out to assess their impact on the outcomes.

5.1. Scale transformation prior to normalisation

Certain normalisation procedures produce the same normalised value of the indicator irrespective of the measurement unit. Applying a normalisation procedure which is not invariant to changes in the measurement unit, however, could result in different outcomes. Below is a simple example with two indicators – temperature and humidity – for two hypothetical countries A and B in 2003 and 2004. The raw data and normalised composites are given in Table 14, where the temperature is first expressed in Celsius and then in Fahrenheit. Each indicator is divided by the value of the leading country and aggregated with equal weights. Using Celsius data normalised based on "distance to the best performer", the level of Country A has increased over time. While the same normalisation and aggregation methods are used, the results in Fahrenheit show a different pattern. The composite indicator for country A now decreases over time.

Table 14. Normalisation based on interval scales

	2003	2004
Country A –Temperature (°C)	35	35.9
Country A –Humidity (%)	75	70
Country B –Temperature (°C)	39	40
Country B –Humidity (%)	50	45
Normalised data in Celsius		
Country A	0.949	0.949
Country B	0.833	0.821
Country A –Temperature (F)	95	96.62
Country A –Humidity (%)	75	70
Country B –Temperature (F)	102.2	104
Country B –Humidity (%)	50	45
Normalised data in Fahrenheit		
Country A	0.965	0.965
Country B	0.833	0.821

The example illustrated above is a case of an *interval scale* (Box 3), based on a transformation f defined as $f: \quad x \to y = \alpha x + \beta; \alpha > 0, \beta \neq 0$, where the variable x is the temperature expressed in Celsius (C) and y is the temperature expressed in Fahrenheit (F). Their relationship is given by: $F = \frac{9}{5}C + 32$. Another common change of measurement unit is the so-called *ratio scale*, which is based on the transformation $f: \quad x \to y = \alpha x; \alpha > 0$. For example, a "length" might be expressed in centimetres (cm) or yards (yd). Their relationship is indeed: 1 yd = 91.44 cm. The normalisation by country leader, not invariant on the *interval scale*, is invariant on the *ratio scale*. This means that

$$\frac{x}{x_{\max}} \neq \frac{ax + \beta}{ax_{\max} + \beta}, \text{ whereas } \frac{x}{x_{\max}} = \frac{ax}{ax_{\max}}.$$

In general, all normalisation methods which are invariant on the *interval scale* are also invariant on the *ratio scale*.

Another transformation of the data, often used to reduce the skewness of (positive) data, is the logarithmic transformation

$$f: \quad x \to y = \log(x); x > 0.$$

When the range of values for the indicator is wide or is positively skewed, the log transformation shrinks the right-hand side of the distribution. As values approach zero they are also penalised, given that after transformation they become largely negative. Expressing the weighted variables in a linear aggregation in logarithms is equivalent to the geometric aggregation of the variables without logarithms. The ratio between two weights indicates the percentage increase in one indicator that would compensate for a one percentage point decline in another indicator. This transformation leads to the attribution of a higher weight for a one-unit increase, starting from a low level of performance, compared to an identical improvement starting from a high level of performance.

The normalisation methods described below are all non-invariant to this type of scale transformation. The user may decide whether or not to use the log transformation before the normalisation, bearing in mind that the normalised data will be affected by the log transformation.

In some circumstances outliers[21] can reflect the presence of unwanted information. An example is offered in the Environmental Sustainability Index, where the variable distributions outside the 2.5 and 97.5 percentile scores are trimmed to partially correct for outliers, as well as to avoid having extreme values overly dominate the aggregation algorithm. That is, any observed value greater than the 97.5 percentile is lowered to match the 97.5 percentile. Any observed value lower than the 2.5 percentile on is raised to the 2.5 percentile. It is advisable first to try to remove outliers and consequently to perform the normalisation, as this latter procedure can be more or less sensitive to outliers.

5.2. Standardisation (or z-scores)

For each individual indicator x_{qc}^t, the average across countries $x_{qc=\bar{c}}^t$ and the standard deviation across countries $\sigma_{qc=\bar{c}}^t$ are calculated. The normalisation formula is $I_{qc}^t = \dfrac{x_{qc}^t - x_{qc=\bar{c}}^t}{\sigma_{qc=\bar{c}}^t}$, so that all I_{qc}^t have similar dispersion across countries. The actual minima and maxima of the I_{qc}^t across countries depend on the individual indicator. For time-dependent studies, in order to assess country performance across years, the average across countries $x_{qc=\bar{c}}^{t_0}$ and the standard deviation across countries $\sigma_{qc=\bar{c}}^{t_0}$ are calculated for a reference year, usually the initial time point, t_0.

5.3. Min-Max

Each indicator x_{qc}^t for a generic country c and time t is transformed in $I_{qc}^t = \dfrac{x_{qc}^t - min_c(x_q^t)}{max_c(x_q^t) - min_c(x_q^t)}$, where $min_c(x_q^t)$ and $max_c(x_q^t)$ are the minimum and the maximum value of x_{qc}^t across all countries c at time t. In this way, the normalised indicators I_{qc} have values lying between 0 (laggard, $x_{qc}^t = min_c(x_q^t)$), and 1 (leader, $x_{qc}^t = max_c(x_q^t)$).

The expression $I_{qc}^t = \dfrac{x_{qc}^t - min_c(x_q^{t_0})}{max_c(x_q^{t_0}) - min_c(x_q^{t_0})}$ is sometimes used in time-dependent studies. However, if $x_{qc}^t > max_c(x_q^{t_0})$, the normalised indicator y_{qc}^t would be larger than 1.

Another variant of the Min-Max method is $I_{qc}^t = \dfrac{x_{qc}^t - min_{t \in T} min_c(x_q^t)}{max_{t \in T} max_c(x_q^t) - min_{t \in T} min_c(x_q^t)}$, where the minimum and maximum for each indicator are calculated across countries and time, in order to take into account the evolution of indicators. The normalised indicators, I_{qc}^t, have values between 0 and 1. However, this transformation is not stable when data for a new time point become available. This implies an adjustment of the analysis period T, which may in turn affect the minimum and the maximum for some individual indicators and hence the values of I_{qc}^t. To maintain comparability between the existing and the new data, the composite indicator for the existing data must be re-calculated.

5.4. Distance to a reference

This method takes the ratios of the indicator x_{qc}^t for a generic country c and time t with respect to the individual indicator $x_{qc=\bar{c}}^{t_0}$ for the reference country at the initial time t_0.

$$I_{qc}^t = \frac{x_{qc}^t}{x_{qc=\bar{c}}^{t_0}}$$

Using the denominator $x_{qc=\bar{c}}^{t_0}$, the transformation takes into account the evolution of indicators across time; alternatively the denominator $x_{qc=\bar{c}}^t$ may be used, with running time t.

A different approach is to consider the country itself as the reference country and calculate the distance in terms of the initial time point as $I_{qc}^t = \dfrac{x_{qc}^t}{x_{qc}^{t_0}}$.

This approach is used in *Concern About Environmental Problems* (Parker, 1991) for measuring the concern of the public in relation to certain environmental problems in three countries (Italy, France and the UK) and in the European Union. An alternative distance for the normalisation could be:

$$y^t_{qc} = \frac{x^t_{qc} - x^{t_0}_{qc=\bar{c}}}{x^{t_0}_{qc=\bar{c}}}$$

which is essentially same as above. Instead of being centred on 1, it is centred on 0. In the same way, the reference country can be the average country, the group leader, or an external benchmark.

5.5. Indicators above or below the mean

This transformation considers the indicators which are above and below an arbitrarily defined threshold, p, around the mean:

$$I^t_{qc} = \begin{cases} 1 & if & w > (1+p) \\ 0 & if & (1-p) \le w \le (1+p) \\ -1 & if & w < (1-p) \end{cases} \qquad where \;\; w = \frac{x^t_{qc}}{x^{t_0}_{qc=\bar{c}}}$$

The threshold p builds a neutral region around the mean, where the transformed indicator is zero. This reduces the sharp discontinuity, from -1 to +1, which exists across the mean value to two minor discontinuities, from -1 to 0 and from 0 to +1, across the thresholds. A larger number of thresholds could be created at different distances from the mean value, which might overlap with the categorical scales. For time-dependent studies to assess country performance over time, the average across countries $x^{t_0}_{qc=\bar{c}}$ would be calculated for a reference year (usually the initial time point t_0). An indicator that moved from significantly below the mean to significantly above the threshold in the consecutive year would have a positive effect on the composite.

5.6. Methods for cyclical indicators

When indicators are in the form of time series the transformation can be made by subtracting the mean over time $E_t\left(x^t_{qc}\right)$ and by then dividing by the mean of the absolute values of the difference from the mean. The normalised series are then converted into index form by adding 100.

$$I^t_{qc} = \frac{x^t_{qc} - E_t\left(x^t_{qc}\right)}{E_t\left(\left|x^t_{qc} - E_t\left(x^t_{qc}\right)\right|\right)}$$

5.7. Percentage of annual differences over consecutive years

Each indicator is transformed using the formula

$$I^t_{qc} = \frac{x^t_{qc} - x^{t-1}_{qc}}{x^{t-1}_{qc}} * 100$$

The transformed indicator is dimension-less.

HANDBOOK ON CONSTRUCTING COMPOSITE INDICATORS: METHODOLOGY AND USER GUIDE – ISBN 978-92-64-04345-9 - © OECD 2008

Table 15. Examples of normalisation techniques using TAI data

Country	Mean years of school (age 15 and above)	Rank *	z-score	Min-Max	distance to reference country (c) ratio c=mean	c=best	c= worst	distance to reference country (c) difference c=mean	c=worst	Above/below the mean (**)	Percentile	Categorical scale
Finland	10	15	0.26	0.59	1.04	0.83	1.41	0.04	0.41	0	65.2	60
United States	12	23	1.52	1.00	1.25	1.00	1.69	0.25	0.69	1	100	100
Sweden	11.4	19	1.14	0.88	1.19	0.95	1.61	0.19	0.61	0	82.6	60
Japan	9.5	12	-0.06	0.49	0.99	0.79	1.34	-0.01	0.34	0	52.2	50
Korea, Rep.	10.8	17	0.76	0.76	1.13	0.90	1.52	0.13	0.52	0	73.9	60
Netherlands	9.4	9	-0.12	0.47	0.98	0.78	1.32	-0.02	0.32	0	39.1	50
UK	9.4	9	-0.12	0.47	0.98	0.78	1.32	-0.02	0.32	0	39.1	50
Canada	11.6	20	1.27	0.92	1.21	0.97	1.63	0.21	0.63	1	87.0	80
Australia	10.9	18	0.83	0.78	1.14	0.91	1.54	0.14	0.54	0	78.3	60
Singapore	7.1	1	-1.58	0.00	0.74	0.59	1.00	-0.26	0.00	-1	4.3	0
Germany	10.2	16	0.38	0.63	1.06	0.85	1.44	0.06	0.44	0	69.6	60
Norway	11.9	22	1.46	0.98	1.24	0.99	1.68	0.24	0.68	1	95.7	100
Ireland	9.4	9	-0.12	0.47	0.98	0.78	1.32	-0.02	0.32	0	39.1	50
Belgium	9.3	8	-0.19	0.45	0.97	0.78	1.31	-0.03	0.31	0	34.8	40
New Zealand	11.7	21	1.33	0.94	1.22	0.98	1.65	0.22	0.65	1	91.3	80
Austria	8.4	6	-0.76	0.27	0.88	0.70	1.18	-0.12	0.18	0	26.1	40
France	7.9	5	-1.08	0.16	0.82	0.66	1.11	-0.18	0.11	0	21.7	40
Israel	9.6	14	0.00	0.51	1.00	0.80	1.35	0.00	0.35	0	60.9	50
Spain	7.3	4	-1.46	0.04	0.76	0.61	1.03	-0.24	0.03	-1	17.4	40
Italy	7.2	3	-1.52	0.02	0.75	0.60	1.01	-0.25	0.01	-1	13.0	20
Czech Rep.	9.5	12	-0.06	0.49	0.99	0.79	1.34	-0.01	0.34	0	52.2	50
Hungary	9.1	7	-0.31	0.41	0.95	0.76	1.28	-0.05	0.28	0	30.4	40
Slovenia	7.1	1	-1.58	0.00	0.74	0.59	1.00	-0.26	0.00	-1	4.3	0

(*) High value = Top in the list
(**) p=20%

Examples of the above normalisation methods are shown in Table 15 using the TAI data. The data are sensitive to the choice of the transformation and this might cause problems in terms of loss of the interval level of the information, sensitivity to outliers, arbitrary choice of categorical scores and sensitivity to weighting.

Sometimes there is no need to normalise the indicators, for example if the indicators are already expressed with the same standard. See, for example, the case of e-Business Readiness (Nardo et al., 2004), where all the indicators are expressed in terms of percentages of enterprises possessing a given infrastructure or using a given ICT tool. In such cases the normalisation would rather obfuscate the issue, as one would lose the information inherent in the percentages.

Box 8. Time distance

The difference between two countries with respect to an indicator is usually measured on the vertical axis as the difference between values of that indicator at a point in time. However there could be a complementary measure of difference which takes time into account, *i.e.* measuring the difference between two countries for a given indicator on the horizontal axis as *time distance* between those countries. For example, the level of female life expectancy of 75 years was reached in Sweden in about 1960 and in the UK in 1970. The time distance is thus 10 years (see Sicherl, 2004). Time distance is a dynamic measure of temporal disparity between two series expressed in units (time) readily comparable across indicators. It requires any of actual time series, benchmarks or projections, thus poor data availability may hamper its use. In formal terms, let x_{qi} be as usual the level of indicator q for country i.

The time distance $S_{ij}(x_q)$ can be written as $S_{ij}(x_q) = T_i(x_q) - T_j(x_q)$, *i.e.* the difference in time which divides country i and country j for the same level of indicator x_q. Time distance can also be applied to calculate a kind of growth rate for time: for each country $S(\Delta x_q) = (T_i(x_q + \Delta x_q) - T_j(x_q)) / \Delta x_q$. For further information see Sicherl (1973).

HANDBOOK ON CONSTRUCTING COMPOSITE INDICATORS: METHODOLOGY AND USER GUIDE – ISBN 978-92-64-04345-9 - © OECD 2008

STEP 6. WEIGHTING AND AGGREGATION

WEIGHTING METHODS

6.1. Weights based on principal components analysis or factor analysis

Principal components analysis, and more specifically factor analysis, groups together individual indicators which are collinear to form a composite indicator that captures as much as possible of the information common to individual indicators. Note that individual indicators must have the same unit of measurement. Each factor (usually estimated using principal components analysis) reveals the set of indicators with which it has the strongest association. The idea under PCA/FA is to account for the highest possible variation in the indicator set using the smallest possible number of factors. Therefore, the composite no longer depends upon the dimensionality of the data set but rather is based on the "statistical" dimensions of the data.

According to PCA/FA, weighting intervenes only to correct for overlapping information between two or more correlated indicators and is not a measure of the theoretical importance of the associated indicator. If no correlation between indicators is found, then weights cannot be estimated with this method. This is the case for the new economic sentiment indicator, where factor and principal components analysis excluded the weighting of individual questions within a sub-component of the composite index (see the supplement B of the Business and Consumer Surveys Result N. 8/9 August/September 2001[22]).

The first step in FA is to check the correlation structure of the data, as explained in the section on multivariate analysis. If the correlation between the indicators is weak, then it is unlikely that they share common factors. The second step is the identification of a certain number of latent factors (fewer than the number of individual indicators) representing the data. Each factor depends on a set of coefficients (loadings), each coefficient measuring the correlation between the individual indicator and the latent factor. Principal components analysis is usually used to extract factors (Manly, 1994[23]). For a factor analysis only a subset of principal components is retained (m), i.e. those that account for the largest amount of the variance.

Standard practice is to choose factors that: (i) have associated eigenvalues larger than one; (ii) contribute individually to the explanation of overall variance by more than 10%; and (iii) contribute cumulatively to the explanation of the overall variance by more than 60%. With the reduced data set in TAI (23 countries) the factors with eigenvalues close to unity are the first four, as summarised in Table 16. Individually they explain more than 10% of the total variance and overall they count for about the 87% of variance.

Table 16. Eigenvalues of TAI data set

	Eigenvalue	Variance (%)	Cumulative variance (%)
1	3.3	41.9	41.9
2	1.7	21.8	63.7
3	1.0	12.3	76.0
4	0.9	11.1	87.2
5	0.5	6.0	93.2
6	0.3	3.7	96.9
7	0.2	2.2	99.1
8	0.1	0.9	100

The third step deals with the rotation of factors (Table 17). The rotation (usually the *varimax rotation*) is used to minimise the number of individual indicators that have a high loading on the same factor. The idea behind transforming the factorial axes is to obtain a "simpler structure" of the factors (ideally a structure in which each indicator is loaded exclusively on one of the retained factors). Rotation is a standard step in factor analysis – it changes the factor loadings and hence the interpretation of the factors, while leaving unchanged the analytical solutions obtained *ex-ante* and *ex-post* the rotation.

Table 17. Factor loadings of TAI based on principal components

	Factor loading				Squared factor loading (scaled to unity sum)			
	Factor 1	Factor 2	Factor 3	Factor 4	Factor 1	Factor 2	Factor 3	Factor 4
Patents	0.07	0.97	0.06	0.06	*0.00*	***0.67***	*0.00*	*0.00*
Royalties	0.13	0.07	-0.07	0.93	*0.01*	*0.00*	*0.00*	***0.49***
Internet	0.79	-0.21	0.21	0.42	***0.24***	*0.03*	*0.04*	*0.10*
Tech exports	-0.64	0.56	-0.04	0.36	*0.16*	***0.23***	*0.00*	*0.07*
Telephones	0.37	0.17	0.38	0.68	*0.05*	*0.02*	*0.12*	***0.26***
Electricity	0.82	-0.04	0.25	0.35	***0.25***	*0.00*	*0.05*	*0.07*
Schooling	0.88	0.23	-0.09	0.09	***0.29***	*0.04*	*0.01*	*0.00*
University	0.08	0.04	0.96	0.04	*0.00*	*0.00*	***0.77***	*0.00*
Expl.Var	2.64	1.39	1.19	1.76				
Expl./Tot	*0.38*	*0.20*	*0.17*	*0.25*				

Note: Expl.Var is the variance explained by the factor and Expl./Tot is the explained variance divided by the total variance of the four factors.

The last step deals with the construction of the weights from the matrix of factor loadings after rotation, given that the square of factor loadings represents the proportion of the total unit variance of the indicator which is explained by the factor. The approach used by Nicoletti *et al.*, (2000) is that of grouping the individual indicators with the highest factors loadings into *intermediate* composite indicators. With the TAI data set there are four *intermediate composites* (Table 17). The first includes *Internet* (with a weight of 0.24), *electricity* (weight 0.25) and *schooling* (weight 0.29).[24] Likewise the second intermediate is formed by *patents* and *exports* (worth 0.67 and 0.23 respectively), the third only by *university* (0.77) and the fourth by *royalties* and *telephones* (weighted with 0.49 and 0.26).

The four intermediate composites are aggregated by assigning a weight to each one of them equal to the proportion of the explained variance in the data set: 0.38 for the first (0.38 = 2.64/(2.64+1.39+1.19+1.76)), 0.20 for the second, 0.17 for the third and 0.25 for the fourth (Table 18).[25] Note that different methods for the extraction of principal components imply different weights, hence different scores for the composite (and possibly different country rankings). For example, if Maximum

HANDBOOK ON CONSTRUCTING COMPOSITE INDICATORS: METHODOLOGY AND USER GUIDE – ISBN 978-92-64-04345-9 - © OECD 2008

Likelihood (ML) were to be used instead of Principal Components (PC), the weights obtained would be as given in Table 18.

Table 18. Weights for the TAI indicators based on maximum likelihood (ML) or principal components (PC) method for the extraction of the common factors

	ML	PC
Patents	0.19	0.17
Royalties	0.20	0.15
Internet	0.07	0.11
Tech exports	0.07	0.07
Telephones	0.15	0.08
Electricity	0.11	0.12
Schooling	0.19	0.14
University	0.02	0.16

6.2. Data envelopment analysis (DEA)

Data Envelopment Analysis (DEA) employs linear programming tools to estimate an *efficiency frontier* that would be used as a benchmark to measure the relative performance of countries.[26] This requires construction of a benchmark (the *frontier*) and the measurement of the distance between countries in a multi-dimensional framework. The following assumptions are made for the benchmark:

(i) positive weights – the higher the value of a given individual indicator, the better for the corresponding country;

(ii) non-discrimination of countries which are the best in any single dimension (individual indicator), thus ranking them equally, and;

(iii) a linear combination of the best performers is feasible, *i.e.* convexity of the frontier.

The distance of each country with respect to the benchmark is determined by the location of the country and its position relative to the frontier. Both issues are represented in Figure 16 for the simple case of four countries and two base indicators which are represented in the two axes. Countries (*a, b, c, d*) are ranked according to the score of the indicators. The line connecting countries *a*, *b* and *c* constitutes the performance frontier and the benchmark for country *d* which lies beyond the frontier. The countries supporting the frontier are classified as the *best performing*, while country *d* is the *worst performing*.

Figure 16.   Data envelopment analysis (DEA) performance frontier

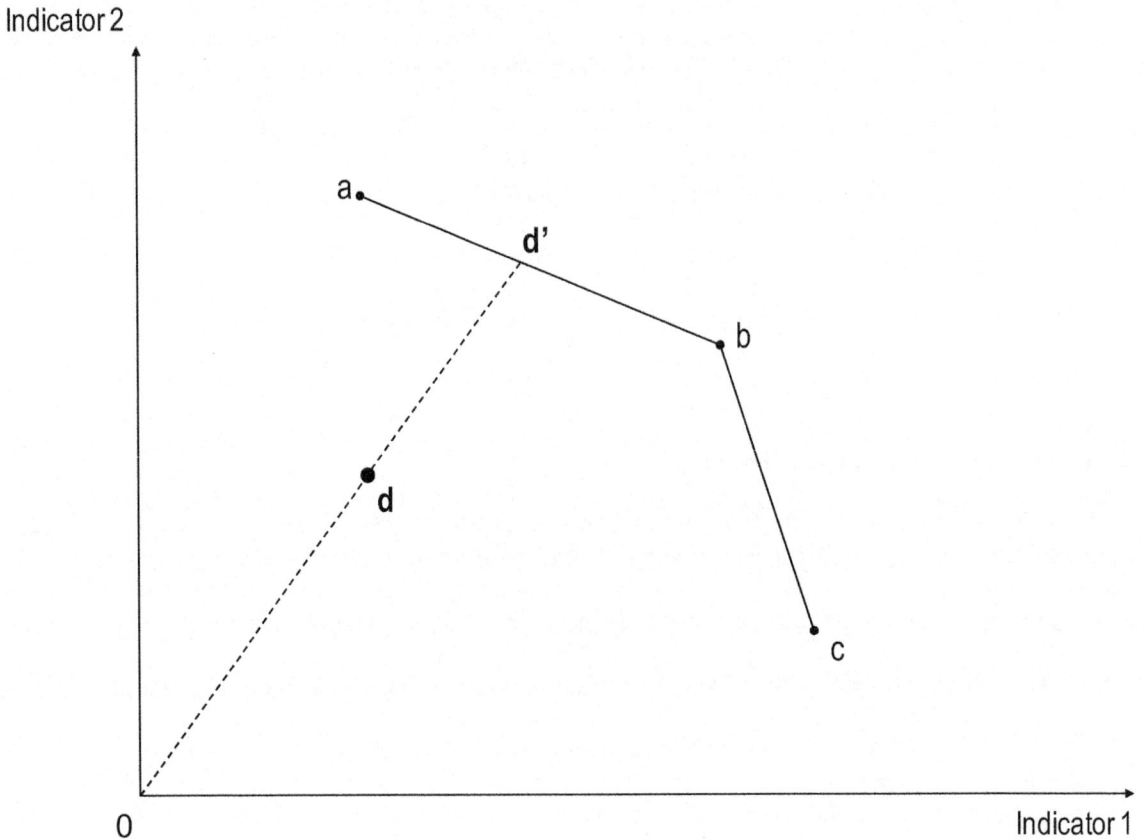

Source : Rearranged from Mahlberg & Obersteiner (2001)

The performance indicator is the ratio of two distances: the distance between the origin and the actual observed point and between the origin and the projected point in the frontier: $\overline{0d}\,/\,\overline{0d'}$. The best performing countries will have a performance score of 1, and the worst, less than one. This ratio corresponds to $(w_{1d}I_{1d} + w_{2d}I_{2d})/(w_{1d}I_{1d}^{*} + w_{2d}I_{2d}^{*})$, where I_{id}^{*} is the frontier value of indicator $i=1,2$, and I_{id} is its actual value (see expression 18 for more than two indicators). The set of weights for each country therefore depends on its position with respect to the frontier, while the benchmark corresponds to the ideal point with a similar mix of indicators (d' in the example). The benchmark could also be determined by a hypothetical decision-maker (Korhonen *et al.*, 2001), who would locate the target in the efficiency frontier with the most preferred combination of individual indicators. This is similar to the budget allocation method (see below) where experts are asked to assign weights (*i.e.* priorities) to individual indicators.

6.3. Benefit of the doubt approach (BOD)

The application of DEA to the field of composite indicators is known as the "benefit of the doubt" approach (BOD) and was originally proposed to evaluate macroeconomic performance (Melyn & Moesen, 1991).[27] In the BOD approach, the composite indicator is defined as the ratio of a country's actual performance to its benchmark performance:

$$CI_c = \frac{\sum_{c=1}^{M} I_{qc} w_{qc}}{\sum_{c=1}^{M} I_{qc}^* w_{qc}} \tag{19}$$

where I_{qc} is the normalised (with the max-min method) score of qth individual indicator (q=1,…,Q) for country c (c=1,…M) and w_{qc} the corresponding weight. Cherchye *et al.*, (2004), the first to implement this method, suggested obtaining the benchmark as the solution of a maximisation problem, although external benchmarks are also possible:

$$I^* = I^*(w) = \underset{I_k, k \in \{1,...,M\}}{arg\,max} \left(\sum_{q=1}^{Q} I_{qk} w_q \right) \tag{20}$$

I* is the score of the hypothetical country that maximises the overall performance (defined as the weighted average), given the (unknown) set of weights w. Note that (i) weights are country specific: different sets of weights may lead to the selection of different countries, as long as no one country has the highest score in all individual indicators; (ii) the benchmark would in general be country-dependent, so there would be no unique benchmark (unless, as before, one particular country were best in all individual indicators), (iii) individual indicators must be comparable, *i.e.* have the same unit of measurement.

The second step is the specification of the set of weights for each country. The optimal set of weights – if such exists – guarantees the best position for the associated country *vis-à-vis* all other countries in the sample. With any other weighting profile, the relative position of that country would be worse. Optimal weights are obtained by solving the following constrained optimisation:

$$CI_c^* = \underset{w_{qc}, q=1,...,Q}{arg\,max} \frac{\sum_{q=1}^{Q} I_{qc} w_{qc}}{\underset{I_k, k \in \{1,...,M\}}{max} \left(\sum_{q=1}^{Q} I_{qk} w_{qc} \right)} \qquad \text{for } c=1,..,M \tag{21}$$

subject to non-negativity constraints on weights.[28]

The resulting composite index will range between zero (worst possible performance) and 1 (the benchmark). Operationally, equation (21) can be reduced to the following linear programming problem by multiplying all the weights with a common factor which does not alter the index value and may then be solved using optimisation algorithms:

$$CI_c^* = \underset{wqc}{arg\,max} \sum_{q=1}^{Q} I_{qc} w_{qc}$$

s.t.

$$\sum_{q=1}^{Q} I_{qk} w_{qk} \leq 1 \tag{22}$$

$$w_{qk} \geq 0$$

$$\forall k = 1,..., M; \forall q = 1,..., Q$$

The result of the BOD approach applied to the TAI example can be seen in Table 19. Weights are given in the first eight columns, while the last column contains the composite indicator values. Finland, the United States and Sweden have a composite indicator value of one, *i.e.* they have the top score in the ranking. This, however, masks a problem of multiple equilibria. In Figure 6 any point between country *a* (*e.g.* Finland) and country *b* (*e.g.* United States) could be an optimal solution for these countries. Thus weights are not uniquely determined. Note also that the multiplicity of solutions is likely to depend upon the set of constraints imposed on the weights of the maximisation problem in (22) – the wider the range of variation of weights, the lower the possibility of obtaining a unique solution.[29] Cherchye *et al.* (2008) propose an application of the BOD approach to the Technology Achievement Index, which imposes restrictions on the pie-shares, instead of restrictions on the weights. The pie-shares are expressed as the ratio of the weighted indicator values over the overall composite indicator score. This application of the BOD is particularly interesting as it directly reveals how the respective pie shares contribute to a composite indicator score and the pie-shares have a unity sum.

Table 19. Benefit of the doubt (BOD) approach applied to TAI

	Patents (weight)	Royalties (weight)	Internet (weight)	Tech. Export (weight)	Telephones (weight)	Electricity (weight)	Schooling (weight)	University (weight)	CI (score)
Finland	0.15	0.17	0.17	0.16	0.19	0.17	0.17	0.19	1
United States	0.20	0.20	0.17	0.21	0.15	0.15	0.21	0.14	1
Sweden	0.18	0.21	0.15	0.19	0.19	0.16	0.20	0.14	1
Japan	0.22	0.15	0.15	0.22	0.22	0.16	0.21	0.15	0.87
Korea	0.22	0.14	0.14	0.22	0.14	0.14	0.22	0.22	0.80
Netherlands	0.22	0.22	0.14	0.22	0.22	0.14	0.14	0.14	0.75
United Kingdom	0.14	0.21	0.14	0.21	0.21	0.14	0.20	0.15	0.71
Canada	0.14	0.14	0.14	0.21	0.21	0.21	0.21	0.14	0.73
Australia	0.13	0.13	0.20	0.13	0.13	0.20	0.20	0.20	0.66
Singapore	0.14	0.14	0.14	0.20	0.20	0.20	0.14	0.20	0.62
Germany	0.22	0.15	0.15	0.22	0.21	0.15	0.22	0.15	0.62
Norway	0.14	0.14	0.20	0.14	0.20	0.20	0.20	0.14	0.86
Ireland	0.14	0.21	0.14	0.21	0.21	0.14	0.20	0.15	0.60
Belgium	0.14	0.16	0.14	0.21	0.19	0.21	0.21	0.14	0.54
New Zealand	0.21	0.14	0.21	0.14	0.14	0.21	0.21	0.14	0.58
Austria	0.22	0.14	0.14	0.22	0.22	0.22	0.14	0.14	0.52
France	0.22	0.14	0.14	0.22	0.22	0.22	0.14	0.14	0.51
Israel	0.21	0.15	0.15	0.22	0.22	0.15	0.22	0.15	0.49
Spain	0.21	0.14	0.14	0.21	0.21	0.14	0.14	0.21	0.34
Italy	0.22	0.14	0.14	0.22	0.22	0.22	0.14	0.14	0.38
Czech Republic	0.22	0.15	0.15	0.22	0.15	0.22	0.22	0.15	0.31
Hungary	0.22	0.14	0.21	0.22	0.14	0.14	0.22	0.15	0.27
Slovenia	0.22	0.14	0.14	0.22	0.22	0.22	0.14	0.14	0.28

Note: Columns 1 to 8: weights, column 9: composite indicator for a given country, n=23 countries.

6.4. Unobserved components model (UCM)

In the Unobserved Components Model (UCM), individual indicators are assumed to depend on an unobserved variable plus an error term – for example, the "percentage of firms using internet in country *j*" depends upon the (unknown) propensity to adopt new information and communication technologies

HANDBOOK ON CONSTRUCTING COMPOSITE INDICATORS: METHODOLOGY AND USER GUIDE – ISBN 978-92-64-04345-9 - © OECD 2008

plus an error term, accounting, for example, for the error in the sampling of firms. Therefore, estimating the unknown component sheds some light on the relationship between the composite and its components. The weight obtained will be set to minimise the error in the composite. This method resembles the well known regression analysis. The main difference lies in the dependent variable, which is unknown under UCM.

Let *ph(c)* be the unknown phenomenon to be measured. The observed data consist in a cluster of $q=1,...,Q(c)$ indicators, each measuring an aspect of *ph(c)*. Let $c=1,...M(q)$ be the countries covered by indicator *q*. The observed score of country *c* on indicator *q*, *I(c,q)* can be written as a linear function of the unobserved phenomenon and an error term, $\varepsilon(c,q)$:

$$I(c,q) = \alpha(q) + \beta(q)[ph(c) + \varepsilon(c,q)] \tag{23}$$

$\alpha(q)$ and $\beta(q)$ are unknown parameters mapping *ph(c)* on *I(c,q)*.

The error term captures two sources of uncertainty. First, the phenomenon can be only imperfectly measured or observed in each country (*e.g.* errors of measurement). Second, the relationship between *ph(c)* and *I(c,q)* may be imperfect (*e.g.* *I(c,q)* may be only a noisy indicator of the phenomenon if there are differences between countries on the indicator). The error term $\varepsilon(c,q)$ is assumed to have a zero mean, $E(\varepsilon(c,q)) = 0$, and the same variance across countries within a given indicator, but a different variance across indicators, $E(\varepsilon(c,q)^2) = \sigma_q^2$; it also holds that $E(\varepsilon(c,q)\varepsilon(i,h)) = 0$ for $c \neq i$ or $q \neq h$.

The error term is assumed to be independent across indicators, given that each individual indicator should ideally measure a particular aspect of the phenomenon independent of others. Furthermore, it is usually assumed that *ph(c)* is a random variable with zero mean and unit variance, and the indicators are normalised using Min-Max to take values between zero and one. The assumption that both *ph(c)* and $\varepsilon(c,q)$ are both normally distributed simplifies the estimation of the level of *ph(c)* in country *c*. This is done by using the mean of the conditional distribution of the unobserved component, once the observed scores are appropriately re-scaled:

$$E[ph(c)/I(c,1),...,I(c,Q(c))] = \sum_{q=1}^{Q(c)} w(c,q) \frac{I(c,q) - \alpha(q)}{\beta(q)} \tag{24}$$

The weights are equal to:

$$w(c,q) = \frac{\sigma_q^{-2}}{1 + \sum_{q=1}^{Q(c)} \sigma_q^{-2}} \tag{25}$$

where *w(c,q)* is a decreasing function of the variance of indicator *q*, and an increasing function of the variance of the other indicators. The weight, *w(c,q)*, depends on the variance of indicator *q* (numerator) and on the sum of the variances of the all other individual indicators, including *q* (denominator). However, since not all countries have data on all individual indicators, the denominator of *w(c,q)* could be country specific. This may produce non-comparability of country values for the composite, as in BOD. Clearly, whenever the set of indicators is equal for all countries, weights will no longer be country specific and comparability will be assured. The variance of the conditional distribution is given by:

$$var[\,ph(c)\,/\,I(c,1),...,I(c,Q(c))] = [\,1 + \sum_{q=1}^{Q(c)} \sigma_q^{-2}\,]^{-1} \qquad (26)$$

and can be used as a measure of the precision of the composite. The variance decreases in the number of indicators for each country, and increases in the disturbance term for each indicator. The estimation of the model could be simplified by the assumption of normality for $ph(c)$ and $\varepsilon(c,q)$. Notice that the unknown parameters to be estimated are $\alpha(q)s$, $\beta(q)s$, and $\sigma_q^2 s$ (hence at least 3 indicators per country are needed for an exactly identified model) so the likelihood function of the observed data based on equation (25) will be maximised with respect to $\alpha(q)s$, $\beta(q)s$, and $\sigma_q^2 s$ and their estimated values substituted back in equations (24) and (25) to obtain the composite indicator and the weights.[30]

6.5. Budget allocation process (BAP)

In the Budget Allocation Process (BAP), experts on a given theme (*e.g.* innovation, education, health, biodiversity, …) described by a set of indicators are asked to allocate a "budget" of one hundred points to the indicator set, based on their experience and subjective judgment of the relative importance of the respective indicators. Weights are calculated as average budgets. The main advantages of BAP are its transparent and relatively straightforward nature and short duration.

It is essential to bring together experts representing a wide spectrum of knowledge and experience to ensure that a proper weighting system is established. Special care should be taken in the identification of the population of experts from which to draw a sample, stratified or otherwise.[31] It is crucial that the selected experts are not specialists for individual indicators, but rather for the given sub-index. For example, a biodiversity index should be handled by biodiversity experts, not by ornithology experts. It is also noteworthy that at the top level, *e.g.* of a sustainable development index composed of economic, social and environmental sub-indices, the "experts" should be those who decide on the relative (political) weight of economic, social and environmental questions, *i.e.* ordinary voters.

The budget allocation process has four different phases:

- Selection of experts for the valuation;
- Allocation of budgets to the individual indicators;
- Calculation of weights;
- Iteration of the budget allocation until convergence is reached (optional).

6.6. Public opinion

From a methodological point of view, opinion polls focus on the notion of "concern". That is, people are asked to express their degree of concern (*e.g.* great or small) about issues, as measured by base indicators. As with expert assessments, the budget allocation method could also be applied in public opinion polls. However, it is more difficult to ask the public to allocate a hundred points to several individual indicators than to express a degree of concern about a given problem.

6.7. Analytic hierarchy process (AHP)

The Analytic Hierarchy Process (AHP) is a widely used technique for multi-attribute decision-making (Saaty, 1987). It facilitates the decomposition of a problem into a hierarchical structure and

HANDBOOK ON CONSTRUCTING COMPOSITE INDICATORS: METHODOLOGY AND USER GUIDE – ISBN 978-92-64-04345-9 – © OECD 2008

assures that both qualitative and quantitative aspects of a problem are incorporated into the evaluation process, during which opinions are systematically extracted by means of pairwise comparisons. According to Forman (1983):

> AHP is a compensatory decision methodology because alternatives that are efficient with respect to one or more objectives can compensate by their performance with respect to other objectives. AHP allows for the application of data, experience, insight, and intuition in a logical and thorough way within a hierarchy as a whole. In particular, AHP as a weighting method enables decision-makers to derive weights as opposed to arbitrarily assigning them.

Weights represent the trade-off across indicators. They measure willingness to forego a given variable in exchange for another. Hence, they are not importance coefficients. It could cause misunderstandings if AHP weights were to be interpreted as importance coefficients (see Ülengin *et al.*, 2001).

The core of AHP is an ordinal pairwise comparison of attributes. For a given objective, the comparisons are made between pairs of individual indicators, asking which of the two is the more important, and by how much. The preference is expressed on a semantic scale of 1 to 9. A preference of 1 indicates equality between two individual indicators, while a preference of 9 indicates that the individual indicator is 9 times more important than the other one. The results are represented in a comparison matrix (Table 20), where $A_{ii} = 1$ and $A_{ij} = 1 / A_{ji}$.

Table 20. Comparison matrix of eight individual TAI indicators

Objective	Patents	Royalties	Internet	Tech exports	Telephone	Electricity	Schooling	University
Patents	1	2	3	2	5	5	1	3
Royalties	1/2	1	2	1/2	4	4	½	3
Internet	1/3	½	1	1/4	2	2	1/5	1/2
Tech. exports	1/2	2	4	1	4	4	1/2	3
Telephones	1/5	1/4	1/2	1/4	1	1	1/5	1/2
Electricity	1/5	¼	1/2	1/4	1	1	1/5	1/2
Schooling	1	2	5	2	5	5	1	4
University	1/3	1/3	2	1/3	2	2	1/4	1

For the example, *patents* is three times more important than *Internet*. Each judgement reflects the perception of the relative contributions (weights) of the two individual indicators to the overall objective (Table 21).

Table 21. Comparison matrix of three individual TAI indicators

Objective	Patents	Royalties	Internet	......
Patents	1	w_P/w_{ROY}	w_P/w_I	
Royalties	w_{ROY}/w_P	1	w_{ROY}/w_I	
Internet	w_I/w_P	w_I/w_{ROY}	1	
....				

The relative weights of the individual indicators are calculated using an eigenvector. This method makes it possible to check the consistency of the comparison matrix through the calculation of the eigenvalues. Figure 17 shows the results of the evaluation process and the weights, together with the corresponding standard deviation.[32]

Figure 17.   Analytical hierarchy process (AHP) weighting of the TAI indicators

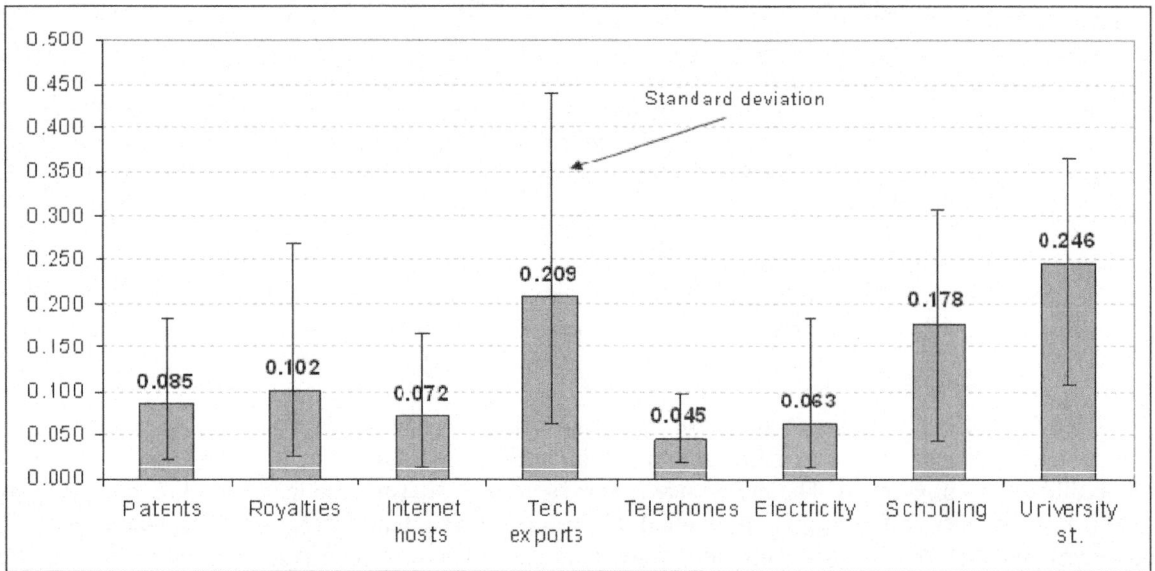

Note. Average weight (bold) and standard deviation.

People's beliefs, however, are not always consistent. For example, if one person claims that A is much more important than B, B slightly more important than C, and C slightly more important than A, his/her judgment is inconsistent and the results are less trustworthy. Inconsistency, however, is part of human nature. It might therefore be adequate to measure the degree of inconsistency in order to make results acceptable to the public. For a matrix of size $Q \times Q$, only $Q–1$ comparisons are required to establish weights for Q indicators. The actual number of comparisons performed in AHP is $Q(Q–1)/2$. This is computationally costly, but results in a set of weights that is less sensitive to errors of judgement. In addition, redundancy allows for a measure of judgment errors, an inconsistency ratio. Small inconsistency ratios – the suggested rule-of-thumb is less than 0.1, although 0.2 is often cited – do not drastically affect the weights (Saaty, 1980; Karlsson, 1998).

6.8. Conjoint analysis (CA)

Merely asking respondents how much importance they attach to an individual indicator is unlikely to yield effective "willingness to pay" valuations. These can be inferred by using conjoint analysis (CA) from respondents' rankings of alternative scenarios (Hair *et al.*, 1995). Conjoint analysis is a decompositional multivariate data analysis technique frequently used in marketing (McDaniel & Gates, 1998) and consumer research (Green & Srinivasan, 1978). If AHP derives the "worth" of an alternative, *summing up* the "worth" of the individual indicators, CA does the opposite, *i.e.* it disaggregates preferences.

This method asks for an evaluation (a preference) of a set of alternative scenarios. A scenario might be a given set of values for the individual indicators. The preference is then decomposed by relating the single components (the known values of individual indicators of that scenario) to the evaluation. Although this methodology uses statistical analysis to treat the data, it relies on the opinion of people (*e.g.* experts, politicians, citizens), who are asked to choose which set of individual indicators they prefer, each person being presented with a different selection of sets to evaluate.

HANDBOOK ON CONSTRUCTING COMPOSITE INDICATORS: METHODOLOGY AND USER GUIDE – ISBN 978-92-64-04345-9 – © OECD 2008

The absolute value (or level) of individual indicators could be varied both within the selection of sets presented to the same individual and across individuals. A preference function would be estimated using the information emerging from the different scenarios. A probability of the preference could therefore be estimated as a function of the levels of the individual indicators defining the alternative scenarios:

$$pref_c = P(I_{1c}, I_{2c}, ..., I_{Qc})\tag{27}$$

where I_{qc} is the level of individual indicator $q=1,...,Q$, for country $c=1,...,M$. After estimating this probability (often using discrete choice models), the derivatives with respect to the individual indicators of the preference function can be used as weights to aggregate the individual indicators in a composite index:

$$CI_c = \sum_{q=1}^{Q} \frac{\partial P}{\partial I_{qc}} I_{qc}\tag{28}$$

The idea is to calculate the total differential of the function P at the point of indifference between alternative states of nature. Solving for the individual indicator q, the marginal rate of substitution of I_{qc} is obtained. Therefore $\partial P/\partial I_{qc}$ (thus the weight) indicates a trade-off – how the preference changes with the change of indicator. This implies compensability among indicators, *i.e.* the possibility of offsetting a deficit in some dimension with an outstanding performance in another. This is an important feature of this method, and should be carefully evaluated vis-à-vis the objectives of the overall analysis. For example, compensability might not be desirable when dealing with environmental issues.

6.9. Performance of the different weighting methods

The weights for the TAI example are calculated using different weighting methods – equal weighting (EW), factor analysis (FA), budget allocation (BAP) and analytical hierarchy process (AHP) (Table 22). The diversity in the weights resulting from applying different methods is notable. Clearly, with each method the various individual indicators are evaluated differently. *Patents*, for example, are worth 17% of the weight according to FA, but only 9% according to AHP. This influences strongly the variability of each country's ranking (Table 23). For example, Korea ranks second with AHP, but only fifth with EW or FA. AHP assigns high weights (more than 20%) to two indicators, *exports* and *university*, for which Korea has higher scores for one or both indicators, compared to the United States, Sweden or Japan. The role of the variability in the weights and their influence on the value of the composite are discussed in the section on sensitivity analysis.

Table 22. TAI weights based on different methods

Equal weighting (EW), factor analysis (FA), budget allocation (BAP), analytic hierarchy process (AHP)

Method	Weights for the indicators (fixed for all countries)							
	Patents	Royalties	Internet	Tech exports	Telephones	Electricity	Schooling	University
EW	0.13	0.13	0.13	0.13	0.13	0.13	0.13	0.13
FA	0.17	0.15	0.11	0.06	0.08	0.13	0.13	0.17
BAP	0.11	0.11	0.11	0.18	0.10	0.06	0.15	0.18
AHP	0.09	0.10	0.07	0.21	0.05	0.06	0.18	0.25

Table 23. TAI country rankings based on different weighting methods

	EW	FA	BOD	BAP	AHP
Finland	1	1	1	1	1
United States	2	2	1	2	3
Sweden	3	3	1	3	4
Japan	4	4	4	5	5
Korea	5	5	6	4	2
Netherlands	6	6	7	8	11
United Kingdom	7	8	9	7	7
Singapore	8	11	12	6	6
Canada	9	10	8	10	10
Australia	10	7	10	11	9
Germany	11	12	11	9	8
Norway	12	9	5	13	16
Ireland	13	14	13	12	12
Belgium	14	15	15	14	13
New Zealand	15	13	14	17	18
Austria	16	16	16	15	15
France	17	17	17	16	14
Israel	18	18	18	18	17
Spain	19	19	20	19	19
Italy	20	20	19	21	21
Czech Republic	21	21	21	22	22
Hungary	22	23	23	20	20
Slovenia	23	22	22	23	23

Note: *e.g.* the United States ranks first according to BOD, second according to EW, FA and BAP, and third according to AHP.

HANDBOOK ON CONSTRUCTING COMPOSITE INDICATORS: METHODOLOGY AND USER GUIDE – ISBN 978-92-64-04345-9 – © OECD 2008

Table 24. Advantages and disadvantages of different weighting methods

Advantages	Disadvantages
Benefit of the doubt (BOD) -- *e.g.* Human Development Index (Mahlberg & Obersteiner, 2001); Sustainable Development (Cherchye & Kuosmanen, 2002); Social Inclusion (Cherchye, *et al.*, 2004); Macro-economic performance evaluation (Melyn & Moesen, 1991; Cherchye 2001); Unemployment (Storrie & Bjurek, 1999; 2000).	
• The indicator is sensitive to national policy priorities, in that the weights are endogenously determined by the observed performances (this is a useful second-best approach whenever the best – full information about true policy priorities – cannot be attained). • The benchmark is not based upon theoretical bounds, but on a linear combination of observed best performances. • Useful in policy arena, since policy-makers could not complain about unfair weighting: any other weighting scheme would have generated lower composite scores. • Such an index could be "incentive generating" rather than "punishing" the countries lagging behind. • Weights, by revealing information about the policy priorities, may help to define trade-offs, overcoming the difficulties of linear aggregations.	• Without imposing constraints on weights (except non-negativity) it is likely to have many of the countries with a composite indicator score equal to 1 (many countries on the frontier). • It may happen that there exists a multiplicity of solutions making the optimal set of weights undetermined (this is likely to happen when $CI=1$). • The index is likely to reward the status quo, since for each country the maximisation problem gives higher weights to higher scores. • The best performer (that with a composite equal to one) will not see its progress reflected in the composite (which will remain stacked to 1). This can be solved by imposing an external benchmark.
Unobserved Components Models -- e.g. Governance indicators (see Kaufmann et al., 1999; 2003)	
• Weights do not depend on *ad hoc* restrictions.	• Reliability and robustness of results depend on the availability of sufficient data. • With highly correlated individual indicators there could be identification problems. • Rewards the absence of outliers, given that weights are a decreasing function of the variance of individual indicators. • If each country has a different number of individual indicators; weights are country–specific.
Budget Allocation -- *e.g.* Employment Outlook (OECD,1999); Composite Indicator on e-Business Readiness (EC, 2004b); National Health Care System Performance (King's Fund., 2001); Eco-indicator 99 (Pré-Consultants NL, 2000) (weights based on survey from experts); Overall Health System Attainment (WHO, 2000) (weights based on survey from experts).	
• Weighting is based on expert opinion and not on technical manipulations. • Expert opinion is likely to increase the legitimacy of the composite and to create a forum of discussion in which to form a consensus for policy action.	• Weighting reliability. Weights could reflect specific local conditions (*e.g.* in environmental problems), so expert weighting may not be transferable from one area to another. • Allocating a certain budget over a too large number of indicators may lead to serious cognitive stress for the experts, as it implies circular thinking. The method is likely to produce inconsistencies for a number of indicators higher than 10. • Weighting may not measure the importance of each individual indicator but rather the urgency or need for political intervention in the dimension of the individual indicator concerned (*e.g.* more weight on Ozone emissions if the expert feels that not enough has been done to tackle them).

Advantages	Disadvantages
Public Opinion – *e.g.* concern about environmental problems Index (Parker, 1991).	
• Deals with issues on the public agenda. • Allows all stakeholders to express their preference and creates a consensus for policy action.	• Implies the measurement of "concern" (see previous discussion on the Budget Allocation). • Could produce inconsistencies when dealing with a high number of indicators (see previous discussion on the Budget Allocation).
Analytic Hierarchy Process -- *e.g.* Index of Environmental Friendliness, (Puolamaa *et al.*, 1996).	
• Can be used both for qualitative and quantitative data. • Transparency of the composite is higher. • Weighting is based on expert opinion and not on technical manipulations. • Expert opinion is likely to increase the legitimacy of the composite and to create a forum of discussion in which to form a consensus for policy action • Provides a measure of the inconsistency in respondents replies	• Requires a high number of pairwise comparisons and thus can be computationally costly. • Results depend on the set of evaluators chosen and the setting of the experiment.
Conjoint Analysis – *e.g.* indicator of quality of life in the city of Istanbul (Ülengin *et al.*, 2001); advocated by Kahn (1998) and Kahn & Maynard (1995) for environmental applications.	
• Weights represent trade-offs across indicators. • Takes into account the socio-political context and the values of respondents.	• Needs a pre-specified utility function and implies compensability. • Depends on the sample of respondents chosen and on how questions are framed. • Requires a large sample of respondents and each respondent may be required to express a large number of preferences. • Estimation process is rather complex.

AGGREGATION METHODS

6.10. Additive aggregation methods

The simplest additive aggregation method entails the calculation of the ranking of each country according to each individual indicator and summation of the resulting rankings, *e.g.* Information and Communication Technologies Index (Fagerberg, 2001). The method is based on ordinal information (the Borda rule). It is simple and independent of outliers. However, the absolute value of information is lost.

$$CI_c = \sum_{q=1}^{Q} Rank_{qc} \quad \text{for } c=1,...,M. \tag{29}$$

The second method is based on the number of indicators that are above and below a given benchmark. This method uses nominal scores for each indicator to calculate the difference between the number of indicators above and below an arbitrarily defined threshold around the mean, *e.g.* the Innovation Scoreboard (European Commission, 2001c).

HANDBOOK ON CONSTRUCTING COMPOSITE INDICATORS: METHODOLOGY AND USER GUIDE – ISBN 978-92-64-04345-9 – © OECD 2008

$$CI_c = \sum_{q=1}^{Q} \cdot sgn\left[\frac{I_{qc}}{I_{EUq}} - (1+p)\right] \text{ for } c=1,...,M. \tag{30}$$

The threshold value p can be arbitrarily set above or below the mean. As with the preceding method, it is simple and unaffected by outliers. However, the interval level information is lost. For example, assume that the value of indicator I for country a is 30% above the mean and the value for country b is 25% above, with a threshold of 20% above the mean. Both country a and country b are then counted equally as 'above average', in spite of a having a higher score than b.

By far the most widespread linear aggregation is the summation of weighted and normalised individual indicators:

$$CI_c = \sum_{q=1}^{Q} w_q I_{qc} \tag{31}$$

with $\sum_q w_q = 1$ and $0 \leq w_q \leq 1$, for all $q=1,..,Q$ and $c=1,...,M$.

Although widely used, this aggregation imposes restrictions on the nature of individual indicators. In particular, obtaining a meaningful composite indicator depends on the quality of the underlying individual indicators and their unit of measurement. Furthermore, additive aggregations have important implications for the interpretation of weights.

When using a linear additive aggregation technique, a necessary and sufficient condition for the existence of a proper composite indicator is *preference independence*: given the individual indicators $\{x_1, x_2,...,x_Q\}$, an additive aggregation function exists if and only if these indicators are mutually preferentially independent (Debreu, 1960; Keeney & Raiffa, 1976; Krantz et al., 1971). [33]

Preferential independence is a very strong condition, as it implies that the trade-off ratio between two variables $S_{x,y}$ is independent of the values of the Q-2 other variables (Ting, 1971).[34] From an operational point of view, this means that an additive aggregation function permits the assessment of the marginal contribution of each variable separately. These marginal contributions can then be added together to yield a total value. If, for example, environmental dimensions are involved, the use of a linear aggregation procedure implies that, among the different aspects of an ecosystem, there are no synergies or conflicts. This appears to be quite an unrealistic assumption (Funtowicz et al., 1990). For example, "laboratory experiments made clear that the combined impact of the acidifying substances SO_2, NO_X, NH_3 and O_3 on plant growth is substantially more severe that the (linear) addition of the impacts of each of these substances alone would be." (Dietz & Van der Straaten, 1992). Additive aggregation could thus result in a biased composite indicator, *i.e.* it would not entirely reflect the information of its individual indicators. The dimension and the direction of the error are not easily determined, and the composite cannot be adjusted properly.

6.11. Geometric aggregation

As discussed above, an undesirable feature of additive aggregations is the implied full compensability, such that poor performance in some indicators can be compensated for by sufficiently high values in other indicators. For example, if a hypothetical composite were formed by inequality, environmental degradation, GDP per capita and unemployment, two countries, one with values 21, 1, 1,

1, and the other with 6,6,6,6, would have equal composites if the aggregation were additive and EW were applied. Obviously the two countries would represent very different social conditions which would not be reflected in the composite. If multi-criteria analysis entails full non-compensability, the use of a geometric aggregation (also called deprivational index) $CI_c = \prod_{q=1}^{Q} x_{q,c}^{w_q}$ is an in-between solution.[35]

In the example above, the first country would have a much lower score on the composite than the second, if the aggregation were geometric (2.14 for the first and 6 for the second). In a benchmarking exercise, countries with low scores in some individual indicators thus would prefer a linear rather than a geometric aggregation. On the other hand, the marginal utility of an increase in the score would be much higher when the absolute value of the score is low: country 1, by increasing the second indicator by 1 unit, would increase its composite score from 2.14 to 2.54, while country 2 would go from 6 to 6.23. In other words, the first country would increase its composite score by 19%, but the second only by 4%. Consequently, a country would have a greater incentive to address those sectors/activities/alternatives with low scores if the aggregation were geometric rather than linear, as this would give it a better chance of improving its position in the ranking.

6.12. On the aggregation rules issue: lessons learned from social choice and multi-criteria decision analysis[36]

The *discrete multi-criterion problem* can be described in the following way: A is a finite set of N feasible actions (or alternatives); M is the number of different points of view or evaluation criteria g_m $i=1, 2, \dots, M$ considered relevant in a policy problem, where the action $\boldsymbol{a}$ is judged to be better than action $\boldsymbol{b}$ (both belonging to the set A) according to the *m-th* point of view if $g_m(a)>g_m(b)$. In this way a decision problem may be represented in a tabular or matrix form. Given the sets A (of alternatives) and G (of evaluation criteria) and assuming the existence of N alternatives and M criteria, it is possible to build an $N \times M$ matrix P called *evaluation or impact matrix* whose typical element p_{ij} $(i=1, 2, \dots, M; j=1, 2, \dots, N)$ represents the evaluation of the *j-th* alternative by means of the *i-th* criterion. The impact matrix may include quantitative, qualitative or both types of information.

In general, in a multi-criteria problem, there is no solution optimising all the criteria at the same time (the so-called *ideal* or *utopia solution*) and therefore *compromise solutions* have to be found.

In sum, the information contained in the impact matrix which is useful for solving the so-called multi-criterion problem is:

- *Intensity of preference* (when quantitative criterion scores are present).

- *Number* of criteria in favour of a given alternative.

- *Weight* attached to each criterion.

- *Relationship* of each alternative to all the other alternatives.

Combinations of this information generate different aggregation conventions, *i.e.* manipulation rules for the available information to arrive at a preference structure. The aggregation of several criteria implies taking a position on the fundamental issue of compensability. *Compensability* refers to the existence of trade-offs, *i.e.* the possibility of offsetting a disadvantage on some criteria by a sufficiently

 HANDBOOK ON CONSTRUCTING COMPOSITE INDICATORS: METHODOLOGY AND USER GUIDE – ISBN 978-92-64-04345-9 – © OECD 2008

large advantage on another criterion, whereas smaller advantages would not do the same. Thus a preference relation is non-compensatory if no trade-off occurs, and is compensatory otherwise. The use of weights with intensity of preference originates in compensatory multi-criteria methods and gives the meaning of trade-offs to the weights. By contrast, the use of weights with ordinal criterion scores originates in non-compensatory aggregation procedures and gives the weights the meaning of importance coefficients (Keeney & Raiffa, 1976; Podinovskii, 1994; Roberts, 1979). [37]

Vansnick (1990) showed that the two main approaches in multi-criteria decision theory, *i.e.* the compensatory and non-compensatory, can be directly derived from the seminal work of Borda (1784) and Condorcet (1785). The study of social choice literature reveals that the various ranking procedures used in multi-criterion methods have their origins in social choice. It is apparent that if the concept of criterion is substituted with that of the individual indicator (or *voter* in social choice parlance), and if we label alternatives as countries, the multi-criterion/social choice problem and the construction of a composite indicator are equivalent from a formal point of view. In conclusion, we can then state that multi-criterion and social choice literature are clearly relevant for understanding the aggregation rules useful for building composite indicators.

A topic to begin with is Arrow's impossibility theorem (Arrow, 1963). This theorem shows that if one defines formally those properties which should hold in the definition of the concept of democracy, a very sad conclusion results, namely that the only political system respecting all those properties would be dictatorship. Arrow & Raynaud (1986, pp. 17-23) have proved that the correct solution of a multi-criterion problem comes from a mono-criterion optimisation. A consequence of this theorem is that no perfect aggregation rule may exist. "Reasonable" ranking procedures must therefore be found. In the context of composite indicators, this circumstance gives rise to two questions: is it possible to find a ranking algorithm consistent with some desirable properties?; and conversely, is it possible to ensure that no essential property is lost?

In social choice, the response to Arrow's theorem has been to search for less ambitious voting structures; it is necessary to retain only a few basic requirements. There are generally three such basic requirements:

1. *Anonymity:* all voters must be treated equally (or, in other terms, all indicators must be equally weighted);

2. *Neutrality:* all alternatives (countries) must be treated equally;

3. *Monotonicity:* greater support for one alternative may not jeopardize its success.

Note that while anonymity is clearly essential in the case of voters, this is not the case in the building of a composite indicator, since equal weighting is usually only one of the possible weighting systems. The consequences of losing anonymity will be discussed further on. The following will examine some ranking procedures hailing directly from the social choice tradition. Emphasis will be put on Arrow's result, in the sense that limitations of these procedures will be elucidated.

Let us start with the first numerical example in Table 25, where 21 individual indicators rank four countries (*a, b, c, d*):

Table 25. 21 indicators and 4 countries

Number of indicators	3	5	7	6
	a	*a*	*b*	*c*
	b	*c*	*d*	*b*
	c	*b*	*c*	*d*
	d	*d*	*a*	*a*

(Rearranged from Moulin, 1988, p. 228)

The first column of the example indicates that three indicators put country *a* in the first place, followed by countries *b*, *c*, and *d*. Suppose that the objective is to find the best country. A first possibility is to apply the so-called *plurality rule*, meaning that the country which is more often ranked first is the 'winner'. Thus in this case, country *a* is chosen, since eight indicators put it in first place. However, looking carefully at the numerical example 1 reveals that *a* is also the country with the strongest opposition, since 13 indicators put it in last place.

It is interesting that this paradox was the starting point of Borda's and Condorcet's research at the end of the 18th century, but the plurality rule corresponds to the most common electoral system in the 21st century – this is a clear example of what Arrow's impossibility theorem means in the real-world implementation of democracy. From the plurality rule paradox two main lessons can be learned:

1.   Good ranking procedures should consider the entire ranking of countries and not only the first position.

2.   It is important to consider not only what a majority of criteria prefer but also what they do not prefer at all.

The Borda solution to the plurality rule paradox is the following scoring rule: given N countries, if a country is ranked last, it receives no points; it receives 1 point if ranked next to last. The scoring process continues like this up to $N-1$ points, awarded to the country ranked first. Of course, the Borda winner is the country with the highest total score.

Let us then apply Borda's rule to the data presented in Table 25. To begin, the information can be presented in a *frequency matrix* fashion, as in Table 26. This shows how many individual indicators put each of the countries into each of the four positions in the ranking and the score with which each position is rewarded. Therefore, according to the first row of the matrix, eight indicators put country *a* into first place; seven, *b*; and six, *c*; whereas no indicator puts *d* first. The sum for each row or each column is always a constant equal to the number of individual indicators (21 in this example).

Table 26. A frequency matrix for the application of Borda's rule

Ranking	Indicators				Points
	a	b	c	d	
1st	8	7	6	0	3
2nd	0	9	5	7	2
3rd	0	5	10	6	1
4th	13	0	0	8	0

By applying Borda's scoring rule, the following results are obtained:

$$a = 8 \times 3 = 24$$
$$b = 5 + 9 \times 2 + 7 \times 3 = 44$$
$$c = 10 + 5 \times 2 + 6 \times 3 = 38$$
$$d = 6 + 7 \times 2 = 20$$

It can be seen that the selected country is now b rather than a. The plurality rule paradox has been solved.

Turning to Condorcet, his rule is based on a pair-wise comparison between all countries considered. For each pair, a *concordance index* is computed by counting how many individual indicators are in favour of each country. In this way an outranking matrix, the elements of which hold the *"constant sum property"*, is built. The pairs whose concordance index is higher than 50% of the indicators are selected. Given the transitivity property, a final ranking is isolated.

To make this procedure even clearer, let us apply it to the data presented in Table 25. The outranking matrix is shown in Table 27; in this case, the constant sum is $e_{ij} + e_{ji} = 21 \quad \forall i \neq j$. According to the first row of this matrix, a is always preferred to b, c, and d by eight indicators.

Table 27. Outranking matrix derived from the Concordet approach

$$
\begin{bmatrix}
 & a & b & c & d \\
a & 0 & 8 & 8 & 8 \\
b & 13 & 0 & 10 & 21 \\
c & 13 & 11 & 0 & 14 \\
d & 13 & 0 & 7 & 0
\end{bmatrix}
$$

In this case, the majority threshold (*i.e.* a number of individual indicators greater than 50% of the indicators considered) is eleven indicators. The pairs with a concordance index higher than 11 are the following:

bPa= 13, bPd=21, cPa=13, cPb=11, cPd=14, dPa=13. Clearly, country c is the Condorcet winner, since it is always preferred to any other country. Country b is preferred to both a and d. Between a and d, d is preferred to a. Thus the final ranking is the following: $c \rightarrow b \rightarrow d \rightarrow a$.

As can be seen, the derivation of a Condorcet ranking may sometimes be a long and complex computation process. Both Borda and Condorcet approaches solve the plurality rule paradox. However, the solutions offered are different. At this point, the question arises: **in the context of composite indicators, can we choose between Borda and Condorcet on any theoretical and/or practical grounds?**

A first question to address is: do Borda and Condorcet rules normally lead to different solutions? Fishburn (1973) proves the following theorem: *there are profiles where the Condorcet winner exists and is never selected by any scoring method.* Moulin (1988, p. 249) proves that "a Condorcet winner (loser) cannot be a Borda loser (winner)". In other words, Condorcet consistent rules and scoring voting rules are deeply different in nature. Their disagreement in practice is in the normal situation. Both approaches must therefore be examined carefully.

Consider the numerical example in Table 28 with 60 indicators and three countries, owed to Condorcet himself (Condorcet, 1785).

Table 28. An original Concordet example

Number of indicators	23	17	2	10	8
	a	b	b	c	c
	b	c	a	a	b
	c	a	c	b	a

The corresponding frequency matrix is shown in Table29.

Table 29. An original Concordet example

Ranking	Indicators			Points
	a	b	c	
1st	23	19	18	2
2nd	12	31	17	1
3rd	25	10	25	0

By applying Borda's scoring rule, the following results are obtained:

$a = 58$, $b = 69$, $c = 53$, thus b is unequivocally selected.

Applying the Condorcet rule, the corresponding outranking matrix is shown below in Table 30.

Table 30. Outranking matrix derived from Table 27

$$\begin{bmatrix} & a & b & c \\ a & 0 & 33 & 25 \\ b & 27 & 0 & 42 \\ c & 35 & 18 & 0 \end{bmatrix}$$

In this case, 60 indicators being used, the concordance threshold is 31. It is: aPb, bPc and cPa, thus, due to the transitive property, a cycle exists and no country can be selected. From this example we might conclude that the Borda rule (or any scoring rule) is more effective, since in this way a country is always selected, while Condorcet sometimes leads to an irreducible state of indecision. However, Borda rules have other drawbacks. This can be seen when analysing the properties of Borda's rule.

Examine again the outranking matrix presented in Table 30. From this matrix it can be seen that 33 individual indicators are in favour of country a, while only 27 are in favour of b. So a legitimate question is why the Borda rule ranks b before a. It is mainly due to the fact that the Borda rule is based on the concept of *intensity* of preference, while the Condorcet rule uses only the *number* of indicators.

In the framework of the Borda rule, and all scoring methods in general, the intensity of preference is measured by the scores given according to the rank positions. This implies that compensability is allowed. Moreover, the rank position of a given country depends on the number of countries considered. This implies that the *mutual preference relation* of a given pair of countries may change according to the countries considered. As a consequence, preference reversal phenomena may easily occur. This problem has been extensively studied by Fishburn (1984). Consider the numerical example presented in Table 31.

Table 31. Fishburn example on Borda rule

Number of indicators	3	2	2
	c	b	a
	b	a	d
	a	d	c
	d	c	b

The corresponding frequency matrix is in Table 32.

Table 32. Frequency matrix derived from Table 31

	Countries				Points
Ranking	a	b	c	d	
1st	2	2	3	0	3
2nd	2	3	0	2	2
3rd	3	0	2	2	1
4th	0	2	2	3	0

By applying Borda's scoring rule, the following results are obtained:
$a = 13$, $b = 12$, $c = 11$, $d = 6$, thus country a is chosen. Now suppose that d is removed from the analysis. Since d was at the bottom of the ranking, nobody should have any reasonable doubt that a is still the best country. To check whether this assumption is correct, the corresponding frequency matrix is presented in Table 33.

Table 33. Frequency matrix derived from Table 31 without country d

Ranking	Countries			Points
	a	*b*	*c*	
1st	2	2	3	2
2nd	2	3	2	1
3rd	3	2	2	0

By applying Borda's scoring rule, the following results are obtained:

$a = 6$, $b = 7$, $c = 8$, thus country c is now preferred. Unfortunately, Borda's rule is fully dependent on irrelevant alternatives and preference reversals can occur with an extremely high frequency. At this point, we need to tackle the issue of when, in the context of composite indicators, it is better to use a Condorcet consistent rule or a scoring method. Given the consensus in the literature that the Condorcet theory of voting is non-compensatory while Borda's is fully compensatory, *a first conclusion is that a Condorcet approach is necessary when weights are to be understood as importance coefficients, while Borda's is desirable when weights are meaningful in the form of trade-offs.*

As we have seen, a basic problem inherent in the Condorcet approach is the presence of cycles, *i.e.* cases where *aPb, bPc* and *cPa* may be found. The probability $\pi\left(N, M\right)$ of obtaining a cycle with N countries and M individual indicators increases with both N and M. Estimations of probabilities of getting cycles can be found in Fishburn (1973, p. 95). Note that these probabilities are estimated under the so-called "*impartial culture assumption*", *i.e.* that voters' opinions do not influence each other. While this assumption is unrealistic in a mass election, it is fully respected in the building of a composite indicator, since individual indicators are supposed to be non-redundant.

Condorcet himself was aware of the problem of cycles in his approach; he built examples to explain it (as in Table 28) and he even came close to finding a consistent rule capable of ranking any number of alternatives when cycles are present. The main attempts to clarify, fully understand and axiomatize Condorcet's approach to solving cycles were made by Kemeny (1959), who made the first intelligible description of the Condorcet approach, and Young & Levenglick (1978), who achieved its clearest exposition and complete axiomatization. For this reason we can call this approach the Condorcet-Kemeny-Young-Levenglick ranking procedure, in short the C-K-Y-L ranking procedure.

Its main methodological foundation is the maximum likelihood concept. The maximum likelihood principle selects as a final ranking that with the maximum pairwise support. This is the ranking which involves the minimum number of pairwise inversions. Since Kemeny (1959) proposes the number of pairwise inversions as a distance to be minimized between the selected ranking and the other individual profiles, the two approaches are perfectly equivalent. The selected ranking is also a median ranking for those composing the profile (in multi-criteria terminology, it is the "compromise ranking" among the various conflicting points of view); for this reason the corresponding ranking procedure is often known as the Kemeny median order.

Condorcet made three basic assumptions:

1. Voters' opinions do not influence each other.
2. Voters all have the same competence, *i.e.* each voter chooses his/her best candidate with a fixed probability p, where $\frac{1}{2} < p < 1$ and p is the same for all voters.

HANDBOOK ON CONSTRUCTING COMPOSITE INDICATORS: METHODOLOGY AND USER GUIDE – ISBN 978-92-64-04345-9 – © OECD 2008

3. Each voter's judgement on any pair of candidates is independent of his/her judgement on any other pair.

As discussed above, assumption 1 always applies for composite indicators. Assumption 2 states that each individual indicator should be weighted equally, which is not always desirable in this context. Indeed, given that complete decisiveness yields to dictatorship, Arrow's impossibility theorem forces us to make a trade-off between decisiveness (an alternative has to be chosen or a ranking has to be made) and anonymity (*i.e.* equal weighting). *As a consequence, the loss of anonymity in favour of decisiveness in this case is even a positive property.* In general, it is essential that no indicator weight constitute more than 50% of the total weights; otherwise the aggregation procedure would become lexicographic in nature, and this individual indicator would become a dictator in Arrow's terminology. Following from this, when indicator weights are derived from different dimensions, the requirement is that no dimension should weigh more than 50% of the total weights (Munda, 2005b).

The third assumption refers to the famous axiom of independence of irrelevant alternatives of Arrow's theorem. The C-K-Y-L ranking procedure naturally does not respect this axiom. However, two considerations have to be observed on this subject.

1. A Condorcet consistent rule always presents smaller probabilities of the occurrence of a rank reversal in comparison with any Borda consistent rule. This is again a strong argument in favour of a Condorcet approach in a multi-criterion framework.
2. The C-K-Y-L ranking procedure is the *"only plausible ranking procedure that is locally stable"*, where *local stability* means that the ranking of countries does not change if only an interval of the full ranking is considered.

Although the theoretical characterization of the C-K-Y-L ranking procedure is not easy, the algorithm *per se* is very simple. The maximum likelihood ranking of countries is the ranking supported by the maximum number of individual indicators for each pairwise comparison, summed over all pairs of countries (see Munda & Nardo, 2007, for more detail). By applying the C-K-Y-L ranking procedure to the numerical example of Table 28 the following six possible rankings with the corresponding scores are obtained.

a	b	c	100
b	**c**	**a**	**104**
c	a	b	86
b	a	c	94
c	b	a	80
a	c	b	76

The ranking $b \rightarrow c \rightarrow a$ is the final result. The original Condorcet problem has been solved in a satisfactory way.

However, note that the computational problem is a clear drawback of this approach. The number of permutations can easily become unmanageable; for example, when ten countries are considered, it is $10!=3,628,800$. To solve this problem it is necessary to use numerical algorithms.

To conclude, consider the numerical example in Table 34 with three countries and three individual indicators (this is the classical example of the Condorcet paradox shown in many textbooks).

Table 34. An unsolvable ranking problem

Number of indicators	1	1	1
	a	c	b
	b	a	c
	c	b	a

By applying the Borda rule, all countries receive a score equal to 3 – no selection is possible. By applying the Condorcet rule, being majority equal to 2/3, the cycle aPb, bPc and cPa is obtained. By applying the C-K-Y-L ranking procedure, three rankings have the greatest support. These are: $a \rightarrow b \rightarrow c$, $b \rightarrow c \rightarrow a$, $c \rightarrow a \rightarrow b$ the cycle remains unsolved.

This example is a perfect manifestation of Arrow's theorem; no decision is possible. To eliminate ties, a larger number of individual indicators, or some indicator weights, would be required. *This is the reason why the use of individual indicator weights is important. Anonymity is lost but decisiveness improves enormously.*

6.13. Non-compensatory multi-criteria approach (MCA)

As in common practice, greater weight could be given to components which are considered more significant in the context of the particular composite indicator (OECD, 2003). Yet it can be shown that when using an additive or a multiplicative aggregation rule, and when individual indicators are expressed as intensities (*e.g.* in pounds, litres or euro) and not as qualities (*e.g.* good, bad, medium) nor in rankings, the substitution rates equal the weights of the variables up to a multiplicative coefficient (Munda & Nardo, 2005).[38] As a consequence, weights in additive aggregations necessarily take the meaning of substitution rates (*trade-offs*) and do not indicate the importance of the associated indicator. This implies a compensatory logic, *i.e.* the possibility of offsetting a disadvantage on some variables by a sufficiently large advantage on others. For example, in the construction of the TAI a compensatory logic (using equal weighting) would imply that it is acceptable to renounce, for example, 2% of *patents* granted to residents, or 2% of *university* enrolment in exchange for a 2% increase in *electricity* consumption.

The implication is the existence of a theoretical inconsistency in the way weights are actually used and their real theoretical meaning. For the weights to be interpreted as "*importance coefficients*" (the greatest weight being placed on the most important "dimension"), non-compensatory aggregation procedures must be used to construct composite indicators (Podinovskii, 1994). This can be done using a non-compensatory multi-criteria approach.

When a number of variables are used to evaluate a set of countries, some may be in favour of one particular country, while others will favour another. As a consequence a conflict among the variables could arise. This conflict can be treated in the light of a non-compensatory logic by taking into account the absence of preferential independence within a discrete non-compensatory multi-criteria approach (NCMC) (Munda, 1995; Roy, 1996; Vincke, 1992).

Given a set of individual indicators $G=\{x_q\}$, $q=1,...,Q$, and a finite set $M=\{c\}$, $c=1,...,M$ of countries, assume that the evaluation of each country c with respect to an individual indicator x_q (*i.e.* the indicator score or variable) is based on an *interval or ratio* scale of measurement. For simplicity's sake, it is also assumed that a higher value in an individual indicator is preferred to a lower, *i.e.* the higher, the better. Further assume the existence of a set of weights $w=\{w_q\}$, $q=1,2,...Q$, with $\sum_{q=1}^{Q} w_q = 1$, interpreted as *importance coefficients*. This information constitutes the impact matrix. As has already been discussed, a non-compensatory rule for ranking countries can be supplied by the C-K-Y-L ranking procedure. For explanatory purposes, consider only five of the countries included in the TAI data set[39] and imagine that equal weights are given to all of the individual indicators (Table 35).

Table 35. Impact matrix for TAI (five countries)

	Patents	Royalties	Internet	Tech exports	Telephones	Electricity	Schooling	University
Finland	187	125.6	200.2	50.7	3.080	4.150	10	27.4
USA	289	130	179.1	66.2	2.997	4.073	12	13.9
Sweden	271	156.6	125.8	59.7	3.096	4.145	11.4	15.3
Japan	994	64.6	49	80.8	3.003	3.865	9.5	10
Korea	779	9.8	4.8	66.7	2.972	3.653	10.8	23.2
weight	1/8	1/8	1/8	1/8	1/8	1/8	1/8	1/8

The mathematical aggregation convention can be divided into two main steps (Munda & Nardo, 2007):

- Pairwise comparison of countries according to the whole set of individual indicators used.

- Ranking of countries in a complete pre-order.

The first step results in a $M \times M$ matrix, E, called *outranking matrix* (Arrow & Raynaud, 1986; Roy, 1996). Any generic element of E: e_{jk}, $j \neq k$ is the result of the pairwise comparison, according to all the Q individual indicators, between countries j and k. Such a global pairwise comparison is obtained by means of equation:

$$e_{jk} = \sum_{q=1}^{Q} (w_q (Pr_{jk}) + \frac{1}{2} w_q (In_{jk}))$$ (32)

where $w_q(Pr_{jk})$ and $w_q(In_{jk})$ are the weights of individual indicators presenting a preference and an indifference relation respectively. In other words, the score of country j is the sum of the weights of individual indicators on which this country does better than country I, as well as – if any – half of the weights for the individual indicators on which the two countries do equally well (32) $e_{jk} + e_{kj} = 1$ clearly holds.

The pairwise comparisons are different from those in the AHP method – which belongs to the set of compensatory multi-criteria methods, together with CA. In the latter, the question to be answered is whether I_q is more important than I_z; here, the question is rather whether I_q is higher for country a or for country b. And if I_q is indeed higher for country a, it is the weight of individual indicator q which enters into the computation of the overall importance of country a, in a manner consistent with the definition of weights as importance measures.

In the TAI example, the pairwise comparison of countries such as Finland and the United States shows that Finland has better scores for the individual indicators – *Internet* (weight 1/8), *telephones* (weight 1/8), *electricity* (weight 1/8) and *university* (weight 1/8). Thus the score for Finland is 4*1/8=0.5, while the complement to one is the score of the US. The resulting outranking matrix is Table 36:

Table 36. Outranking impact matrix for TAI (five countries)

	Finland	USA	Sweden	Japan	Korea
Finland	0	0.5	0.375	0.75	0.625
USA	0.5	0	0.5	0.625	0.625
Sweden	0.625	0.5	0	0.75	0.625
Japan	0.25	0.375	0.25	0	0.75
Korea	0.375	0.375	0.375	0.25	0

According to C-K-Y-L, the ranking of countries with the highest likelihood is that supported by the maximum number of individual indicators for each pairwise comparison, summed over all pairs of countries considered. More formally, the outranking matrix E is composed of all the $M(M–1)$ pairwise comparisons. Call R the set of all $M!$ possible complete rankings of alternatives, $R=\{r_S\}$, $s=1,2,..., M!$.

For each r_S, compute the corresponding score φ_s as the summation of e_{jk} over all the $\binom{M}{2}$ pairs j,k of alternatives. That is, $\varphi_s = \sum e_{jk}$ where $j \neq k$, $s = 1,2,...M!$ and $e_{jk} \in r_s$. The final ranking ($r*$) is the solution of:

$$r* \Leftrightarrow \varphi_* = \max \sum e_{jk} \qquad \text{where } e_{jk} \in R \qquad (33)$$

In the TAI example, the number of permutations obtained from five countries is 120: the first five are listed in Table 37. For example, the score of the first ranking (USA, Sweden, Finland, Japan and Korea) is obtained as follows: according to the impact matrix, the comparison of the USA with the other countries yields 0.5 against Finland and Sweden and 0.625 against Japan and Korea (overall 2.25). The comparison for Sweden yields 0.625 against Finland and Korea and 0.75 against Japan (overall 2). Finland obtains 0.625 against Korea and 0.75 against Japan (overall 1.375). Finally Japan obtains 0.75 against Korea. The final score of this ranking is then equal to 2.25+2+1.375+0.75=6.375.

Table 37. Permutations obtained from the outranking matrix for TAI and associated score

USA	Sweden	Finland	Japan	Korea	**6.375**
Sweden	Finland	USA	Japan	Korea	**6.375**
Sweden	USA	Finland	Japan	Korea	**6.375**
Finland	USA	Sweden	Japan	Korea	6.125
Finland	Sweden	USA	Japan	Korea	6.125
USA	Finland	Sweden	Japan	Korea	6.125

According to expression (33) the final ranking will be the permutation(s) with the highest score. In this example the first three permutations have the highest overall score, and thus all those can be considered as a winning ranking.

HANDBOOK ON CONSTRUCTING COMPOSITE INDICATORS: METHODOLOGY AND USER GUIDE – ISBN 978-92-64-04345-9 - © OECD 2008

This aggregation method has the advantage of overcoming some of the problems raised by additive or multiplicative aggregations, *e.g.* preference dependence, the use of different ratio or interval scales to express the same indicator and the meaning of trade-offs taken to the weights. With this method, moreover, qualitative and quantitative information can be treated jointly. In addition, it does not need any manipulation or normalisation to assure the comparability of individual indicators. The drawbacks, on the other hand, include the dependence of irrelevant alternatives, *i.e.* the possible presence of cycles/rank reversal in which in the final ranking, country *a* is preferred to *b*, *b* is preferred to *c* but *c* is preferred to *a* (the same problem highlighted for AHP with indicators). Furthermore, information on intensity of preference of variables is never utilised: even though the difference between values on an indicator for two countries might be quite large, a very small difference could also produce the same ranking.[40]

6.14. Performance of the different aggregation methods

The type of aggregation employed is strongly related to the method used to normalise raw data (*Step 5*). In particular, Ebert & Welsch (2004) have shown that the use of linear aggregations yields meaningful composite indicators only if data are all expressed on a partially comparable interval scale (*i.e.* temperature in Celsius or Fahrenheit) of type $f : x \rightarrow \alpha x + \beta_i$, $\alpha > 0$ (*i.e.* α fixed, but β_i varying across sub indicators) or on a fully comparable interval scale (β constant); Non-comparable data measured on a ratio scale (*i.e.* kilograms and pounds) $f : x \rightarrow \alpha_i x$ where $\alpha_i > 0$ (*i.e.* α_i varying across individual indicators) can only be meaningfully aggregated by using geometric functions, provided that x is strictly positive. In other terms, except in the case of indicators measured on a different ratio scale, the measurement scale must be the same for all indicators when aggregating. Thus, care should be taken when indicators measured on different scales coexist in the same composite. The normalisation method should be properly used to remove the scale effect.

Table 38. TAI country rankings by different aggregation methods

	LIN	NCMC	GME
Finland	1	3	2
United States	2	1	1
Sweden	3	2	3
Japan	4	4	4
Korea, Rep.	5	9	16
Netherlands	6	8	5
United Kingdom	7	5	6
Singapore	8	12	18
Canada	9	11	13
Australia	10	9	14
Germany	11	7	8
Norway	12	6	11
Ireland	13	13	7
Belgium	14	17	9
New Zealand	15	15	17
Austria	16	15	12
France	17	14	10
Israel	18	18	15
Spain	19	20	19
Italy	20	19	21
Czech Republic	21	21	23
Hungary	22	23	22
Slovenia	23	22	20

Table 38 highlights the dependence of rankings on the aggregation methods used (in this case linear, geometric and based on the multi-criteria technique for the TAI data set with 23 countries). Although in all cases equal weighting is used, the resulting rankings are very different. For example, Finland ranks first according to the linear aggregation, second according to the geometric aggregation and third according to the multi-criteria. Note that Korea ranks sixteenth with GME, while its ranking is much higher according to the other two methods, while the reverse is true for Belgium.

HANDBOOK ON CONSTRUCTING COMPOSITE INDICATORS: METHODOLOGY AND USER GUIDE – ISBN 978-92-64-04345-9 – © OECD 2008

STEP 7. UNCERTAINTY AND SENSITIVITY ANALYSIS

Sensitivity analysis is considered a necessary requirement in econometric practice (Kennedy, 2003) and has been defined as the modeller's equivalent of orthopaedists' X-rays.

Composite indicator development involves stages where subjective judgements have to be made: the selection of individual indicators, the treatment of missing values, the choice of aggregation model, the weights of the indicators, *etc*. All these subjective choices are the *bones* of the composite indicator and, together with the information provided by the numbers themselves, shape the message communicated by the composite indicator.

Since the quality of a model also depends on the soundness of its assumptions, good modelling practice requires that the modeller provide an evaluation of the confidence in the model, assessing the uncertainties associated with the modelling process and the subjective choices taken. This is what sensitivity analysis does: it performs the 'X-rays' of the model by studying the relationship between information flowing in and out of the model.

More formally, sensitivity analysis is the study of how the variation in the output can be apportioned, qualitatively or quantitatively, to different sources of variation in the assumptions, and of how the given composite indicator depends upon the information fed into it. Sensitivity analysis is thus closely related to uncertainty analysis, which aims to quantify the overall uncertainty in country rankings as a result of the uncertainties in the model input. A combination of uncertainty and sensitivity analysis can help to gauge the robustness of the composite indicator ranking, to increase its transparency, to identify which countries are favoured or weakened under certain assumptions and to help frame a debate around the index.

Below is described how to apply uncertainty and sensitivity analysis to composite indicators. Our synergistic use of uncertainty and sensitivity analysis has recently been applied for the robustness assessment of composite indicators (Saisana *et al.*, 2005a; Saltelli *et al.*, 2008) and has proven to be useful in dissipating some of the controversy surrounding composite indicators such as the Environmental Sustainability Index (Saisana *et al.*, 2005b) . Note that the structure of the uncertainty and sensitivity analysis discussed below in relation to the TAI case study is only illustrative. In practice the set-up of the analysis will depend upon which sources of uncertainty and which assumptions the analyst considers relevant for a particular application. In the TAI case study we focus on five main uncertainties/assumptions: inclusion/exclusion of one indicator at a time, imputation of missing data, different normalisation methods, different weighting schemes and different aggregation schemes.

Let *CI* be the index value for country *c, c=1,...,M,*

$$CI_c = f_{rs}\left(I_{1,c}, I_{2,c}, ... I_{Q,c}, w_{s,1}, w_{s,2}, ... w_{s,Q}\right) \tag{34}$$

according to the weighting model f_{rs}, $r = 1,2,3$, $s = 1,2,3$, where the index *r* refers to the aggregation system (LIN, GME, NCMC) and index *s* refers to the weighting scheme (BAP, AHP, BOD). The index is based on *Q* normalised individual indicators $I_{1,c}, I_{2,c}, ... I_{Q,c}$ for that country and scheme-dependent weights $w_{s,1}, w_{s,2}, ... w_{s,Q}$ for the individual indicators. The most frequently used normalisation methods for the individual indicators are based on the Min-Max (35) standardised (36), or on the raw indicator values (37).

$$\begin{cases} I_{q,c} = \dfrac{x_{q,c} - \min(x_q)}{range(x_q)} & \quad (35) \\[3mm] I_{q,c} = \dfrac{x_{q,c} - mean(x_q)}{std(x_q)} & \quad (36) \\[3mm] I_{q,c} = x_{q,c} & \quad (37) \end{cases}$$

where $I_{q,c}$ is the normalised and $x_{q,c}$ is the raw value of the individual indicator x_q for country c.

Note that the Min-Max method (35) can be used in conjunction with all the weighting schemes (BAP, AHP and BOD) and for all aggregation systems (LIN, GME, NCMC). The standardised value (36) can be used with weighting schemes (BAP, AHP) for aggregation systems (LIN, NCMC). And the raw indicator value (37)can be used with weighting schemes (BAP, AHP) for aggregation systems (GME, NCMC).

The rank assigned by the composite indicator to a given country, *i.e.* $Rank(CI_c)$ is an output of the uncertainty/sensitivity analysis. The average shift in country rankings is also explored. This latter statistic captures the relative shift in the position of the entire system of countries in a single number. It can be calculated as the average of the absolute differences in countries' ranks with respect to a reference ranking over the M countries:

$$\bar{R}_S = \frac{1}{M}\sum_{c=1}^{M}\left|Rank_{ref}(CI_c) - Rank(CI_c)\right| \qquad (38)$$

The reference ranking for the TAI analysis is the original rank given to the country by the original version of the index. The investigation of $Rank(CI_c)$ and $\bar{R}_S$ is the scope of the uncertainty and sensitivity analysis.[41]

7.1. General framework

The analysis is conducted as a single Monte Carlo experiment, *e.g.* by exploring all uncertainty sources simultaneously to capture all possible synergy effects among uncertain input factors. This involves the use of triggers, *e.g.* the use of uncertain input factors to decide which aggregation system and weighting scheme to adopt. A discrete uncertain factor, which can take integer values between 1 and 3, is used for the aggregation system and similarly for the weighting scheme. Other trigger factors are generated to select those indicators to be omitted, the editing scheme, the normalisation scheme and so on, until a full set of input variables is available to compute $Rank(CI_c), \bar{R}_S$.

7.2. Uncertainty analysis (UA)

Various components of the CI construction process can introduce uncertainty into the output variables, $Rank(CI_c)$ and $\bar{R}_S$. The UA is essentially based on simulations that are carried out on various equations that constitute the underlying *model*. The uncertainties are transferred into a set of

HANDBOOK ON CONSTRUCTING COMPOSITE INDICATORS: METHODOLOGY AND USER GUIDE – ISBN 978-92-64-04345-9 - © OECD 2008

scalar input factors, such that the resulting $Rank(CI_c)$ and $\overline{R}_S$ are non-linear functions of the uncertain input factors, and the estimated probability distribution (pdf) of $Rank(CI_c)$ and $\overline{R}_S$. Various methods are available for evaluating output uncertainty. The following is the Monte Carlo approach, which is based on multiple evaluations of the model with k randomly selected model input factors. The procedure has three steps:

- Assign a pdf to each input factor X_i, $i = 1,2...k$. The first input factor, X_1, is used for the selection of the editing scheme (for the second TAI analysis only):

X_1	Estimation of missing data
1	Use bivariate correlation to impute missing data
2	Assign zero to missing datum

The second input factor, X_2, is the trigger to select the normalisation method.

X_2	Normalisation
1	Min-Max (equation (35))
2	Standardisation (equation (36))
3	None (equation (37))

Both X_1 and X_2 are discrete random variables. In practice they are generated by drawing a random number ζ, uniformly distributed between $[0,1]$, and applying the so-called *Russian roulette algorithm*, e.g. for X_1, select 1 if $\zeta \in [0,0.5)$ and 2 if $\zeta \in [0.5,1]$. Uncertain factor X_3 is generated to select which individual indicator, if any, should be omitted.

ζ	X_3, excluded individual indicator
$[0, \dfrac{1}{Q+1})$	None ($X_3 = 0$) all indicators are used
$[\dfrac{1}{Q+1}, \dfrac{2}{Q+1})$	$X_3 = 1$
...	...
$[\dfrac{Q}{Q+1}, 1]$	$X_3 = Q$

That is, with probability $\dfrac{1}{Q+1}$, no individual indicator will be excluded, while with probability $[1-\dfrac{1}{Q+1}]$, one of the Q individual indicators will be excluded with equal probability. Clearly, the probability of $X_3 = 0$ could have been made larger or smaller than $\dfrac{1}{Q+1}$ and the values $X_3 = 1, 2, \ldots Q$ could have been sampled with equal probability. A scatter plot based sensitivity analysis would be used to track which indicator affects the output the most when excluded. Recall also that whenever an indicator is excluded, the weights of the other factors are scaled to unity sum to make the composite index comparable with either BAP or AHP. When BOD is selected the exclusion of individual indicators leads to a re-execution of the optimisation algorithm.

Trigger X_4 is used to select the aggregation system:

X_4	Aggregation Scheme
1	LIN
2	GME
3	NCMC

Note that when LIN is selected the composite indicators are computed as:

$$CI_c = \sum_{q=1}^{Q} w_{sq} I_{q,c} \tag{39}$$

while when GME is selected they are:

$$CI_c = \prod_{q=1}^{Q} \left(I_{q,c} \right)^{w_{sq}} \tag{40}$$

When NCMC is selected the countries are ranked directly from the outscoring matrix.

X_5 is the trigger to select the weighting scheme:

X_5	Weighting Scheme
1	BAP
2	AHP
3	BOD

The last uncertain factor, X_6, is used to select the expert. In this experiment, there are 20 experts. Once an expert has been selected at runtime via the trigger X_6, the weights assigned by that expert (either for the BAP or AHP schemes) are assigned to the data. Clearly the selection of the expert has no bearing when BOD is used ($X_5 = 3$). However, this uncertain factor would be generated in each individual Monte Carlo simulation, given that the row dimension of the Monte Carlo sample (*constructive dimension*) should be fixed in a Monte Carlo experiment, *i.e.* even if some of the sampled factors are active in a particular run, they will nevertheless be generated by the random sample generation algorithm. The constructive dimension of the Monte Carlo experiment, the number of random

HANDBOOK ON CONSTRUCTING COMPOSITE INDICATORS: METHODOLOGY AND USER GUIDE – ISBN 978-92-64-04345-9 – © OECD 2008

numbers to be generated for each trial, is hence $k = 6$. Note that alternative arrangements of the analysis would have been possible.

- Generate randomly N combinations of independent input factors $\mathbf{X}^l$, $l = 1,2,...N$ (a set $\mathbf{X}^l = X_1^l, X_2^l, ..., X_k^l$ of input factors is called a sample). For each trial sample $\mathbf{X}^l$ the computational model can be evaluated, generating values for the scalar output variable Y^l, where Y^l is either $Rank(CI_c)$, the value of the rank assigned by the composite indicator to each country, or $\overline{R}_S$, the averaged shift in countries' ranks.

-. Close the loop over l, and analyse the resulting output vector $\mathbf{Y}^l$, with $l = 1, ..., N$.

The generation of samples can be performed using various procedures, such as simple random sampling, stratified sampling, quasi-random sampling or others (Saltelli *et al.*, 2008; Saltelli *et al.* 2004). The sequence of $\mathbf{Y}^l$ gives the pdf of the output Y. The characteristics of this pdf, such as the variance and higher order moments, can be estimated with an arbitrary level of precision related to the size of the simulation N.

7.3. Sensitivity analysis using variance-based techniques

A necessary step when designing a sensitivity analysis is to identify the output variables of interest. Ideally these should be relevant to the issue addressed by the model. It has been noted earlier that composite indicators may be considered as models. When several layers of uncertainty are present simultaneously, a composite indicator could become a non-linear, possibly non-additive model. As argued by practitioners (Chan *et al.*, 2000; EPA, 2004; Saltelli *et al.*, 2008), with non-linear models, robust, "model-free" techniques should be used for sensitivity analysis. Sensitivity analysis using variance-based techniques are model-free and display additional properties convenient in the present analysis, such as the following:

- They allow an exploration of the whole range of variation of the input factors, instead of just sampling factors over a limited number of values, *e.g.* in fractional factorial design (Box *et al.*, 1978);

- They are quantitative, and can distinguish main effects (first order) from interaction effects (higher order);

- They are easy to interpret and to explain;

- They allow for a sensitivity analysis whereby uncertain input factors are treated in groups instead of individually;

- They can be justified in terms of rigorous settings for sensitivity analysis.

To compute a variance-based sensitivity measure for a given input factor X_i, start from the fractional contribution to the model output variance, *i.e.* the variance of Y, where Y is either a country's rank, $Rank(CI_c)$, or the overall shift in countries ranking with respect to a reference ranking, $\overline{R}_S$, due to the uncertainty in X_i:

$$V_i = V_{X_i}(E_{\mathbf{X}_{-i}}(Y|X_i))$$

(41)

Fix factor X_i, *e.g.* to a specific value x_i^* in its range, and compute the mean of the output Y averaging over all factors but factor X_i: $E_{\mathbf{X}_{-i}}(Y|X_i = x_i^*)$. Then take the variance of the resulting function of x_i^* over all possible x_i^* values. The result is given by equation (41) where the dependence on x_i^* has been dropped. V_i is a number between 0 (when X_i does not make a contribution to Y at the first order), and $V(Y)$, the unconditional variance of Y when all factors other than X_i are non-influential at any order. Note that the following is always true:

$$V_{X_i}(E_{\mathbf{X}_{-i}}(Y|X_i)) + E_{X_i}(V_{\mathbf{X}_{-i}}(Y|X_i)) = V(Y)$$

(42)

where the first term of equation (42) is called a main effect, and the second, the residual. An important factor should have a small residual, *e.g.* a small value of $E_{X_i}(V_{\mathbf{X}_{-i}}(Y|X_i))$. This is intuitive as the residual measures the expected reduction in variance that would be achieved if X_i were fixed. Rewrite this as $V_{\mathbf{X}_{-i}}(Y|X_i = x_i^*)$, a variance conditional on x_i^*. Then the residual $E_{X_i}(V_{\mathbf{X}_{-i}}(Y|X_i))$ is the expected value of such conditional variance, averaged over all possible values of x_i^*. This would be small if X_i were influential. A first-order sensitivity index is obtained through normalising the first-order term by the unconditional variance:

$$S_i = \frac{V_{X_i}(E_{\mathbf{X}_{-i}}(Y|X_i))}{V(Y)} = \frac{V_i}{V(Y)}$$

(43)

One can compute conditional variances corresponding to more than one factor, *e.g.* for two factors X_i and X_j, the conditional variance would be $V_{X_iX_j}(E_{\mathbf{X}_{-ij}}(Y|X_i, X_j))$, and the variance contribution of the second-order term would become:

$$V_{ij} = V_{X_iX_j}(E_{\mathbf{X}_{-ij}}(Y|X_i, X_j)) - V_{X_i}(E_{\mathbf{X}_{-i}}(Y|X_i)) - V_{X_j}(E_{\mathbf{X}_{-j}}(Y|X_j))$$

(44)

where clearly V_{ij} is different from zero only if $V_{X_iX_j}(E_{\mathbf{X}_{-ij}}(Y|X_i, X_j))$ is larger than the sum of the first-order term relative to factors X_i and X_j.

When all k factors are independent from one another, the sensitivity indices can be computed using the following decomposition formula for the total output variance $V(Y)$:

$$V(Y) = \sum_i V_i + \sum_i \sum_{j>i} V_{ij} + \sum_i \sum_{j>i} \sum_{\substack{l>j \\ j>i}} V_{ijl} + \ldots + V_{12\ldots k}$$

(45)

Terms above the first order in equation (45) are known as interactions. A model without interactions among its input factors is said to be *additive*. In this case, $\sum_{i=1}^{k} V_i = V(Y)$, $\sum_{i=1}^{k} S_i = 1$ and the first-order

HANDBOOK ON CONSTRUCTING COMPOSITE INDICATORS: METHODOLOGY AND USER GUIDE – ISBN 978-92-64-04345-9 – © OECD 2008

conditional variances of equation (41) are all needed to decompose the model output variance. For a non-additive model, higher order sensitivity indices, responsible for interaction effects among sets of input factors, have to be computed. However, higher order sensitivity indices are usually not estimated, since in a model with k factors, the total number of indices (including the S_i's) to be estimated would be as high as $2^k - 1$. Instead a more compact sensitivity measure is used. The total effect sensitivity index concentrates on a single term for all the interactions, involving a given factor X_i. For example, for a model of $k=3$ independent factors, the three total sensitivity indices would be:

$$S_{T1} = \frac{V(Y) - V_{X_2 X_3}(E_{X_1}(Y|X_2, X_3))}{V(Y)} = S_1 + S_{12} + S_{13} + S_{123} \tag{46}$$

And analogously:

$$S_{T2} = S_2 + S_{12} + S_{23} + S_{123}$$
$$\tag{47}$$
$$S_{T3} = S_3 + S_{13} + S_{23} + S_{123}$$

The conditional variance $V_{X_2 X_3}(E_{X_1}(Y|X_2, X_3))$ in equation (46) can be written in general terms as $V_{\mathbf{X}_{-i}}(E_{X_i}(Y|\mathbf{X}_{-i}))$ (Homma & Saltelli, 1996). This is the total contribution to the variance of Y due to non-X_i, i.e. to the k-1 remaining factors, such that $V(Y) - V_{\mathbf{X}_{-i}}(E_{X_i}(Y|\mathbf{X}_{-i}))$ includes all terms. In general, $\sum_{i=1}^{k} S_{Ti} \geq 1$.

The total effect sensitivity index can also be written as:

$$S_{Ti} = \frac{V(Y) - V_{\mathbf{X}_{-i}}(E_{X_i}(Y|\mathbf{X}_{-i}))}{V(Y)} = \frac{E_{\mathbf{X}_{-i}}(V_{X_i}(Y|\mathbf{X}_{-i}))}{V(Y)} \tag{48}$$

For a given factor X_i a significant difference between S_{Ti} and S_i signals an important interaction role for that factor in Y. Highlighting interactions among input factors helps to improve our understanding of the model structure. Estimators for both (S_i, S_{Ti}) are provided by a variety of methods reviewed in Chan et al., (2000). Here the method of Sobol' (1993), in the improved version of Saltelli (2002), is used. The method of Sobol' uses quasi-random sampling of the input factors. The pair (S_i, S_{Ti}) gives a fairly good description of the model sensitivities, which for the improved Sobol' method is of $n(k+2)$ model evaluations, where n represents the sample size required to approximate the multi-dimensional integration implicit in the E and V operators above to a plain sum. n can vary in the hundred-to-thousand range.

When the uncertain input factors X_i are dependent, the output variance cannot be decomposed, as in equation (45) The S_i, S_{Ti} indices, defined by (43) and (48) are still valid sensitivity measures for X_i, though their interpretation has changed, e.g. S_i could carry over the effects of other factors which may be positively or negatively correlated to X_i (see Saltelli & Tarantola, 2002), while S_{Ti} can no longer be meaningfully decomposed into main effect and interaction effects. The S_i, S_{Ti}, in the case of non-independent input factors, could also be interpreted as "settings" for sensitivity analysis.

A description of two settings linked to S_i, S_{Ti} is discussed below.[42]

Factor Prioritisation (FP) Setting. Suppose a factor that, once "discovered" in its true value and then fixed, would reduce V(Y) the most. The true values for the factors, however, are unknown. The best choice would be the factor with the highest S_i, regardless of whether the model is additive or the factors are independent.

Factor Fixing (FF) Setting. Can one fix a factor [or a subset of input factors] at any given value over their range of uncertainty without significantly reducing the variance of the output? Only those (sets of) factors whose S_{Ti} is zero can be fixed.

The extended variance-based methods, including the improved version of Sobol', for both dependent and independent input factors, are implemented in the freely distributed software SIMLAB (Saltelli *et al.*, 2004).

7.3.1. Analysis 1

The first analysis is run without imputation, i.e. by censoring all countries with missing data. As a result, only 34 countries, in theory, may be analysed. Other countries from rank 24 onwards (in the original TAI) are also dropped, *e.g.* Hong Kong, as this is the first country with missing data. The analysis is restricted to the set of countries whose rank is not altered by the omission of missing records. The uncertainty analysis for the remaining 23 countries is given in Figure 18 for the ranks, with countries ordered by their original TAI position, ranging from Finland (rank=1) to Slovenia (rank=23). Note that the choice of ranks, instead of composite indicator values, is dictated by the use of the NCMC aggregation system.

The width of the $5^{th} - 95^{th}$ percentile bounds and the ordering of the medians (black hyphen) are often at odds with the ordering of the original TAI (grey hyphen). For several countries, *e.g.* United Kingdom or Belgium, the median rank is equal to the original TAI rank (overlap of black and grey hyphen in Figure 18). Although the difference between the groups of leaders and laggards can still be observed, there are considerable differences between the new and the original TAI. If the uncertainty within the system were a true reflection of the status of knowledge and the (lack of) consensus among experts on how TAI should be built, it would have to be concluded that TAI is not a robust measure of countries' technology achievement.

HANDBOOK ON CONSTRUCTING COMPOSITE INDICATORS: METHODOLOGY AND USER GUIDE – ISBN 978-92-64-04345-9 – © OECD 2008

Figure 18.   Uncertainty analysis of TAI country rankings

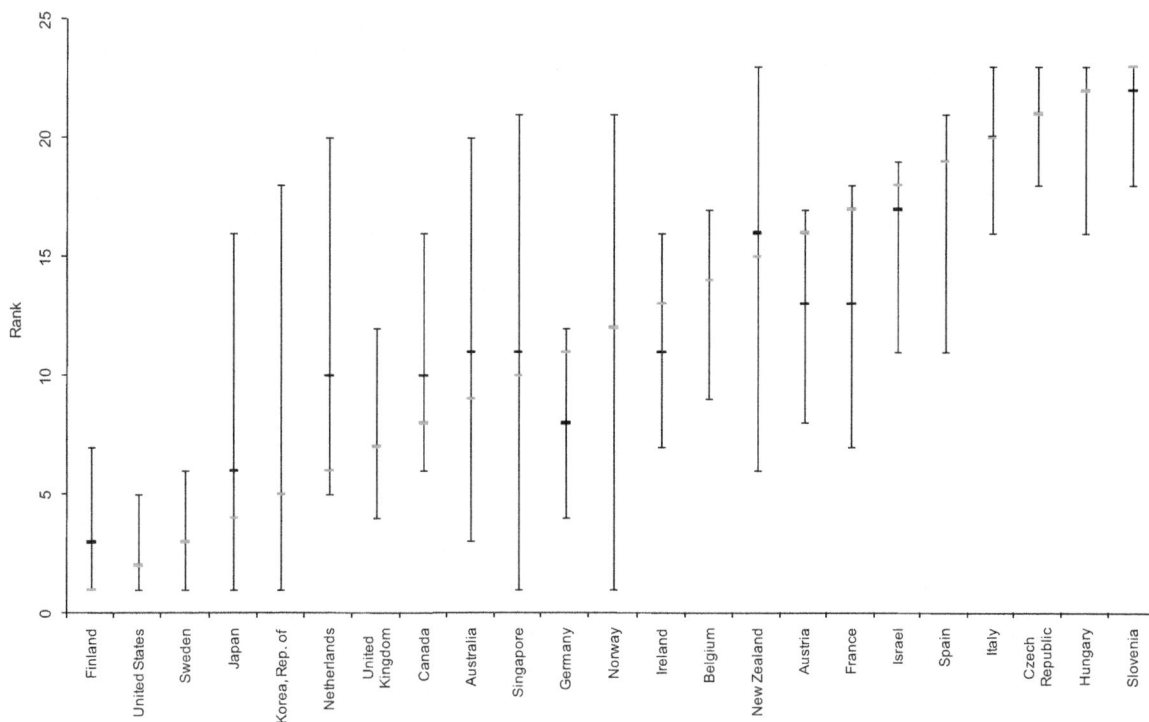

Note: Results show the country rankings according to the original TAI 2001 (light grey marks), the median (black mark) and the corresponding 5th and 95th percentiles (bounds) of the distribution of the MC-TAI for 23 countries. Uncertain input factors: normalisation method, inclusion/exclusion of a individual indicator, aggregation system, weighting scheme, expert selection. Countries are ordered according to the original TAI values.

Figure 19 shows the sensitivity analysis based on the first-order indices. The total variance in each country's rank is presented along with the part that can be decomposed according to the first-order conditional variances. The aggregation system, followed by the inclusion/exclusion of individual indicators and expert selection, is the most influential input factors. The countries with the highest total variance in ranks are the middle-of-the-table countries, while the leaders and laggards in technology achievement have low total variance. The non-additive, non-linear part of the variance that is not explained by the first-order sensitivity indices ranges from 35% for the Netherlands to 73% for the United Kingdom, while for most countries it exceeds 50%. This underlines the necessity of computing higher order sensitivity indices that capture the interaction effect among the input factors.

Figure 19. Sobol' sensitivity measures of first-order TAI results

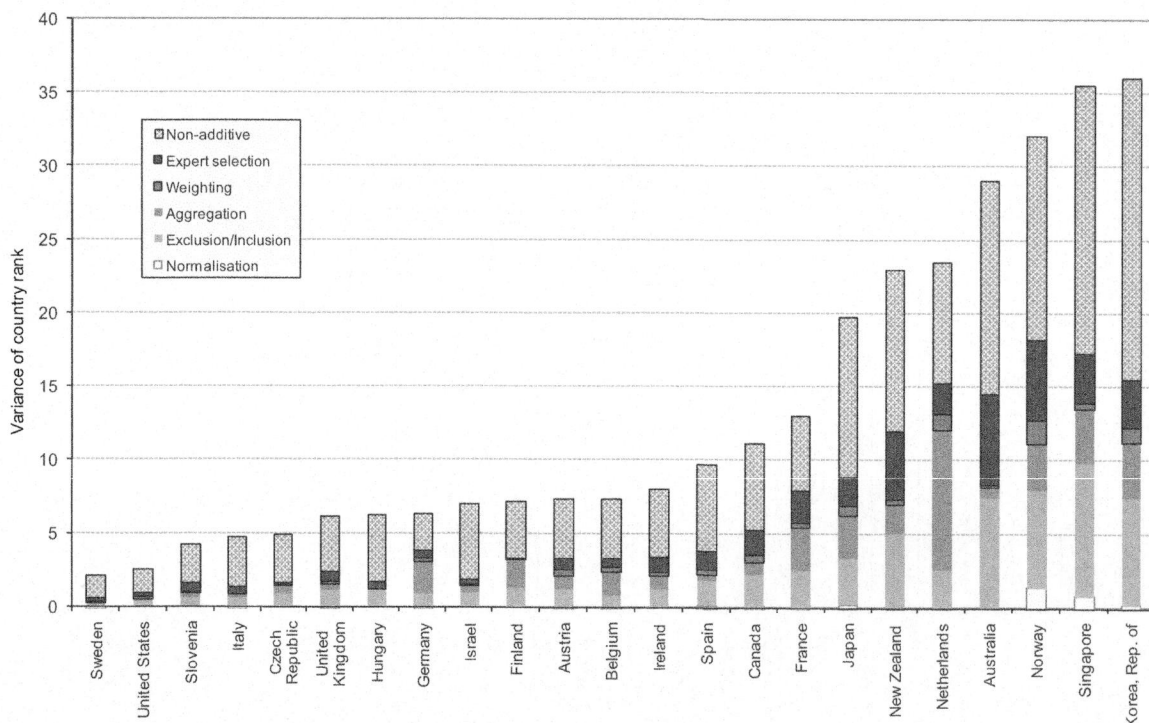

Note: Results based on first-order indices. Decomposition of country variance according to the first-order conditional variances. Aggregation system, followed by the inclusion/exclusion of individual indicator and expert selection, are the most influential input factors. The part of the variance that is not explained by the first-order indices is noted as non-additive. Countries are ordered in ascending order of total variance.

Figure 20 shows the total effect sensitivity indices for the variance of each country's rank. The total effect sensitivity indices concentrate on one single term for all the interactions involving each input factor. The indices add up to a number greater than 1 due to the interactions which seem to exist among the identified influential factors.

If the TAI model were additive with no interactions between the input factors, the non-additive part of the variance in Figure 19 would have been zero. In other words, the first-order sensitivity indices would have summed to 1, and the sum of the total effect sensitivity indices would have been 1. Yet the sensitivity indices show the high degree of non-linearity and additivity for the TAI model and the importance of the interactions. The high effect of interactions for the Netherlands, which also has a large percentile bound, is further explored. Figure 21 shows that the Netherlands is favoured by the combination of "geometric mean system" with "BAP weighting", and not favoured by the combination of "Multi-criteria system" with "AHP weighting". This is a clear interaction effect. In-depth analysis of the output data reveals that, as far as inclusion/exclusion is concerned, it is the exclusion of the individual indicator *royalties* which leads to a deterioration in the Netherlands' rank under any aggregation system.

HANDBOOK ON CONSTRUCTING COMPOSITE INDICATORS: METHODOLOGY AND USER GUIDE – ISBN 978-92-64-04345-9 – © OECD 2008

Figure 20.   Sobol' sensitivity measures of TAI total effect indices

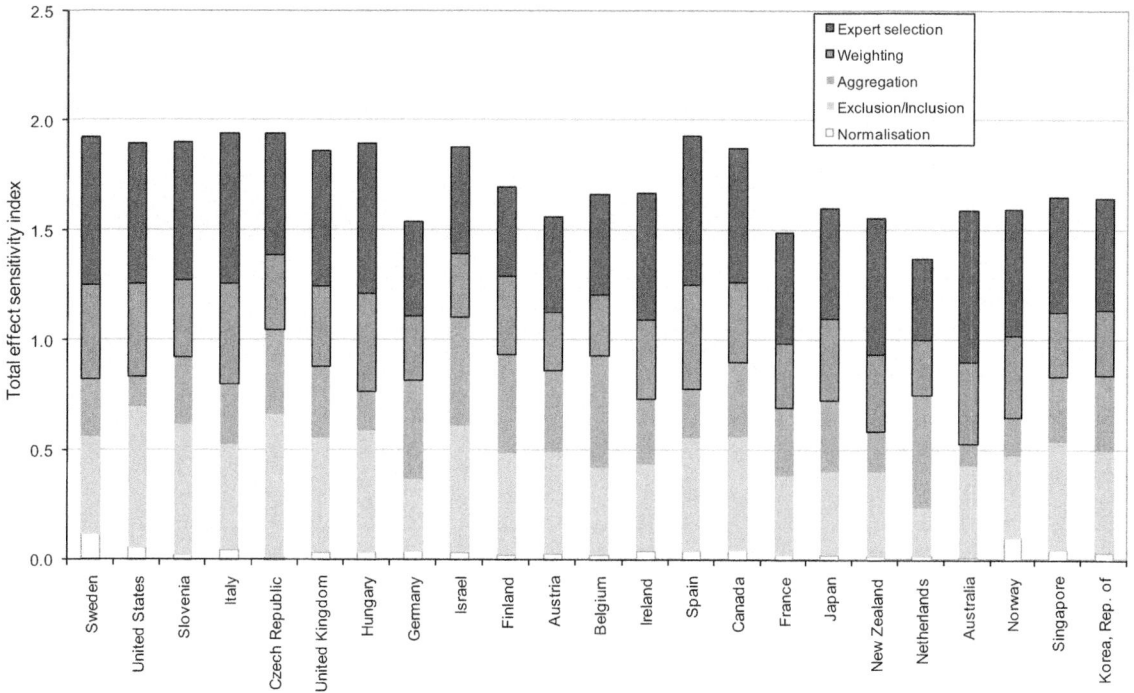

Figure 21.   Netherlands' ranking by aggregation and weighting systems

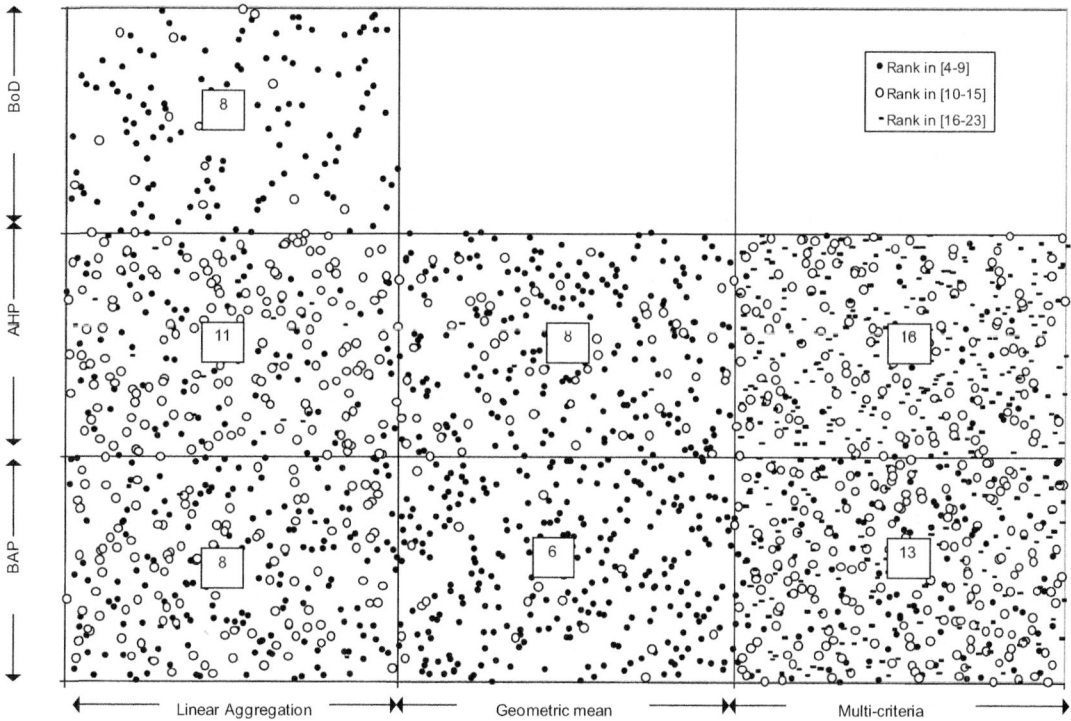

Figure 22 shows the histogram of values for the average shift in the rank of the output variable (equation (38)) with respect to the original TAI rank. The mean value is almost three positions, with a standard deviation slightly above one position. The input factors – the aggregation system plus inclusion/exclusion at the first order – affect this variable the most (Table 39). When the interactions are considered, both weighting scheme and expert choice become important. This effect can be seen in Figure 23. In some cases the average shift in country's rank when using NCMC can be as great as nine places.

Table 39. Sobol' sensitivity measures of first order and total effects on TAI results

Input Factors	First order (S_i)	Total effect (S_{T_i})	$S_{T_i} - S_i$
Normalisation	0.000	0.008	0.008
Exclusion/Inclusion of an indicator	0.148	0.435	0.286
Aggregation system	0.245	0.425	0.180
Weighting Scheme	0.038	0.327	0.288
Expert selection	0.068	0.402	0.334
Sum	0.499	1.597	

Note: Average shift in countries' rank with respect to the original TAI. Significant values are underlined.

Figure 22.   Uncertainty analysis for TAI output variable

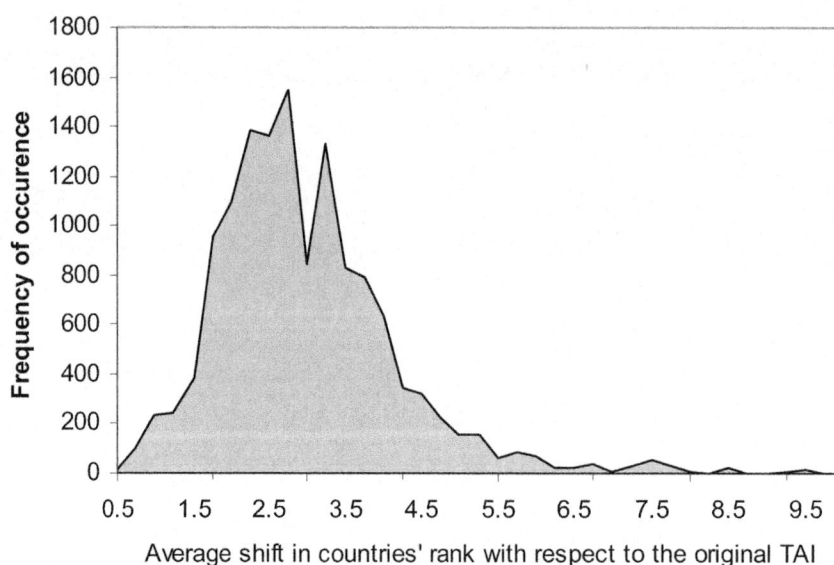

Average shift in countries' rank with respect to the original TAI

Note: Average shift in countries' ranks with respect to the original TAI. Uncertain input factors: normalisation method, inclusion-exclusion of an indicator, aggregation system, weighting scheme, expert selection.

 HANDBOOK ON CONSTRUCTING COMPOSITE INDICATORS: METHODOLOGY AND USER GUIDE – ISBN 978-92-64-04345-9 - © OECD 2008

Figure 23.   Average shift in TAI country rankings by aggregation and weighting combinations

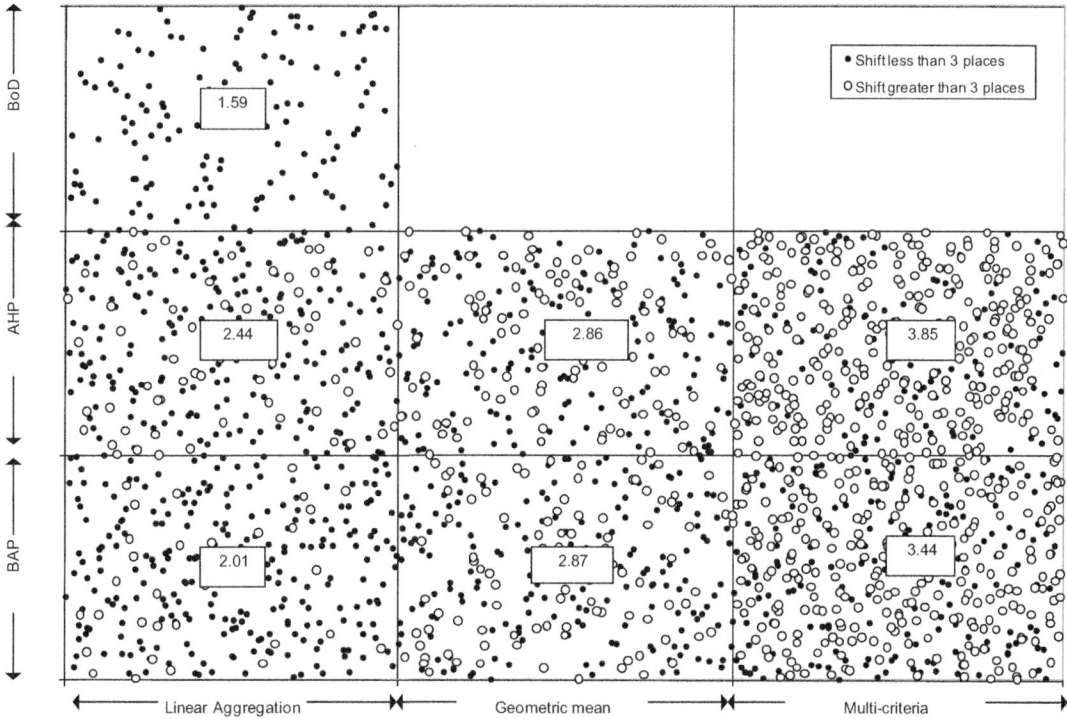

Note: Average shift in countries' rank with respect to the original TAI for different combinations of aggregation system and weighting scheme. Average value per case is indicated in the box.

7.3.2. Analysis 2

In this analysis it is assumed that the TAI stakeholders have agreed on a linear aggregation system. In fact, it might be argued that the choice of the aggregation system is to some extent dictated by the use of the index and by the expectation of its stakeholders. For instance, if stakeholders believe that the system should be non-compensatory, NCMC would be adopted. Eventually, this would lead on average to a medium-to-good performance, which is worth more to a country than a performance which is very good on some individual indicators and bad in others. A GME approach would follow the progress of the index over time in a scale-independent fashion.

Given these considerations, the second analysis is based on the LIN system, as in the original TAI. The uncertainty analysis plot (Figure 24) shows much more robust behaviour in the index, with fewer inversions of rankings, when median-TAI and original TAI are compared. With regard to sensitivity, the uncertainty arising from imputation does not seem to make a significant contribution to the output uncertainties, which are also dominated by weighting, inclusion/exclusion and expert selection. Even when, as in the case of Malaysia, imputation by bivariate approach leads to an unrealistic number of patents being imputed for this country (234 patents granted to residents per million people), the uncertainty in its rank is still insensitive to imputation. The sensitivity analysis results for the average shift in rank output variable (equation (38)) is shown in Table 40. Interactions are now between expert selection and weighting, and considerably less with inclusion/exclusion.

Figure 24.   Uncertainty analysis of TAI country rankings

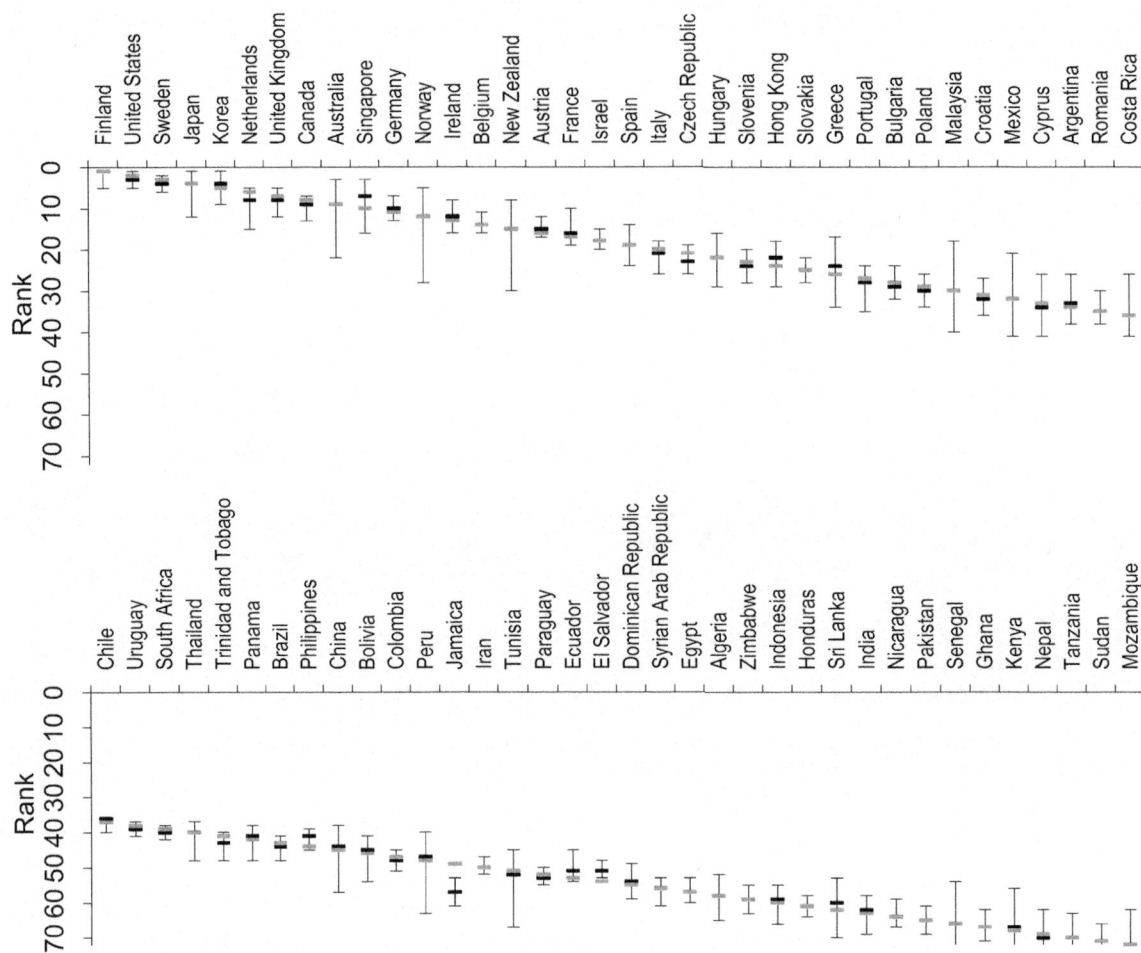

Note: Uncertainty analysis results showing country ranks according to the original TAI 2001 (light grey marks), the median (black mark) and the corresponding 5th and 95th percentiles (bounds) of the distribution of the MC-TAI for 72 countries. Uncertain input factors: imputation, normalisation method, inclusion/exclusion of an individual indicator, weighting scheme, expert selection. A linear aggregation system is used. Countries are ordered according to the original TAI values.

Table 40. Sobol' sensitivity measures and average shift in TAI rankings

Input Factors	First order (S_i)	Total effect (S_{T_i})	$S_{T_i} - S_i$
Imputation	0.001	0.005	0.004
Normalisation	0.000	0.021	0.021
Exclusion/Inclusion of an indicator	0.135	0.214	0.078
Weighting Scheme	0.212	0.623	0.410
Expert selection	0.202	0.592	0.390
Sum	0.550	1.453	

Note: Significant values are underlined.

HANDBOOK ON CONSTRUCTING COMPOSITE INDICATORS: METHODOLOGY AND USER GUIDE – ISBN 978-92-64-04345-9 - © OECD 2008

The use of one strategy versus another in indicator building might lead to a biased picture of country performance, depending on the severity of the uncertainties. As shown by the preceding analyses, if the constructors of the index disagree on the aggregation system, it is highly unlikely that a robust index will emerge. If uncertainties exist in the context of a well-established theoretical framework, *e.g.* if a participatory approach within a linear aggregation scheme is favoured, the resulting country rankings could be fairly robust in spite of the uncertainties.

Neither imputation nor normalisation significantly affect countries' rankings when uncertainties of higher order are present. In the current set-up, the uncertainties of higher order are expert selection and weighting scheme (second analysis). *A fortiori* normalisation does not affect output when the very aggregation system is uncertain (first analysis). In other words, when the weights are uncertain, it is unlikely that normalisation and editing will affect the country ranks.

The aggregation system is of paramount importance. It is recommended that indicator developers agree on a common approach. Once the system is fixed, it is the choice of aggregation methods and of experts which – together with indicator inclusion/exclusion – dominate the uncertainty in the country ranks. However, note that even in the second analysis, when the aggregation system is fixed, the composite indicator model is strongly non-additive, which reinforces the case for the use of the quantitative, Monte Carlo based approach to robustness analysis.

STEP 8. BACK TO THE DETAILS

Establishing a relationship between cause and effect is notoriously difficult; the widely accepted statement "correlation does not mean causality" has to be borne in mind. Practically, however, in the absence of a genuine theory on "what causes what", the correlation structure of the data set can be of some help in at least excluding causal relationships between variables (but not necessarily between the theoretical constructs of which the variable is a manifestation). However, a distinction should be made between spatial data (as in the case of TAI) and data which also have a time dimension (*e.g.* GDP of EU countries from 1970 to 2005). In this latter case causality can be tested using tools such as the Granger test (see *e.g.* Greene, 2002). The case of spatial data is more complicated, but tools such as Path Analysis and Bayesian Networks (the probabilistic version of path analysis) could be of some help in studying the many possible causal structures and removing those which are strongly incompatible with the observed correlations.

Path analysis, conceived by the biologist S. Wright in the 1920s, is an extension of regression analysis in which many endogenous and exogenous variables can be analysed simultaneously (Wright, 1934). Consider the following example in Figure 25. Variables A and B have a direct effect on variable D. Variable B also has a direct effect on variable C, which in turn has a direct effect on D. Therefore the effect of B on D is caused directly by B but also by the effect of B on C. p_{AD} is the path coefficient relating A to D whereas r_{BA} is the correlation coefficient of the pair of variables A, B (see Box 7 for a definition of correlation coefficient).

Path analysis consists in a set of multiple regressions. In this case the equations to estimate would be:

$$D = p_{AD}A + p_{BD}B + p_{CD}C + \varepsilon_1$$
$$C = p_{BC}B + \varepsilon_2$$

Therefore, the standardized regression coefficients emerging from this estimation (*i.e.* the coefficients of the model in which the variables are expressed as z-scores) will be used as path coefficients. The total effect of A on D will be the sum of the direct effect represented by the path coefficient relating A to D and of the indirect effect through its correlation with B: $r_{AD} = p_{AD} + (r_{BA} \cdot p_{BD})$. A high value of r_{AD} corroborates the relationship between A and D, whereas a low value would point to the absence of a linear relationship (at least as far the data analysed are concerned). Note that the arrows in a path analysis reflect an hypothesis about causality. However, the resulting path coefficients or correlations only reflect the pattern of correlation found in the data. Path analysis cannot be used to infer causality, given its confirmatory nature: the causal relationship has to be modelled in advance.[43] In other terms, path analysis cannot tell us which of two distinct path diagrams is to be preferred, whether the correlation between A and B represents a causal effect of A on B, of B on A, or mutual dependence on another variable C, or some mixture of these. This technique is based on a number of assumptions (those usually made in regression analysis), including: (i) the linearity of the relationship between variables; (ii) the absence of interaction effects between variables (called additivity, see also the preferential independence of the multi-criteria methodology); (iii) recursivity (all arrows flow one way with no feedback looping); and (iv) an adequate sample size (Kline, 1998, recommends 10 to 20 times as many cases as parameters to estimate). For a comprehensive list see Pedhazur (1982); the seminal article on path analysis is Wright (1934).

Figure 25.   Simple example of path analysis

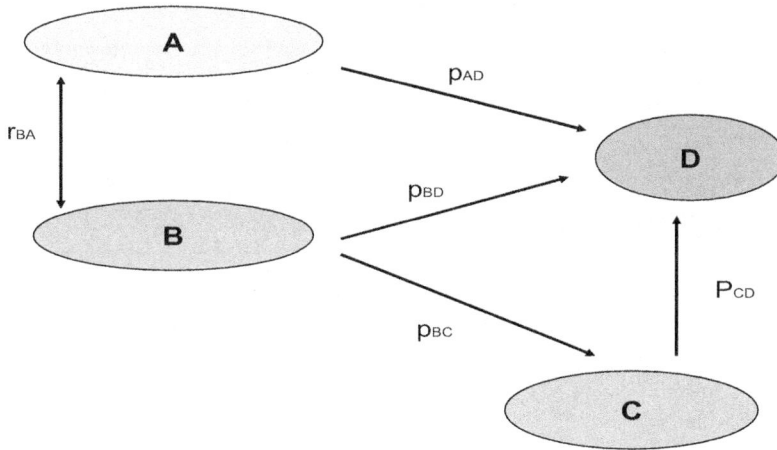

The standardised regression coefficients (beta values) for the TAI example reveal that Internet and patents have by far the strongest influence on the variance in the TAI scores (beta > 0.35), followed by royalties, university, exports and schooling (Figure 26). Two indicators, *telephones* and *electricity*, appear not to be influential on the variance in the TAI scores.

Figure 26.   Standardised regression coefficients for the TAI

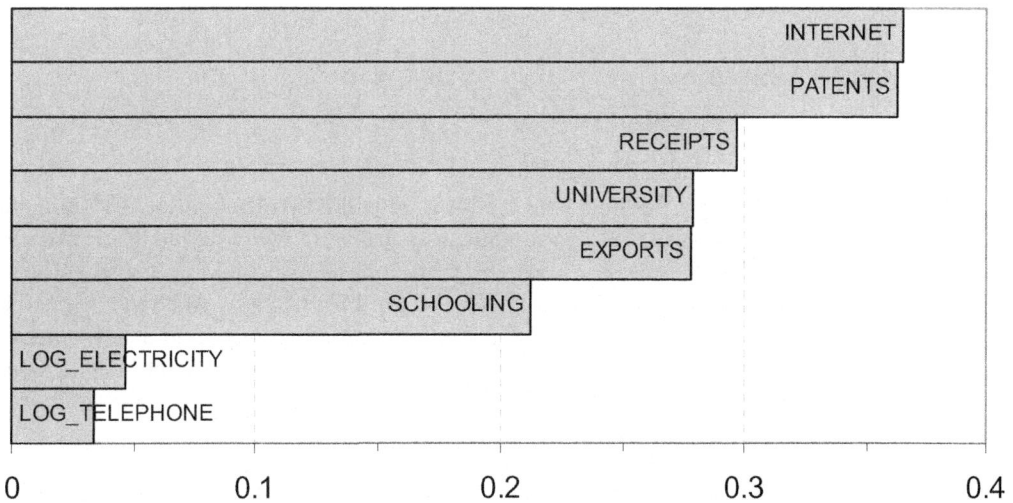

All standardised regression coefficients are significant ($p < 0.01$, $R^2 = 0.9996$, $n = 23$)

Table 41. Impact of eliminating two indicators from the TAI example

	TAI (Original, 8 indicators)	TAI 6 (Excluding telephones and electricity)	Absolute Difference (TAI-TAI6)
Finland	1	1	0
United States	2	2	0
Sweden	3	3	0
Japan	4	4	0
Korea	5	5	0
Netherlands	6	6	0
United Kingdom	7	7	0
Canada	8	9	1
Australia	9	10	1
Singapore	10	8	2
Germany	11	11	0
Norway	12	12	0
Ireland	13	13	0
Belgium	14	14	0
New Zealand	15	15	0
Austria	16	16	0
France	17	17	0
Israel	18	18	0
Spain	19	19	0
Italy	20	22	2
Czech Republic	21	21	0
Hungary	22	20	2
Slovenia	23	23	0

To test the implications of these findings, one could exclude the two least influential indicators from the TAI data set. Even in this scenario, TAI6, the indicators are weighted equally. Table 41 shows that the TAI6 version, which excludes *telephones* and *electricity*, produces a ranking that is identical to the original TAI for 18 of the 23 countries. Minor shifts are observed for Canada, Australia (1 position shift) and Singapore, Italy and Hungary (2 positions). Thereafter, in a parsimonious approach, the indicators on *telephones* and *electricity* would be excluded, as they do not have an impact on either the variance of the TAI scores or on the TAI ranking.

Although this type of analysis cannot determine the TAI's capacity to capture the concept of technological achievement, it is fair to say that the TAI encompasses distinct and important dimensions. However, not every indicator adds a crucial component to the index, which is reflected in the inferiority of the indicator *telephones* and *electricity*, while others (*e.g. Internet* and *patents*) are highly influential on the variance of the TAI scores. The path analysis results, based on the standardised regression coefficients and the bivariate correlations between the indicators as explained above, are shown in Table 42.

HANDBOOK ON CONSTRUCTING COMPOSITE INDICATORS: METHODOLOGY AND USER GUIDE – ISBN 978-92-64-04345-9 – © OECD 2008

Table 42. Path analysis results for TAI: total effect impact of the indicators on the TAI scores

Patents	13.5%
Royalties	16.2%
Internet	13.9%
Tech exports	6.1%
Telephones (logarithm)	15.8%
Electricity (logarithm)	10.6%
Schooling	13.1%
University	10.8%

There appears to be no dominance issue in the TAI example, as seven of the eight indicators contribute more than 10% each to the overall TAI scores. The indicator on *exports* makes the smallest contribution (6.1%). Yet this indicator was found to be influential on the variance of the TAI scores.

In the 1970s factor analysis and latent variables enriched path analysis, giving rise to the field of **Structural Equation Modelling** (SEM, see Kline, 1998). SEM is an extension of the general linear model that simultaneously estimates relationships between multiple independent, dependent and latent variables. The idea is again that interrelations in a set of linear relationships can be examined using the variance and covariance of the variables, but the advantages of SEM are its generality (it includes path analysis and multivariate regression as special cases) and the possibility of including latent variables or factors as nodes. This is particularly useful when working with composite indicators, given that in most cases the available indicators only imperfectly measure theoretical concepts.

In the Composite Learning Index developed by the Canadian Council of Learning (http://www.ccl-cca.ca/CCL/Reports/CLI/), for example, the social and economic benefits of learning are considered a latent variable since they can be only imperfectly measured by indicators such as crime rate, population health or unemployment rate. SEM combines measurement and regression techniques. Measurement techniques such as factor analysis and item response theory are used to relate latent variables to the observed indicators (the measurement model), whereas regression techniques are used to relate indicators. In the Composite Learning Index the aggregation of sub-indices into a composite and the dependence of socio-economic benefits on learning is captured by the multivariate regression, whereas the disaggregation of learning into social-economic outcomes takes the form of a measurement model.

Note that this complex architecture is used to estimate (recursively) the weights used to compute the Composite Learning Index. More generally, SEM can be viewed as a confirmatory procedure making it possible to (i) determine that the pattern of covariances in the data is consistent with the model specified; (ii) specify and test alternative models and determine which has the best fit; (iii) use SEM results to change the structure of the model. However, as David Garson has remarked: "Regardless of the approach, SEM cannot itself draw causal arrows in models or resolve causal ambiguities".[44]

Bayesian networks can also give some indication of which path diagram is more likely to be supported by the data. Bayesian networks are graphical models encoding probabilistic relationships between variables. Nodes (A, B, C and D in our example above) are not restricted to random variables (as in path analysis) and can represent any kind of variable: a measured parameter or a latent variable.

If SEM stems from the classical (or frequentist) approach based on sampling distributions, Bayesian networks rely on a subjective concept of probability. The prior density function of the graph reflects the odds the analyst would give to the structure of nodes and arrows. The prior distribution, when combined with the data via Bayes' theorem, produces a posterior distribution. This posterior, in short a weighted average of the prior density and of the conditional density (conditional on the data), is the output of

Bayesian analysis. (Note that the output of classical analysis is rather a point estimate.) Bayesian networks can be used for several purposes: (i) to explore all possible combinations of a given set of nodes in order to find the most likely structure; (ii) to see how the different evidence (the data available) modifies the probability of each given node; (iii) to lean the probability distribution of the parameters of the model, given the graph structure, the use of Bayesian networks is becoming increasingly common in bioinformatics, artificial intelligence and decision-support systems;[45] however, their theoretical complexity and the amount of computer power required to perform relatively simple graph searches make them difficult to implement in a convenient manner.

HANDBOOK ON CONSTRUCTING COMPOSITE INDICATORS: METHODOLOGY AND USER GUIDE – ISBN 978-92-64-04345-9 – © OECD 2008

CONCLUDING REMARKS

COMPOSITE INDICATORS: BETWEEN NARRATIVE AND ANALYSIS

The construction of a composite indicator is not a straightforward process. It involves assumptions which have to be assessed carefully to avoid resulting in a product of dubious analytic rigour.

In the present work an attempt has been made to map the effect of each assumption on the quality of the aggregation, and to draft a stylised "checklist" for the practitioner to follow in the construction process. We have emphasised the need for an explicit conceptual framework for the index and the usefulness of multivariate analysis prior to the aggregation of the individual indicators. Also reviewed were the tools available for imputation of missing observations, the methodologies for weighting and aggregation, and the testing of the robustness of the composite using uncertainty and sensitivity analysis. The present work is perhaps timely, as it seems to respond to an increasing interest in these measures. The table below shows the number of hits obtained by searching for "composite indicators" through Google (taken here as a proxy of overall diffusion of the concept) and Scholar Google (taken as a proxy of academic interest).

	Google	Scholar Google
October 2005	~ 35,500	992
June 2006	~ 80,800	1,440
September 2007	~ 2 million	167,000

We alluded in the introduction to the controversy surrounding the use of these measures, pitting aggregators against non-aggregators. The authors of this Handbook believe that individual variables and quantitative analyses (*e.g.* cost-benefit, multi-criteria) might be more relevant than aggregate measures for policy formulation, while an aggregate index might be useful to make a argument for action, *e.g.* positioning relation to the relative performance of a country, when this is of use in political discourse. Distilling the "pros" described in Section I to their essence, it might be argued that the construction of CIs is driven by the need for advocacy, for which the rationale can mainly be identified in the generation of narratives to support the subject of the advocacy (Saltelli, 2007). As pointed out in *The Financial Times*: "[…] Economists are often accused, justly, of thinking that what cannot be counted does not count. In this case *[the construction of CIs]*, economists are trying to count what - many would say - cannot be counted. The alternatives, however, are worse. Either we ignore this fact or we make subjective guesses." (12 July, 2007).

At the same time, there is abundant literature on the *analytic* problems associated with even well established statistical indices such as GDP, which we do not review here (see Rifkin, 2004, p.70 and following, for a discussion). This literature hardly seems to dent the rather universal acceptance of GDP. This suggests that a given constituency may come to accept an aggregate measure (and reach compromise on weighting) on an index to be used to benchmark best practice, but such acceptance cannot be taken for granted. On the other hand, a composite indicator of countries' scholastic achievement or competitiveness, such as the OECD's PISA (2004) or the World Economic Forum's

World Competitiveness Index, may lead to a valuable soul-searching exercise within constituencies of countries, even if disagreement exists over the measures themselves.

On the same grounds a composite indicator may prove unfit to further a given cause. If a composite indicator were to exacerbate disagreement among stakeholders, who would otherwise have been willing to accept a scoreboard, *i.e.* an un-aggregated list of the same variables, then there would be little point in insisting on aggregation.

Acknowledging the limitations of composite indicators but focusing on their potentiality, Mahbub ul Haq (the pioneer of the Human Development Index) states that "*For any useful policy index, some compromises must be made.*" (Haq, 1995, p. 59). When questioned on the data reliability/quality of the HDI, Haq said that it should be used to improve data quality, rather than to abandon the exercise. In fact, all the debate on development and public policy and media attention would not have been possible if the idea had been aborted at the level of indicators, without progressing to a composite indicator. The HDI estimates and ranking have persuaded many countries to invest more resources and effort in preparing better statistical series.

The point of these considerations is that subjectivity and fitness need not be antithetical. They are in fact both at play when constructing and adopting a composite indicator, where inter-subjectivity may be at the core of the exercise, such as when participative approaches to weight negotiations are adopted. Thus these apparently conflicting properties might underpin the suitability of CIs for advocacy purposes. This is perhaps the opinion of Mario Monti, the former EU Commissioner for Competition, who, in describing the internal market scoreboard and indices developed by the European Commission, notes:

> […] it is a pity that attempts to use even comparatively bland measures - such as the "naming and shaming" of laggards - have been dropped. In other areas, such as the implementation of single-market legislation or state-aid controls, "scoreboards" have played a useful role in bringing peer pressure to bear on national decision-makers. (Monti, 2005)

While the interplay between composite indicators and narratives is clear, the usefulness of composite indicators for analytic purposes should not be discounted. To illustrate, Sapir (2005), in making the case for a taxonomy of EU economic models among Mediterranean, Nordic, Anglo-Saxon and Continental, makes use of a plot of "strictness of employment protection legislation" (a composite), versus unemployment benefits. Similarly, Nicoletti and others make use of factor analysis in the analysis of, for example, product market regulation in OECD countries (Nicoletti *et al.*, 2000). Another example can be found in the work of Amartya Sen. Sen was initially opposed to composite indicators but was eventually convinced by their ability to represent his concept of 'Capabilities' ('the range of things that a person could do and be in her life,' Sen, 1989) in the UN Human Development Index.

It might be contended that we are witnessing an growing appetite in the economically literate press for statistic-based narratives. The media coverage of events such as the publishing of the World Economic Forum's World Competitiveness Index and Environmental Sustainability Index, the OECD's PISA study, not to mention more specialised measures such as Transparency International's Corruption Index or the Center for Global Development's Commitment to Development Index, among many others, is evidently on the rise (see also the table above). A telling remark along these lines comes from from Pisani-Ferry and Sapir:

> […] civil societies learn from the experience of others. Such policy learning can be enhanced by initiatives that facilitate cross country comparison and benchmarking. A telling example in this respect is […] PISA.

 HANDBOOK ON CONSTRUCTING COMPOSITE INDICATORS: METHODOLOGY AND USER GUIDE – ISBN 978-92-64-04345-9 – © OECD 2008

[...] peer pressure and benchmarking should be integral parts of the political process that underpins Lisbon 2. Transparency benefits the democratic process as it empowers national electorates to review the performance of their own governments and it helps focus the debate on key areas of underperformance. The use of league tables facilitates this process.

It is also evident that analysis-based narratives such as those supported by composite indicators would gain in effectiveness if citizens' statistical and economic literacy could be increased. Amartya Sen remarks that:

[...] the ability to exercise freedom may, to a considerable extent, be directly dependent on the education we have received, and thus the development of the educational sector may have foundational connections with the capability-based approach.

REFERENCES

Anderberg M.R. (1973), *Cluster Analysis for Applications*, New York: Academic Press, Inc.

Arrow K.J. (1963), *Social choice and individual values*, 2nd edition, Wiley, New York.

Arrow K.J. and Raynaud H. (1986), *Social choice and multicriterion decision making*, M.I.T. Press, Cambridge.

Bandura R. (2006), *A Survey of Composite Indices Measuring Country Performance: 2006 Update*, United Nations Development Programme – Office of Development Studies, available at http://www.thenewpublicfinance.org/background/Measuring%20country%20performance_nov2006%20update.pdf

Binder D.A. (1978), Bayesian Cluster Analysis, *Biometrika*, 65: 31-38.

Borda J.C. de (1784), Mémoire sur les élections au scrutin, in *Histoire de l' Académie Royale des Sciences,* Paris.

Boscarino J.A., Figley C.R., and Adams R.E. (2004), Compassion Fatigue following the September 11 Terrorist Attacks: A Study of Secondary Trauma among New York City Social Workers, *International Journal of Emergency Mental Health*, Vol. 6, 2: 1-10.

Box G., Hunter W. and Hunter J. (1978), *Statistics for experimenters*, New York: John Wiley and Sons.

Brand D.A., Saisana M., Rynn L.A., Pennoni F., Lowenfels A.B. (2007), Comparative Analysis of Alcohol Control Policies in 30 Countries, *PLoS Medicine*, 0759 April 2007, Vol. 4, 4, e151: 0752-0759, www.plosmedicine.org

Bryant F.B., and Yarnold P.R. (1995), Principal components analysis and exploratory and confirmatory factor analysis. In Grimm and Yarnold, *Reading and understanding multivariate analysis*. American Psychological Association Books.

Center for Global Development's *Commitment to development index*, http://www.cgdev.org/

Chan K., Tarantola S., Saltelli A. and Sobol' I.M. (2000), Variance based methods. In *Sensitivity Analysis* (eds, Saltelli A., Chan K., Scott M.) 167-197. New York: John Wiley & Sons.

Chantala K, Suchindran C., (2003) Multiple Imputation for Missing Data. SAS OnlineDocTM: Version 8.

Charnes A., Cooper W.W., Lewin A.Y., and Seiford L.M. (1995), *Data Envelopment Analysis: Theory, Methodology and Applications*. Boston:Kluwer.

Chatfield, C., Collins, A.J. (1980), *Introduction to Multivariate Analysis*, Chapman and Hall.

Cherchye L. (2001), Using data envelopment analysis to assess macroeconomic policy performance, *Applied Economics*, 33: 407-416

Cherchye L. and Kuosmanen T. (2002), Benchmarking sustainable development: a synthetic meta-index approach, *EconWPA* Working Papers.

Cherchye, L., Moesen W. and Van Puyenbroeck T. (2004), Legitimately Diverse, Yet Comparable: on Synthesising Social Inclusion Performance in the EU, *Journal of Common Market Studies*, 42: 919-955.

Cherchye, L., Moesen, W., Rogge, N., van Puyenbroeck, T., Saisana, M., Saltelli, A., Liska, R., Tarantola, S. (2008), Creating composite indicators with DEA and robustness analysis: the case of the Technology Achievement Index, *Journal of the Operational Research Society,* 59, 239-251.

Condorcet, Marquis de (1785), *Essai sur l'application de l'analyse à la probabilité des décisions rendues à la probabilité des voix*, De l' Imprimerie Royale, Paris.

Cortina J.M. (1993), What is coefficient alpha? An examination of theory and applications, *Journal of Applied Psychology*, 78, 1: 98-104

Cronbach L. J. (1951), Coefficient alpha and the internal structure of tests, *Psychometrika*, 16: 297-334.

Davis J. (1986), *Statistics and Data Analysis in Geology*, John Wiley & Sons, Toronto.

Debreu G. (1960), Topological methods in cardinal utility theory, in Arrow K.J., Karlin S. and Suppes P. (eds.) *Mathematical methods in social sciences*, Stanford University Press, Stanford.

Dempster A.P. and Rubin D.B. (1983), *Introduction* (pp.3-10), in *Incomplete Data in Sample Surveys* (vol. 2): Theory and Bibliography (Madow W.G., Olkin I. and Rubin D.B., eds.) New York: Academic Press.

De Soete, G., Heiser, W.J. (1993), A latent class unfolding model for analyzing single stimulus preference ratings. *Psychometrika* 58, 545-565.

Dietz F.J. and van der Straaten J. (1992), Rethinking environmental economics: missing links between economic theory and environmental policy, *Journal of Economic Issues*, Vol. XXVI,1: 27-51.

Dunteman G.H. (1989), *Principal components analysis*, Thousand Oaks, CA: Sage Publications, Quantitative Applications in the Social Sciences Series, No. 69.

Ebert U. and Welsch H. (2004), Meaningful environmental indices: a social choice approach, *Journal of Environmental Economics and Management*, Vol. 47: 270-283.

Efron, B. (1987), Better bootstrap confidence intervals (with discussion). *J. Amer. Statist. Assoc.* 82, 171-200.

Efron, B., Tibshirani, R. (1991), Statistical data analysis in the computer age. *Science* 253, 390-395.

Efron, B., Tibshirani, R. (1993), *An Introduction to the Bootstrap*, CHAPMAN & HALL/CRC, Boca Raton

EPA, Environmental Protection Agency (2004), Council for Regulatory Environmental Modeling (CREM), "Draft Guidance on the Development, Evaluation, and Application of Regulatory Environmental Models", http://www.epa.gov/osp/crem/library/CREM%20Guidance%20Draft%2012_03.pdf.

European Commission (2000), *Business Climate Indicator*, DG ECFIN, Brussels.

European Commission (2001a), *Summary Innovation Index*, DG ENTR, Brussels.

European Commission (2001b), *Internal Market Scoreboard*, DG MARKT, Brussels.

European Commission (2001c), *European Innovation Scoreboard*, DG ENTR, Brussels.

European Commission (2004a), *Economic Sentiment Indicator*, DG ECFIN, Brussels, http://europa.eu.int/comm/economy_finance/index_en.htm

European Commission (2004b), *Composite Indicator on e-business readiness*, DG JRC, Brussels.

Everitt B.S. (1979), Unresolved Problems in Cluster Analysis, *Biometrics*, 35: 169-181.

Fagerberg J. (2001), in Lundvall B. and Archibugi D. (eds.) *Europe at the crossroads: The challenge from innovation-based growth in the Globalising Learning Economy*, Oxford Press.

Feldt L.S., Woodruffe D.J., and Salih F.A. (1987), Statistical Inference for Coefficient Alpha, *Applied Psychological Measurement*, 11,1: 93-103.

Fishburn P.C. (1973), *The theory of social choice*, Princeton University Press, Princeton.

Fishburn P.C. (1984), Discrete mathematics in voting and group choice, *SIAM Journal of Algebraic and Discrete Methods,* 5: 263-275.

Forman E.H. (1983), The analytic hierarchy process as a decision support system, *Proceedings of the IEEE Computer society.*

Freudenberg M. (2003), Composite indicators of country performance: a critical assessment, OECD, Paris.

Fukuda-Parr K.S. (2003) *Readings in Human Development*. Oxford University Press, Oxford.

Funtowicz S.O., Munda G., Paruccini M. (1990), The aggregation of environmental data using multicriteria methods, *Environmetrics*, Vol. 1(4): 353-36.

Gall M. (2007) Indices of social vulnerability to natural hazards: A comparative evaluation, PhD dissertation, Department of Geography, University of South Carolina.

Gentle J.E.; Härdle W. and Mori, Yuichi (eds.) (2004): *Handbook of Computational Statistics: Concepts and Methods*, Springer.

Golub G.H. and van der Vorst, H.A. (2000), Eigenvalue computation in the 20th century, *Journal of Computational and Applied Mathematics*, Vol. 123 (1-2).

Gorsuch R. L. (1983), *Factor Analysis*. Hillsdale, NJ: Lawrence Erlbaum. Orig. ed. 1974.

Green S.B., Lissitz R.W., and Mulaik S.A.(1977), Limitations of coefficient alpha as an index of test unidimensionality, *Educational and Psychological Measurement*, 37: 827-838.

Green P.E., and Srinivasan V. (1978), Conjoint analysis in consumer research: issues and outlook, *Journal of Consumer Research* 5: 103-123.

Greenacre, M. J., (1984), *Theory and applications of correspondence analysis*. Academic Press, London.

Greenacre, M.J., (1993), *Correspondence analysis in practice*, Academic Press, London.

Greene, William H. (2002), *Econometric Analysis*, Prentice Hall, 5th Edition.

Hair J.F., Anderson R.E., Tatham R.L., and Black W.C. (1995), *Multivariate data analysis with readings*, fourth ed. Prentice Hall, Englewood Cliffs, NJ.

Hair J.F., Black W.C., B.J., Babin, Anderson R.E. and R.L.,Tatham (2006), *Multivariate data analysis*, sixth edition, Pearson Prentice Hall, Upper Saddle River, NJ.

Haq M. (1995), *Reflections on Human Development*, Oxford University Press, New York.

Hartigan J.A. (1975), *Clustering Algorithms*, New York: John Wiley & Sons, Inc.

Hatcher L. (1994), *A step-by-step approach to using the SAS system for factor analysis and structural equation modeling*. Cary, NC: SAS Institute. Focus on the CALIS procedure.

Hattie J. (1985), Methodology Review: Assessing unidimensionality of tests and items, *Applied Psychological Measurement*, 9, 2: 139-164.

Heiser, W.J. (1993), Clustering in low-dimensional space. In: Opitz, O., Lausen, B. and Klar, R., Editors, 1993. Information and Classification., Springer, Berlin, 162-173.

Homma T. and Saltelli A. (1996), Importance measures in global sensitivity analysis of model output, *Reliability Engineering and System Safety*, 52(1), 1-17.

Hutcheson G. and Sofroniou N.(1999), *The multivariate social scientist: Introductory statistics using generalized linear models*, Thousand Oaks, CA: Sage Publications.

Jackson, D.A. (1993), Stopping rules in principal component analysis a comparison of heuristical and statistical approaches, *Ecology* 74 (1993), 2204–2214.

Jacobs R., Smith P. and Goddard M. (2004), Measuring performance: an examination of composite performance indicators, Centre for Health Economics, *Technical Paper Series* 29.

Jencks S.F., Huff E.D. and Cuerdon T. (2003), Change in the quality of care delivered to Medicare beneficiaries, 1998-1999 to 2000-2001, *Journal of the American Medical Association*, 289(3): 305-12.

Johnson R., Wichern D.W., (2002), *Applied Multivariate Statistical Analysis*, 5th edition, Prentice Hall.

Jolliffe I.T. (1986), *Principal component analysis*. New York: Springer.

Kahn J.R and Maynard P. (1995), Conjoint Analysis as a Method of Measuring Use and Non-Use Values of Environmental Goods, paper presented at the American Economic Association.

Kahn J.R (1998), Methods for aggregating performance indicators, mimeo, University of Tennessee.

Kaiser H.F. and J. Rice,(1974), Little jiffy, mark IV, *Educational and Psychological Measurement* 34, 111-117.

Karlsson J. (1998), A systematic approach for prioritizing software requirements, PhD. Dissertation n. 526, Linkoping, Sverige.

Kaufmann D., Kraay A., and Zoido-Lobatón P. (1999), Aggregating Governance Indicators, Policy Research Working Papers, World Bank, http://www.worldbank.org/wbi/governance/working_papers.html

Kaufmann D., Kraay A., and Zoido-Lobatón P. (2003), Governance matters III: governance Indicators for 1996-2002, mimeo, World Bank.

Keeney R. and Raiffa H. (1976), *Decision with multiple objectives: preferences and value trade-offs*, Wiley, New York.

Kemeny J. (1959), Mathematics without numbers, *Daedalus*, 88: 571-591.

Kennedy P. (2003), *A guide to Econometrics*, 5th edition, MIT Press.

Kim, J.,Mueller, C.W. (1978), *Factor analysis: Statistical methods and practical issues*, Sage Publications, Beverly Hills, California, pp.88.

King's Fund (2001), *The sick list 2000, the NHS from best to worst*, http://www.fulcrumtv.com/sick%20list.htm

Kline R.B. (1998), *Principles and practice of structural equation modelling*, NY: Guilford Press. Covers confirmatory factor analysis using SEM techniques. See esp. Ch. 7.

Knapp, T. R., Swoyer, V. H. (1967), Some empirical results concerning the power of Bartlett's test of the significance of a correlation matrix. *American Educational Research Journal*, 4, 13-17.

Korhonen P., Tainio R., and Wallenius J. (2001), Value efficiency analysis of academic research, *European Journal of Operational Research*, 130: 121-132.

Krantz D.H., Luce R.D., Suppes P. and Tversky A. (1971), *Foundations of measurement, vol. 1, Additive and polynomial representations*, Academic Press, New York.

Lawley D. N. and Maxwell A. E. (1971), *Factor analysis as a statistical method*, London: Butterworth and Co.

Little R.J.A. and Schenker N. (1994), Missing Data, in Arminger G., Clogg C.C., and Sobel M.E.(eds.) *Handbook for Statistical Modeling in the Social and Behavioral Sciences,* pp.39-75, New York: Plenum.

Little R.J.A (1997), Biostatistical Analysis with Missing Data, in Armitage P. and Colton T. (eds.) *Encyclopaedia of Biostatistics*, London: Wiley.

Little R.J.A. and Rubin D.B. (2002), *Statistical Analysis with Missing Data*, Wiley Interscience, J. Wiley & Sons, Hoboken, New Jersey.

Mahlberg B. and Obersteiner M. (2001), *Remeasuring the HDI by data Envelopment analysis*, Interim report IR-01-069, International Institute for Applied System Analysis, Laxenburg, Austria.

Manly B. (1994), *Multivariate statistical methods*, Chapman & Hall, UK.

Massart D.L. and Kaufman L. (1983), *The Interpretation of Analytical Chemical Data by the Use of Cluster Analysis*, New York: John Wiley & Sons, Inc.

McDaniel C. and Gates R. (1998), *Contemporary Marketing Research*. West Publishing, Cincinnati, OH.

McLachlan G., (2004), *Discriminant Analysis and Statistical Pattern Recognition*, NY: Wiley-Interscience, Wiley Series in Probability and Statistics.

Melyn W. and Moesen W.W. (1991), Towards a synthetic indicator of macroeconomic performance: unequal weighting when limited information is available, *Public Economic research Paper* 17, CES, KU Leuven.

Miller M.B. (1995), Coefficient Alpha: a basic introduction from the perspectives of classical test theory and structural equation modelling, *Structural Equation Modelling*, 2, 3: 255-273.

Milligan G.W. and Cooper M.C. (1985), An Examination of Procedures for Determining the Number of Clusters in a Data Set, *Psychometrika*, 50: 159-179.

Moldan B., Billharz S. and Matravers R. (1997), *Sustainability Indicators: Report of the Project on Indicators of Sustainable Development*, SCOPE 58. Chichester and New York: John Wiley & Sons.

Monti M. (2005), Toughen up EU reform agenda and make it count, Financial Times, Published: March 21 2005.

Moulin H. (1988), *Axioms of co-operative decision making,* Econometric Society Monographs, Cambridge University Press, Cambridge.

Munda G. (1995), *Multicriteria evaluation in a fuzzy environment*, Physica-Verlag, Contributions to Economics Series, Heidelberg.

Munda G. (2005a), Multi-Criteria Decision Analysis and Sustainable Development, in Figueira J., Greco S. and Ehrgott M. (eds.), *Multiple-criteria decision analysis. State of the art surveys,* Springer International Series in Operations Research and Management Science, New York, pp. 953-986.

Munda G. (2005b), "Measuring sustainability": a multi-criterion framework, *Environment, Development and Sustainability*, Vol. 7 (1): 117-134.

Munda G. and Nardo M. (2005), Constructing Consistent Composite Indicators: the Issue of Weights, EUR 21834 EN, Joint Research Centre, Ispra.

Munda G. and Nardo M. (2007), Non-compensatory/Non-Linear composite indicators for ranking countries: a defensible setting, Forthcoming in *Applied Economics.*

Munda G. (2007), *Social multi-criteria evaluation,* Springer-Verlag, Heidelberg, New York, Economics Series.

Nardo M., Tarantola S., Saltelli A., Andropoulos C., Buescher R., Karageorgos G., Latvala A. and Noel F. (2004), The e-business readiness composite indicator for 2003: a pilot study, *EUR* 21294.

Nelsen R.B., (1999), *An Introduction to Copulas* (ISBN 0-387-98623-5).

Nicoletti G., Scarpetta S. and Boylaud O. (2000), Summary indicators of product market regulation with an extension to employment protection legislation, *OECD, Economics department working papers* No. 226, ECO/WKP(99)18. http://www.oecd.org/eco/eco.

Nilsson R. (2000), Confidence Indicators and Composite Indicator", *CIRET* conference, Paris, 10-14 October 2000

Nunnaly J. (1978), *Psychometric theory*, New York: McGraw-Hill.

OECD (1999), *Employment Outlook*, Paris.

OECD (2003), *Quality Framework and Guidelines for OECD Statistical Activities*, www.oecd.org/statistics.

OECD (2004), *Learning for Tomorrow's World - First Results from PISA 2003*, Programme for International Student Assessment, http://www.pisa.oecd.org/dataoecd/1/60/34002216.pdf.

OECD (2007), *Data and Metadata Reporting and Presentation Handbook*, available at http://www.oecd.org/dataoecd/46/17/37671574.pdf).

Parker J. (1991), Environmental reporting and environmental indices, PhD Dissertation, Cambridge, UK.

Pedhazur E. J. (1982), *Multiple regression in behavioral research*, 2nd edition, NY Holt.

Pré Consultants (2000), *The Eco-indicator 99. A damage oriented method for life cycle impact assessment.* http://www.pre.nl/eco-indicator99/ei99-reports.htm

Podinovskii V.V. (1994), Criteria importance theory, *Mathematical Social Sciences*, 27: 237-252.

Puolamaa M., Kaplas M. and Reinikainen T. (1996), *Index of Environmental Friendliness. A methodological study*, Eurostat.

Raykov T. (1998), Cronbach's Alpha and Reliability of Composite with Interrelated Non-homogenous Items, *Applied Psychological Measurement*, 22: 375-385.

Rifkin J. (2004), *The European Dream*, Tarcher-Penguin, New York.

Roberts F. S. (1979), *Measurement theory with applications to decision making, utility and the social sciences*, Addison-Wesley, London.

Rosen R. (1991), *Life Itself: A Comprehensive Inquiry into Nature, Origin, and Fabrication of Life*. Columbia University Press.

Roy B. (1996), *Multicriteria methodology for decision analysis*, Kluwer, Dordrecht.

Saaty T. L. (1980), *The Analytic Hierarchy Process*, New York: McGraw-Hill.

Saaty R.W. (1987), The analytic hierarchy process: what it is and how it is used, *Mathematical Modelling*, 9: 161-176.

Saisana M. and Tarantola S. (2002), *State-of-the-art report on current methodologies and practices for composite indicator development*, EUR 20408 EN, European Commission-JRC: Italy.

Saisana M., Tarantola S. and Saltelli A. (2005a), Uncertainty and sensitivity techniques as tools for the analysis and validation of composite indicators, *Journal of the Royal Statistical Society* A, 168(2), 307-323.

Saisana M., Nardo M. and Saltelli A. (2005b), Uncertainty and Sensitivity Analysis of the 2005 Environmental Sustainability Index, in Esty D., Levy M., Srebotnjak T. and de Sherbinin A. (2005) Environmental Sustainability Index: Benchmarking National Environmental Stewardship. New Haven: Yale Center for Environmental Law and Policy, pp.75-78.

Saltelli A., Ratto M., Andres T., Campolongo F., Cariboni J., Gatelli D. Saisana M., and Tarantola S. (2008), *Global Sensitivity Analysis*. The Primer, John Wiley & Sons.

Saltelli A. (2007) Composite indicators between analysis and advocacy, *Social Indicators Research*, 81: 65-77.

Saltelli A., Tarantola S., Campolongo F. and Ratto M. (2004), *Sensitivity Analysis in practice, a guide to assessing scientific models*, New York: John Wiley & Sons. Software for sensitivity analysis is available at http://www.jrc.ec.europa.eu/uasa/prj-sa-soft.asp.

Saltelli A. (2002), Making best use of model valuations to compute sensitivity indices, *Computer Physics Communications*, 145: 280-297.

Saltelli A. and Tarantola S. (2002), On the relative importance of input factors in mathematical models: safety assessment for nuclear waste disposal, *Journal of American Statistical Association*, 97 (459): 702-709.

Sapir A. (2005), Globalisation and the Reform of European Social Models, http://www.bruegel.org/.

Sen A. (1989), Development as Capabilities Expansion, *Journal of Development Planning*, 19: 41-58.

Sharpe A. (2004), *Literature Review of Frameworks for Macro-indicators*, Centre for the Study of Living Standards, Ottawa, CAN.

Sicherl P., (1973), Time Distance as a Dynamic Measure of Disparities in Social and Economic Development, *Kyklos*, XXVI, 3.

Sicherl, P., (2004), Time distance – a missing perspective in comparative analysis. *eWisdom, Journal for Comparative Research*, 2a: 11-30

Sobol' I.M. (1993), Sensitivity analysis for non-linear mathematical models, *Mathematical Modelling & Computational Experiment* 1: 407-414.

Spath H. (1980), *Cluster Analysis Algorithms*, Chichester, England: Ellis Horwood.

Storrie D. and Bjurek H. (1999), Benchmarking European labour market performance with efficiency frontier technique, *Discussion Paper* FS I 00-2011.

Storrie D. and Bjurek H. (2000), *Benchmarking the basic performance indicators using efficiency frontier techniques*, Report presented to the European commission, DG employment and social affairs.

Tabachnick, B., Fidell L. (1989), *Using Multivariate Statistics*, Harper & Row Publishers, New York, pp.746.

Tarantola S., Jesinghaus J. and Puolamaa M. (2000), *Global sensitivity analysis: a quality assurance tool in environmental policy modelling.* In Saltelli A., Chan K., Scott M. (eds.) *Sensitivity Analysis*, pp. 385-397. New York: John Wiley & Sons.

Tarantola S., Saisana M., Saltelli A., Schmiedel F. and Leapman N. (2002), *Statistical techniques and participatory approaches for the composition of the European Internal Market Index 1992-2001*, EUR 20547 EN, European Commission: JRC-Italy.

Tarantola S., Liska R., Saltelli A., Leapman N., Grant C. (2004), The Internal Market Index 2004, EUR 21274 EN, European Commission: JRC-Italy

Ting H.M. (1971), *Aggregation of attributes for multiattributed utility assessment*, Technical report n. 66, Operations Research Center, MIT Cambridge Mass.

Transparency International's *Corruption Index,* http://www.transparency.org/cpi/2004/cpi2004.en.html#cpi2004

Trufte E.R. (2001), *The Visual Display of Quantitative Information.* Graphic Press, Connecticut, USA, 2nd edition (first edition 1981).

Ülengin B., Ülengin F. and Güvenç Ü. (2001), A multidimensional approach to urban quality of life: the case of Istanbul, *European Journal of Operational Research*, 130: 361-374.

United Nations (1992, 1999, 2000, 2001), *Human Development Report.* United Kingdom: Oxford University Press. http://www.undp.org

U.K. Government (2004), *Sustainable Development Indicators in Your Pocket 2004.*

Vansnick J. C. (1990), Measurement theory and decision aid, in Bana e Costa C.A. (ed.), *Readings in multiple criteria decision aid,* Springer-Verlag, Berlin, pp. 81-100.

Vermunt J.K. and Magidson J. (2005), Factor Analysis with categorical indicators: A comparison between traditional and latent class approaches. In A. Van der Ark, M.A. Croon and K. Sijtsma (eds), *New Developments in Categorical Data Analysis for the Social and Behavioral Sciences*, 41-62. Mahwah: Erlbaum.) Available at http://spitswww.uvt.nl/~vermunt/vanderark2004.pdf

Vichi M. and Kiers H. (2001), Factorial k-means analysis for two-way data, *Computational Statistics and Data Analysis*, 37(1): 49-64.

Vincke P. (1992), *Multicriteria decision aid*, Wiley, New York.

Ward, J.H (1963), Hierarchical Grouping to optimize an objective function. *Journal of American Statistical Association*, 58(301), 236-244.

Watanabe S., (1960), Information theoretical analysis of multivariate correlation, *IBM Journal of Research and Development* 4: 66-82.

Willmott C.J. (1982), Some comments on the evaluation of model performance, *Bulletin of the American Meteorological Society* 63: 1309-1313.

Willmott C.J., Ackleson S.G., Davis R.E, Feddema J.J., Klink K.M., Legates D.R., O'Donnel J., and Rowe C.M. (1985), Statistics for the evaluation and comparison of models, *Journal of Geophisical Research* 90: 8995-9005.

WHO (2000), *Overall Health System attainment*. http://www.who.int/whr2001/2001/archives/2000/en/contents.htm

Wright S. (1934), *The method of path coefficients* Annals of Mathematical Statistics, Vol. 5: 161-215.

Young H.P. and Levenglick A. (1978), A consistent extension of Condorcet's election principle, SIAM *Journal of Applied Mathematics*, 35: 285-300.

Zimmermann H.J. and Zysno P. (1983), Decisions and evaluations by hierarchical aggregation of information, *Fuzzy Sets and Systems*, 10: 243-260

HANDBOOK ON CONSTRUCTING COMPOSITE INDICATORS: METHODOLOGY AND USER GUIDE – ISBN 978-92-64-04345-9 – © OECD 2008

APPENDIX: TECHNOLOGY ACHIEVEMENT INDEX

Table A.1 List of individual indicators of the Technology Achievement Index

Indicator	Unit	Definition
CREATION OF TECHNOLOGY		
PATENTS	Patents granted per 1 000 000 people	Number of patents granted to residents, to reflect the current level of invention activities (1998)
ROYALTIES	US $ per 1 000 people	Receipts of royalty and license fees from abroad per capita, so as to reflect the stock of successful innovations of the past that are still useful and hence have market value (1999)
DIFFUSION OF RECENT INNOVATIONS		
INTERNET	Internet hosts per 1 000 people	Diffusion of the Internet, which is indispensable to participation in the network age (2000)
EXPORTS	%	Exports of high and medium technology products as a share of total goods exports (1999)
DIFFUSION OF OLD INNOVATIONS		
TELEPHONES	Telephone lines per 1 000 people (log)	Number of telephone lines (mainline and cellular), which represents old innovation needed to use newer technologies and is also pervasive input to a multitude of human activities (1999)
ELECTRICITY	kWh per capita (log)	Electricity consumption, which represents old innovation needed to use newer technologies and is also pervasive input to a multitude of human activities (1998)
HUMAN SKILLS		
SCHOOLING	Years	Mean years of schooling (age 15 and above), which represents the basic education needed to develop cognitive skills (2000)
UNIVERSITY	%	Gross enrolment ratio of tertiary students enrolled in science, mathematics and engineering, which reflects the human skills needed to create and absorb innovations (1995-1997)

Table A.2 Raw data for the individual indicators of the Technology Achievement Index

		PATENTS	ROYALTIES	INTERNET	EXPORTS	TELEPHONES (log)	ELECTRICITY (log)	SCHOOLING	UNIVERSITY
1	Finland	187	125.6	200.2	50.7	3.08	4.15	10	27.4
2	United States	289	130	179.1	66.2	3.00	4.07	12	13.9
3	Sweden	271	156.6	125.8	59.7	3.10	4.14	11.4	15.3
4	Japan	994	64.6	49	80.8	3.00	3.86	9.5	10
5	Korea, Rep. of	779	9.8	4.8	66.7	2.97	3.65	10.8	23.2
6	Netherlands	189	151.2	136	50.9	3.02	3.77	9.4	9.5
7	United Kingdom	82	134	57.4	61.9	3.02	3.73	9.4	14.9
8	Canada	31	38.6	108	48.7	2.94	4.18	11.6	14.2
9	Australia	75	18.2	125.9	16.2	2.94	3.94	10.9	25.3
10	Singapore	8	25.5	72.3	74.9	2.95	3.83	7.1	24.2
11	Germany	235	36.8	41.2	64.2	2.94	3.75	10.2	14.4
12	Norway	103	20.2	193.6	19	3.12	4.39	11.9	11.2
13	Ireland	106	110.3	48.6	53.6	2.97	3.68	9.4	12.3
14	Belgium	72	73.9	58.9	47.6	2.91	3.86	9.3	13.6
15	New Zealand	103	13	146.7	15.4	2.86	3.91	11.7	13.1
16	Austria	165	14.8	84.2	50.3	2.99	3.79	8.4	13.6
17	France	205	33.6	36.4	58.9	2.97	3.80	7.9	12.6
18	Israel	74	43.6	43.2	45	2.96	3.74	9.6	11
19	Spain	42	8.6	21	53.4	2.86	3.62	7.3	15.6
20	Italy	13	9.8	30.4	51	3.00	3.65	7.2	13
21	Czech Republic	28	4.2	25	51.7	2.75	3.68	9.5	8.2
22	Hungary	26	6.2	21.6	63.5	2.73	3.46	9.1	7.7
23	Slovenia	105	4	20.3	49.5	2.84	3.71	7.1	10.6
24	Hong Kong, China (SAR)	6		33.6	33.6	3.08	3.72	9.4	9.8
25	Slovakia	24	2.7	10.2	48.7	2.68	3.59	9.3	9.5
26	Greece			16.4	17.9	2.92	3.57	8.7	17.2
27	Portugal	6	2.7	17.7	40.7	2.95	3.53	5.9	12
28	Bulgaria	23		3.7	30	2.60	3.50	9.5	10.3
29	Poland	30	0.6	11.4	36.2	2.56	3.39	9.8	6.6
30	Malaysia			2.4	67.4	2.53	3.41	6.8	3.3
31	Croatia	9		6.7	41.7	2.63	3.39	6.3	10.6
32	Mexico	1	0.4	9.2	66.3	2.28	3.18	7.2	5
33	Cyprus			16.9	23	2.87	3.54	9.2	4
34	Argentina	8	0.5	8.7	19	2.51	3.28	8.8	12
35	Romania	71	0.2	2.7	25.3	2.36	3.21	9.5	7.2
36	Costa Rica		0.3	4.1	52.6	2.38	3.16	6.1	5.7
37	Chile		6.6	6.2	6.1	2.55	3.32	7.6	13.2
38	Uruguay	2		19.6	13.3	2.56	3.25	7.6	7.3
39	South Africa		1.7	8.4	30.2	2.43	3.58	6.1	3.4
40	Thailand	1	0.3	1.6	48.9	2.09	3.13	6.5	4.6
41	Trinidad and Tobago			7.7	14.2	2.39	3.54	7.8	3.3

HANDBOOK ON CONSTRUCTING COMPOSITE INDICATORS: METHODOLOGY AND USER GUIDE – ISBN 978-92-64-04345-9 – © OECD 2008

		PATENTS	ROYALTIES	INTERNET	EXPORTS	TELEPHONES (log)	ELECTRICITY (log)	SCHOOLING	UNIVERSITY
42	Panama			1.9	5.1	2.40	3.08	8.6	8.5
43	Brazil	2	0.8	7.2	32.9	2.38	3.25	4.9	3.4
44	Philippines		0.1	0.4	32.8	1.89	2.65	8.2	5.2
45	China	1	0.1	0.1	39	2.08	2.87	6.4	3.2
46	Bolivia	1	0.2	0.3	26	2.05	2.61	5.6	7.7
47	Colombia	1	0.2	1.9	13.7	2.37	2.94	5.3	5.2
48	Peru		0.2	0.7	2.9	2.03	2.81	7.6	7.5
49	Jamaica		2.4	0.4	1.5	2.41	3.35	5.3	1.6
50	Iran, Islamic Rep. of	1			2	2.12	3.13	5.3	6.5
51	Tunisia		1.1		19.7	1.98	2.92	5	3.8
52	Paraguay		35.3	0.5	2	2.14	2.88	6.2	2.2
53	Ecuador			0.3	3.2	2.09	2.80	6.4	6
54	El Salvador		0.2	0.3	19.2	2.14	2.75	5.2	3.6
55	Dominican Republic			1.7	5.7	2.17	2.80	4.9	5.7
56	Syrian Arab Republic				1.2	2.01	2.92	5.8	4.6
57	Egypt		0.7	0.1	8.8	1.89	2.94	5.5	2.9
58	Algeria				1	1.73	2.75	5.4	6
59	Zimbabwe			0.5	12	1.56	2.95	5.4	1.6
60	Indonesia			0.2	17.9	1.60	2.51	5	3.1
61	Honduras				8.2	1.76	2.65	4.8	3
62	Sri Lanka			0.2	5.2	1.69	2.39	6.9	1.4
63	India	1		0.1	16.6	1.45	2.58	5.1	1.7
64	Nicaragua			0.4	3.6	1.59	2.45	4.6	3.8
65	Pakistan			0.1	7.9	1.38	2.53	3.9	1.4
66	Senegal			0.2	28.5	1.43	2.05	2.6	0.5
67	Ghana				4.1	1.08	2.46	3.9	0.4
68	Kenya			0.2	7.2	1.04	2.11	4.2	0.3
69	Nepal			0.1	1.9	1.08	1.67	2.4	0.7
70	Tanzania, U. Rep. of				6.7	0.78	1.73	2.7	0.2
71	Sudan				0.4	0.95	1.67	2.1	0.7
72	Mozambique				12.2	0.70	1.73	1.1	0.2

Note: The first 23 countries are used as case study in the Handbook. Units are given in Table A.1.

ENDNOTES

[1] Mansky (2004, Measuring Expectations, *Econometrica* vol. 72, pp. 1329-1376) notes, however: "Economists have long been hostile to subjective data. Caution is prudent, but hostility is not warranted. The empirical evidence cited in this article shows that, by and large, persons respond informatively to questions eliciting probabilistic expectations for personally significant events. ... The unattractive alternative to measurement is to make unsubstantiated assumptions" (p.1370).

[2] The Human Development Index uses Min-Max normalisation method; it is also the default behaviour of the Dashboard of Sustainability.

[3] Colours need to be chosen (1) so that graphics communicate for colour-blind persons, and (2) so that graphics continue to communicate when they are printed in black and white.

[4] The label "composite indicators" has not of universal acceptance. Sometimes CI are known as composite indexes while in the measurement literature the term indicator is reserved for observable or directly measurable variables.

[5] The transitive property states that if *aPb* and *bPc*, then *aPc*.

[6] In decision theory literature, this concept of weights as importance coefficients is usually referred to as *symmetrical importance*, that is *"... if we have two non-equal numbers to construct a vector in R^2, then it is preferable to place the greatest number in the position corresponding to the most important criterion."* (Podinovskii, 1994, p. 241).

[7] This Section is heavily based on Munda (2007, Chapter 4).

[8] The median is the value that divides in two equal parts the distribution of the random variable.

[9] The mode is the value with the highest frequency.

[10] A variant of unconditional mean imputation is the fill-in via conditional mean. The regression approach is one possible method. Another common method (called imputing means within adjustment cells) is to classify the data for the individual indicator with some missing values in classes and to impute provisionally the missing values of that class with the sample mean of the class. The sample mean (across all classes) is then calculated and substituted as final imputation value.

[11] If the observed variables are dummies for a categorical variable, then the prediction $\hat{x}_{ih}$ are respondent means within classes defined by the variable and the method reduces to that of imputing means with adjustment cells.

[12] Define $SSE = \sum_i (x_{ih} - \hat{x}_{ih})^2$, $SST = \sum_i (x_{ih} - \bar{x}_h)^2$, then $R^2 = 1 - (SSE / SST)$, $MSE = SSE / (M - r - k)$, where k is the number of coefficients in the regression and $(M-r)$ the number of observations. $RMS = \sum_i (\hat{x}_{ih} - \bar{x}_h)^2$ and $C_k = (SSE_k / MSE) - (M - r) + 2k$

where the SSE_k is computed from a model with only k coefficients and MSE is computed using all available regressors.

[13] Other iterative methods include the Newton-Raphson algorithm and the scoring method. Both involve a calculation of the matrix of second derivatives of the likelihood, which, for complex patterns of incomplete data, can be a very complicated function of θ. As a result these algorithms often require algebraic manipulations and complex programming. Numerical estimation of this matrix is also possible but careful computation is needed.

[14] For NMAR mechanisms one needs to make assumptions on the missing-data mechanism and to include them in the model (see Little & Rubin, 2002, Ch. 15).

[15] The technique of PCA was first described by Karl Pearson in 1901. A description of practical computing methods came much later from Hotelling in 1933. For a detailed discussion on the PCA, *see* Jolliffe (1986), Jackson (1991) and Manly (1994). Social scientists may also find the shorter monograph by Dunteman (1989) helpful.

[16] For reasons of clarity in this section we substitute the indexing $q=1,...Q$ with the indexing $i=1,...,Q$ and $j=1,...,Q$.

[17] Golub, Gene H. & van der Vorst, Henk A. (2000): Eigenvalue computation in the 20th century, *Journal of Computational and Applied Mathematics*, Vol. 123, Iss. 1-2. and Gentle, James E.; Härdle, Wolfgang; Mori, Yuichi (Eds.) (2004): *Handbook of Computational Statistics: Concepts and Methods*, Springer.

[18] Euclidean distances can be greatly influenced by variables that have the largest values. One way around this problem is to standardise the variables.

[19] The name is based on the route that follows the grid of roads, as in most American cities it is not possible to go directly between two points.

[20] The Bartlett test is valid under the assumption that data are a random sample from a multivariate normal distribution. A different version of the Bartlett test is also used to test that k samples have equal variance. For details see http://www.itl.nist.gov/div898/handbook/eda/section3/eda357.htm

[21] In a sample of n observations it is possible for a limited number to be so far separated in value from the remainder that they give rise to the suspicion that they may be from a different population, or that the sampling technique is at fault. Such values are called outliers (F.H.C. Marriott, 1990, *A dictionary of statistical terms*, Longman Scientific & Technical, 5th edition, p.223). Eurostat employs this definition of outlier.

[22] http://europa.eu.int/comm/economy_finance/publications/european_economy/2001/b2001_0809_en.pdf

[23] Other methods are available, *e.g.* the Maximum Likelihood or the Principal Factor centroids. Note that these methods usually supply very different weights especially when the sample size of FA is small.

[24] Weights are normalized squared factor loadings, *e.g.* $0.24 = (0.79^2)/2.64$, which is the portion of the variance of the first factor explained by the variable *Internet*.

[25] To preserve comparability final weights could be rescaled to sum up to one.

[26] DEA has also been used in production theory (for a review see Charnes *et al.*, 1995).

[27] We present the method as it has been used in Cherchye *et al.* (2004) and Cherchye & Kuosmanen (2002).

28   Additional constraints could be imposed. Country-specific restrictions to reflect prior information can also be added. Note that constraints should not be given to the absolute value of weights but should be placed on the relative weights. The result of this approach is therefore relative weights or trade-offs to be legitimately used in linear and geometric aggregations.

29   In our example we imposed the requirement that each individual indicator should take at least 10% and no more than 15% of the total weight.

30   Maximum likelihood estimation requires the normality assumption. Without this assumption a method of moments can be applied. For a discussion of the method and its applicability see Kaufmann *et al.* (1999).

31   In 1991, 400 German experts were asked to allocate a budget to several environmental indicators related to an air pollution problem. The results were consistent, although the experts came from opposing social spheres like the industrial and the environmental sectors (Jesinghaus, in Moldan & Billharz, 1997).

32   The exercise was carried out at the JRC through interviewing experts in the field.

33   A subset of indicators Y is *preferentially independent* of Y^C (the complement of Y) only if any conditional preference among elements of Y, holding all elements of Y^C fixed, remain the same, regardless of the levels at which Y^C are held. The variables $x_1, x_2, ..., x_Q$ are *mutually preferentially independent* if every subset Y of these variables is preferentially independent of its complementary set of evaluators.

34      $\dfrac{\partial S_{x,y}}{\partial z} = 0$, $\forall x, y \in Y, \forall z \in Y^C$, see the note above.

35   Compensability of aggregations is widely studied in fuzzy set theory, for example Zimmermann & Zysno (1983) use the geometric operator $\left(\prod_q I_q \right)^{(1-\gamma)} (1 - \prod_q (1 - I_q))^{\gamma}$ where γ is a parameter of compensation: the larger γ, the higher the degree of compensation between operators (in our case individual indicators).

36   This section is heavily based on Chapter 6 of Munda (2007).

37   In decision theory literature, this concept of weights is usually referred to as *symmetrical importance*, that is, "... *if we have two non-equal numbers to construct a vector in R^2, then it is preferable to place the greatest number in the position corresponding to the most important criterion.*" (Podinovskii, 1994, p. 241).

38   Suppose that country a is evaluated according to some criteria/individual indicators $(x_1(a),...,x_Q(a))$, then the *substitution rate at a* of individual indicator j with respect to individual indicator r (taken as a reference) is the amount $S_{jr}(a)$ such that country b, whose evaluations are: $x_l(a) = x_l(b), \forall l \neq j, r; x_j(b) = x_j(a) - 1$; and $x_r(b) = x_r(a) + S_{jr}(a)$ is indifferent to country a. Therefore, $S_{jr}(a)$ is the amount which must be added to the reference individual indicator in order to compensate the loss of one unit on individual indicator j, keeping the others constant. While for additive aggregations the substitution rate is constant, in the multiplicative aggregation it is proportional to the relative score of the indicator with respect to the others.

39   Data are not normalized. Normalization does not change the result of the multi-criteria method whenever it does not change the ordinal information of the data matrix.

[40]   To prevent this problem it is possible to set thresholds of this type: if the difference between two countries in the indicator I is more than x%, then give to the country with the highest score a much higher weight. If the difference is less than x%, give nearly the same weight. However, more precision comes at the expenses of *ad hoc* threshold and weighting values.

[41]   The multi-criteria approach MCA produces ranks for countries. The focus of the analysis thus is $Rank(CI_c)$ rather than the raw value of the index CI_c.

[42]   For proof, see Saltelli *et al.*, 2004.

[43]   Furthermore, no programme can take into account variables that are not included in an analysis.

[44]   Garson, *Structural Equation Modeling*, http://www2.chass.ncsu.edu/garson/pa765/structur.htm. This webpage also contains a useful bibliography for Structural Equation Models. LISREL, AMOS and EQS are statistical packages performing SEM.

[45]   Introductory information on Bayesian Networks can be found in Jensen (1996, Springer), *Introduction to Bayesian Networks*, and Neapolitan (2001, Chapmann and Hall), *Learning Bayesian networks*.

OECD PUBLICATIONS, 2, rue André-Pascal, 75775 PARIS CEDEX 16
PRINTED IN FRANCE
(30 2008 25 1 P) ISBN 978-92-64-04345-9 – No. 56327 2008